Maryland Street

Pat Jourdan

I have been observing and these are my reactions.
William Langland, *Piers Plowman*

I've got to ask what happened.
You don't have to answer, but I've got to ask.
Carl Hiaasen, *Stormy Weather* p 131

You need all these things. The things that are not there.
Jon Rappoport

Also by Pat Jourdan

Poetry
The Bedsit Girl
The Bedsit
Ainnir Anthology
Turpentine
The Cast-Iron Shore
Liverpool Poets 2008
Citizeness

Short Stories
Average Sunday Afternoons
Taking the Field
Rainy Pavements
The Fog Index

Novels
Finding Out
A Small Inheritance

Maryland Street

Pat Jourdan

for
Amelia Hull-Hewitt,   Hunter Jourdan & Inigo Jourdan

Contents

Bytes

The computer turned up supposed relatives all over the place, from every century and race. They tumbled out of the screen in hordes. None of them matched or made sense.

April 1810
M. Martineau for an attempt to shoot Mr Manget, was whipped and branded and forever banished (sic) the Colony, which sentence he bore in a manner that evinced a mind of no common stamp. It is reported that he is a nephew of the late General Martineau.

1881 Residents of Union Workhouse, Shaw Heath, Stockport, Cheshire:
Agnes Martineau, 4, F, inmate
Patrick Martineau, 3, M, inmate
Patrick Martineau, Unmarried, M, inmate, Cotton Blowing Room hand (CM), born in Ireland.

They became faint images, still trying to be seen:
1851 Folio 78a H0107/2263
Chorley Enumeration District 1c
Homer? Martineau? Lodger ???   36 Ireland
Bridget Martineau? Daur of Above 9 Ireland
Thomas Martineau? Son of Above   4   Ireland

They fell out into infinity, leaving these last traces, like fingerprints of people who could not hold onto the side of a bridge any longer, plummeting into an ocean; still foreign, wherever they may have drowned, leaving only a name.

Traces

You can hold an entire street in your head, complete against that inner screen stretching across your forehead, an endless film that outlasts external seasons and centuries. An entire street, its uneven paving slabs, its random lamp-posts, the black iron circles of the coal-hole covers with their sturdy lacework, the prim black railings surrounding each basement area, the low wide steps to each black door, the sameness, the everyday reality and its reassurance.

Held forever, it waits to be unreeled and spun out, its dark reality and its hidden, dashing colours within. There's times when you want to smooth a city out like a feverish child and tell it everything's going to be all right tomorrow. There are a lot of tears below those paving stones and behind those bricks.

You can be homesick for places that don't even exist.

The census-man called at the bootblack's home, as all the boys had not been counted. He knew he must call back again and again as they were out all day working down town. Criss-crossing from street to street, he worked his way up Copperas Hill from door to door. His new boots still hurt a bit, but he was grateful for them in this rain. At least this doorway was a single dwelling, too many houses were a warren of different families cramped together. He knocked on the shabby door, painted black but needing more attention now. An oldish woman answered the door, another Irishwoman; the district was full of them. He began the questioning again. She was unable to write or read, like so many of them, so he led her carefully through the questions. It was a serious and important job.

"Martineau," she said, "My husband was Martin Martineau. I am a widow-woman now. My son, George lives with me, and my daughter and her two children too." Henry Latimer wrote this down

10

in his flowing copperplate exactly as he heard it. After Judith, the householder, born in Ireland, he asked if there were any children at school. This was often a fiction, with children roaming the streets begging or running after any means of getting a ha'penny. What Judith had actually said was from the Irish – Mártin Óg – quite clearly, Young Martin. Old Martin had been left back in Galway, back in the tree-deep lane, back with the wind and rain and lack of hope. And now their surname had been changed into a French name without Judith knowing. From here on they had been renamed and by the time it was found out generations later, no one cared to change it. When her son George returned from work that evening, Judith told him that the census-man had been round. He was worn out after walking up from Hotham Street and the French polishing warehouse where other Irishmen worked .

"We have all been entered into his book. They asked where we were all born and I only had to say Ireland, not our real townland. And I had to give our ages, too." George gave a slight smile,

"Who on earth would be interested in all that? At least you did not let him into the house."

"He said the next census would be in ten years. Mary's children will be grown by then."

"If God spares us."

"True." Her daughter Mary had ended up back at home with two children after the death of her young husband. They got by with her doing some needlework and by letting out the two small back rooms to lodgers. Judith turned back to the fire where the blackened kettle was spitting as its lid rose and fell with the pressure of bubbling boiling water. Carefully measuring the water into the warmed teapot, Judith poured it onto the already-used tea leaves. Frugality was their only way of getting-by, for the time being.

1

They called her Mary because her Mother was dying and so was the baby.

"It was the only name I could think of," Celi said when Mary complained as a teenager about the ordinariness of the name. "You were at the point of death so I threw some water over you and roughly baptised you. Then the midwife did a quick form of baptism and by that time your Father had got hold of a priest and you were properly baptised there in the maternity hospital." Three times baptised; three times nearly dead; a wonderful start to life in this world. But it was the commonest girls' name of all; that was why Mary was ashamed of it.

Her first memory was of the inside of a pram with a zigzag Greek key pattern on the black ribbon edging round the hood. She could look out from this hideaway, with its own special smell.

Taken home to her grandparent's, Mary stayed with them while Celi was given treatment for TB at the sanatorium on the Wirral. Eventually Nannie could not cope with the nappies any more and Mary was sent across to the other grandmother. It was the start of a constant ring-around, being shuffled from one house to another while her Father stayed on in the empty house, going next-door into his own mother's for meals. Celi came back now and again for visits; it was a muddled, hectic time, the war taking everyone's attention and energy. The adults already had too much to worry about.

As her Father, Vin, had a weak heart and was in a reserved occupation at Cammell Laird's shipyards, he had to serve during the war as a Special Constable.

He was alone on fire duty down town at Whitechapel one night when incendiary bombs on Paradise Street hit a chemist's shop next door to Horne Brothers, the men's outfitters. A fire engine, plugged into a hydrant found only a dribble of water, as the mains came through Prescott Street, so they had to pack up and go away, defeated. The fire gradually spread at the back of the outfitters, with a startling spontaneous combustion from the chemists into the Kodak shop. Luckily Vin was at Bunney's corner when the entire building went up in a giant explosion.

With this, the Salvage Corps came along. Luckily it had begun to rain but it was too late as the fire had spread along by Stoniers, the Glass Co and had reached Williams Pianos. The Salvage Corps then pushed all the pianos into the pouring rain, strings bursting and a mish-mash of discordant music adding to the din. It was everything that Shostakovitch would have written, clashing warfare made into music. He walked along to the Bear's Paw, next to the Irish Linen Co, which was blazing away to hell. The doorman and liveryman were pouring water on the frontage helplessly. That night Lewis's, Blacklers and the Liverpool Museum were all bombed out. Town was being destroyed street by street.

At home, Celi, and little Mary were huddled on mattresses under the stairs with Nannie and Julie, as they could not risk even going across to the convent shelter in the raging firestorm.

Then, on the fifth of May, 1941, St Lukes church was attacked down Leece Street. The all-clear had gone. Vin was not on duty, but he went out to see what was happening.

"I've got to see this, it's too close, though you'd think I've seen enough fires in my time." Celi went out with him in the street, holding the year-old baby in her arms to watch from the corner of South Hunter Street. The sky was tinged red. Duke street was on fire, the Gas Offices in flames, with no sign of help anywhere about until a National Fire Service engine came along from St Helens.

"Yes, we've had to come all this way from St Helens,you wouldn't believe it, but there's no spares left." This was at a quarter to six in the morning, already light as a spring day. "I'm waiting to 6.30 to assemble," the chief fireman said.

"I live up the road, come in for a cup of tea," Vin said, Then you'd better make tracks to meet your mates." Celi was not too pleased, but they managed to stretch the tea leaves and milk for extra persons. There was St Lukes still blazing away down the hill. The fire-watcher on duty had beat it home, defeated.

13

"I don't blame him," the chief fireman sagely remarked, "There's no saving all that lot now." The bells came clattering down, the spring sky still red with flames and sparks from the roof-beams wildly spreading upwards .

The city had to reclaim whatever buildings were left and as soon as possible, Blacklers and Lewis's took over every empty shop in Bold Street. And with half the country shut down, like this, the Americans came into the war later that year.

From the window of number eleven's upstairs living room, Nannie could see silver barrage balloons in the sky over the Radium Hospital. They had got used to the sirens which produced headaches to add to the panic and the wide sweep of the 'All Clear' siren afterwards with the dread of what they would see after yet another air raid.

2

It is a blank. Nothing happened, everything happened. They were still able to use the convent shelter in the cellars beneath the refectory and had to walk through the grounds and the school playground back to the empty house. The war took over their sleep and their daytime.

Mary cried so loudly once that Nannie came in from her part of the house, hurrying through the sitting room and told Celi that the child could be heard all over the street, what on earth was wrong?

Another time, Celi was bathing the baby-girl beside the living room fire, the only heat in the house and one by one, Julie, Grandpa, Nannie, Julie and even Joe came in until there were no chairs left and they sat staring until Celi, overcome, began to cry.

But Celi's TB had erupted again and there was a hotch-potch arrangement of Mary being sent to live with various relatives-both grandmothers and even friends from Celi's working days at

14

Littlewoods offices. Mary was shuffled round from one house to another while Celi stayed in the Sanatorium. It was all a mystery.

3

Presents at the end of a pink cot, crawling towards them by the inner yellow-papered window of Auntie Julie's bedroom in number eleven, along the top corridor.Then other relatives and places to stay, Mary went from one to the other.

Fawn gaiters, how clever adults are and Aunty Kay is helping me with a button hook because there are so many buttons to go into loops, all up my legs, it is almost a hundred, like wearing a snake. Cousin Lucy has the same gaiters too. They keep the cold out. Once winter arrives everything changes and you could be attacked by this sharp icy air all over the house, but it is even worse out in the street. Life is mysterious but you have to be obedient, or it all goes wrong and you get strange illnesses.

Sitting on the kneelers at St Philip Neri's on Sundays, I am waiting for the money-plate to come round and I can put a penny on it. Every now and again, all the In Memoriam cards fall out of someone's prayerbook and slip onto the floor. I am the quickest to pick them up for the embarrassed adults. We go to Mass through the snow, even when there are no trams or buses or cars along Catherine Street. It is a mortal sin to miss Sunday Mass, the world has these guidelines and Sundays are special, the streets are quiet and empty. This is called our Parish and we belong here.

It is a wonderful feeling to be going through a city like this, being wheeled in a pram. At home the fire dries out our shoes and we have fried bread and tea, with baby milk for me.

4

"Come on now, hurry up, I want the table now, Julie. You finished,? D'y'ear me?"

"Yes, Mum. Here, Mary, you get a pencil and add your message to Mummy. Down here, now. Hold the pencil like this."

This is for Mummy. I can't see her to talk to yet. But they send this to her. I wonder what she looks like and what she does with this when she gets it. I wonder how they send messages on these pieces of paper. What does my message mean? I'll make this message very big and black. Here's the line coming all the way down and now I've got to fill up this corner too. I hope Mummy understands all this, it's very hard to do.

"Hasn't she finished yet? Hurry up, dearie, dinner's ready

"Yes, Nannie, I've finished now." *Did I see her this year? I can't remember. I must ask them. They remember things like that, about days on the big calendar over there. How do they work it out?* "Nannie, what's a calendar for?"

"It's for telling you what day it is. Mind out, the fat's hot." The smell of Sunday's joint, roast potatoes and boiled vegetables filled the room, seeping down even into the lino. *They squash Auntie Julie's school papers off the table-cover and onto a chair in the corner by the window and put on the big white tablecloth over the green fringed cover with the ink-stain that I did. They always remember to tell me that, as if I didn't know it. Daddy is somewhere around. I don't see him much , only his shoes, because he is very tall and big. And I don't think he picks me up much because I don't remember his face. Sometimes when he is working late he sits round in his shirt sleeves because I can remember the white of the shirt all showing. But I never know what his job is, no one ever tells me. Nannie washes the clothes at the sink and puts them through the big mangle that trundles all heavy, all rollers and wheels; it should have been a hurdy-gurdy, painted yellow. Or sometimes it all goes off to*

16

the laundry. His shirts are special, but Grandpa wears old shirts under his work overalls. Uncle Joe is away at the war flying planes somewhere. His bedroom is upstairs along the corridor.

Nannie did everything but didn't say much. Grandpa said even less; he was always coughing. When he came in at the door downstairs he started to cough, it echoed all up the hallway, with the sound of his feet on the lino-covered stairs. Then his boots sounded outside the living room door and then he would sit and cough for a solid five minutes right beside the door on a big chair before they could say anything. In time they became used to it and went on as usual but at first they used to sit quiet and listen to him.

Today was special. Auntie Julie was taking her down Mount Pleasant and they were going to the back of a little down-at-heel general stores run by two sisters in Brownlow Hill. Long grey hair, dirty faces and flowered dresses and stained pinnies, the two indistinguishable elderly sisters sold all types of tinned food and bottles of milk. They were let in behind the mahogany counter, through a drab velvet curtain and in the gloomy back room was an old couch, a fireplace with a kettle murmuring on the hob and there, a bitch lay with seven pups swarming about, all beautiful, small and black and white. The sisters looked embarrassed at all this teeming life at their feet.. Auntie Julie helped Mary choose and so they took Whiskey, called after the Bell's Irish whiskey advert on the front of the Liverpool Echo, *"Whiskey, black or white,"* and brought her home.

It was in preparation for moving back into number nine when her Mother was due to return. The house was crowded with visitors. Mary couldn't remember her properly and, in the fuss, went to the wrong person, a lady who had brought Celi back from the sanatorium. The two women both wore similar black coats and hats. They were all standing in the back kitchen, and Mary was confused in all the fuss, not having seen her mother for a long time. The group of women were gossiping and laughing. Suddenly Celi was there and there was a different feeling about the place. Mary was more used to living with Auntie Julie next-door in number eleven, her bed was next to hers and she kissed Mary in the mornings before she went to work. It was a wrench to part from her shared room.

17

Now Mary was returned to the other part of the house.. Originally it had been the servants' quarters and was less grand, with the living room and back kitchen having black and red tiled floors, and both rooms had large ranges for cooking. As her own bedroom, originally the cook's room over the back kitchen, was too damp to sleep in, Mary was put in a cot in her parents' bedroom.

Things got harder now because it was the middle of the war and rationing ruled each mealtime. Mary was caught going into Nannie's walk-in pantry and choosing a cake and saying "It's my's," inventing the possessive because what else could a child do, there was no other way of acquiring anything in the way adults could, with their anarchic possibilities and their strange money. And with cousin Lucy, she could spit on a finger, put it on a favoured cake or slice of pie and say " It's mine now, I've put my spit on it." A sign uncrossable, made of liquid spit, better than words or any label, Lucy and Mary both understood it perfectly.

A red picture. The room is all red with his anger, it fills right up to the ceiling. I am standing at the table where he is sitting laying out his stamps in his extra-tidy fashion. I can just see the edge of the table, just level with it and his angry face above. He is livid. It is something about a vest that I have not put on, or put it on back to front or a liberty bodice or something I have forgotten or misunderstood. I have cried so much that now I am choking and snot is running down my face. Behind me, Mummy is upset too, she is crying and she is saying,

" But, Vin, but." All I can hear is this 'but.' " Vin, do stop it, she's upset enough." He is very angry with both of us and she seems to have done something wrong too. He thumps the table with his fist but it makes the stamps jump up so he stops. Mummy is beginning to cry more too, she has found a handkerchief. I am snuffling and still sobbing but my mind is has got out of my head and is looking out at it all and he looks very silly sitting there laying down the law and I am getting cold standing here. She and me together, standing here crying, why is it like this? Eventually she ushers me upstairs to the cold bedroom that I share with them. There is an extra room off theirs, which is called my bedroom, but they say it is too damp and

cold to use in the wintertime and so I have a bed beside their wardrobe.

But I prefer my own room and remember it. It is bedtime. The room is black. The only light comes from the night-light lit beside the statue of the Holy Child of Prague on the fretwork bracket up on the wall. It is in a red votive glass and the flame flickers in the draughts. The gaslight is hardly ever lit in my bedroom. The gas pipe comes out from the wall like an arm and can give a jet of light with its delicate filigree of the white mantle.

Sometimes I am there, sometimes in a bed in their room when the weather is freezing.

Mid mornings and the grate had to be black-leaded every day. There was a cat, which used to sit on the hob, but it died or ran away. The fire was essential to the functioning of the house; it heated the water. To have a bath in the summer meant lighting a good roaring fire. Cinders and ash were the currency; coal was essential, a bucket or two each day. The edges of the top of the grate were burnished silver; they rusted every day. While Celi scoured the top edge with emery-paper and blackened the rest of the range, Mary played on the large brass-edged fireguard. Laid flat, it was a sleigh. She was in Russia, dashing across the snow, sleigh bells jangling merrily. The dog joined in though the green wires caught her claws. At the side of the fireplace was a hook, high up. A pair of scissors hung on it together with the dog's collar and lead.

Mummy has taken something else down from the hook. It's the cane. She looks at it coldly and looks at me.

"Well, we won't be needing this now." It tapers gently to a point, like a delicate walking-stick. It was for me and the dog, I know that. It means fear, and the dog and myself share it. But I cannot remember it being used. Have I forgotten? The dog cowers and goes underneath the chair. Mummy looks at me in a strange way.

There are strange illnesses with new names. I am spread-eagled, undressed, across Mummy's lap, Nannie is sitting in the other fireside chair, Daddy is doing his stamps at the table. Mummy is shoving a sliver of soap up my backside to cure a bout of constipation. The dog looks up at me. I know this is not right, but

19

can't say anything to change it. Auntie Julie is there as well in the background, advising what to do as usual, but I feel awkward and out of place and don't know why they are making this happen. I am smaller than them.

At some unknown time, Celi had a clean-up. Something about it 'being time.' And there they were, walking up Maryland Street with the shopping and right there up the street, looking out of the school's nursery class windows were all Mary's favourite toys. Her Teddy and Blue Rabbit and Golliwog were all the other side of the glass, on the school's windowsill, already belonging to another world, already mixed in with other teddies and bunnies, and already belonging to other children who would be hurt if they were taken away. Mummy said not to make a fuss, she was a big girl now and the children needed them more. A few days later, the little figures had disappeared and she never saw them again, even when she joined the school.

5

It was time for the interview for the Demonstration School, with Mary taken across the road by Auntie Julie as Mummy was away again having treatment, wherever the sanatorium was. Up the big steps and into a tall room, very, like a tram laid on its end, very small with tall windows in both walls. Sister Monica sat at a gigantic roll-top desk. She held a large book with names and figures., the ledger of admissions.

They are talking about people they know and seem to know each other quite well. I don't. The room is very high and I am like a marble at the bottom of it. I don't want a headmistress with cracked hands. She had shaken hands with me and said I was coming to her school. I don't want a headmistress who is old with scratchy hands.

After playtime, mornings or afternoons, Sister Monica, who was fond of her border of lupins between the upper and lower playgrounds would wander slowly along it, as if talking to each flower. But at playtime, little boys sped across the top playground, playing at war, their arms stretched out wide, being aeroplanes. They banged into each other, pretending to be shot down and cannonaded into girls who were nonchalantly wandering about. Luckily all the boys left at seven years old, but were replaced yearly by just as enthusiastic fighters. They left and the girls and boys staying behind were not told where they went, until they reappeared, older, and wearing long trousers. At nine years old, the girls went upstairs to the Big Girls, which was almost grown up.

Sister Monica soon became a friend. Mary was often decoyed into her office, colouring in pictures for her in the remains of a dinner-time. As Mary filled in the black outlines of Nativity scenes or Angels or Saints with bright blue and red and green – the spread of coloured pencils was enthralling; she still wondered what on earth the pictures were used for.

"We know you are a good little artist," Sister Monica said. "We talk about you in community, how you like colouring-in."

Smell, large windows, desks, toilets outside. Concrete corridor floors of grey but with some diamond spattering in them which glinted, sparkling like chipped stars after the cleaners mopped them with Jeyes Fluid, its rich peppery-ginger smell. They began right at four o'clock, swirling the milky disinfectant across the corridors. The lovely smell of hot disinfectant coming up the glinty grey stairs from the canteen basement spread throughout the school.

Along the corridor, glass tanks of goldfish were arranged on the classroom window cills, fronds of underwater greenery waving about as the fish glided through. Each classroom had a large brass latch, regularly polished by the cleaners. The only stark reminder of reality was the mop and bucket kept in the babies' class as the youngsters of five were often likely to wet them selves. Unfortunately the only toilets were outside and entire classes were led out, in all weathers, halfway through each morning and afternoon. The whitewashed cubicles were often unusable because of being fouled by children who had not been able to use a toilet without help, so that the general trip was often a repulsive experience.

Upstairs were the Big Girls, who had a different playtime. They also had four indoor toilets and a proper cloakroom. They left school and went to work and had babies. You went upstairs at nine years old.

Best friend, Margaret Sullivan, golden ringlets and a sunny nature, someone to giggle with.

Teachers, Miss Phillips, always cheerful, who got married and mixed them all up because now she had to be called Mrs McCracken., Miss Mc Ginty, who went off to London and broke her heart, Miss Young, large, white-haired, plump,always in flowered dresses, Miss Gill, thin, grey haired bun, lilac or mauve dress and matching jacket. Rests in the afternoon after dinner-time on camp beds with scratchy blankets "Heads down" on the desks with elbows folded. Tommy Ball made her laugh and Miss Young slapped them both across the knuckles with a ruler, a big fat woman not understanding their interaction. Adults needed to stay apart from children; they did not understand, which was why they hit you.

Brown gymslips and yellow blouses. Navy blue for the Central School and bottle green for the High School; each of the schools could recognise each other in any of the streets around.

Starting school meant that there was now too much to do. God, for instance, and colouring in.

It was very easy to learn at first:

WhomadeyouGodmademeWhydidGodmakeyouGodmademe toknowHimloveHimandserveHiminthisworldandtobehappywithHimf oreverinthenext.

Forever-in-the-next sounded a wonderful place. To begin with they learned two questions a week from the catechism. There were 370 questions, all in a little twopenny ha'penny book which they had to buy. It would take years and years to learn all this but then they would know everything.

At dinnertime they said the Angelus while it rang out from the convent chapel and added Grace Before Meals (for those who went home at the dinner-hour.) It sounded as though the meals were 'gifts from Thy holy mountain' which made sense. The secular equivalent was the the One O' Clock Gun sounding from Bidston Hill Observatory which designated lunchtime for factories, with sometimes ships' sirens joining in.

Before afternoon lessons, Grace After Meals was said, which included the faithful departed resting in peace. The connection between dinnertime and the dead was unclear; they needed no food. Each mid-morning Liverpool Education Committee lorries arrived with metal tins and trays, and industrial-strength custard in metal jugs. The dinner-ladies helped to take them down to the canteen. "It looks like sick" was only needed to be said once for an entire table to start giggling. It slid down the sides of the slabs of apple pie or plum pie or mince pie or rhubarb pie according to season.

Mary went home for dinner as it was only ten yards away. About a third of every class went home, collected and walked back by Mothers, grannies or neighbours. But at Christmas they all tried to stay to the special Christmas dinner and joined the dinner-money queue on Monday at teacher's desk. Fourpence a day made it 1/8pence a week, noted down in a separate register by the teacher. The potatoes had white string in them and blue scabs; the custard had lumps like marbles, but the rich smell of chicken and sage and onion stuffing wafted up from the basement canteen and the yard-long mince pies in their Education Committee metal cooking tins were exciting.

As Christmas approached everywhere in the school was decorated with the swarf of Reece's milk-bottling factory near the Pro-Cathedral. From lightshade to lightshade and corner of every classroom and corridor, the endless shimmering ribbons shone and tinkled, the regular OOOO in their centres showing where the bottletops had been stamped out.

Over the terms towards Christmas they became a factory too. They made Jumping Jacks with concertina legs and arms, crinoline lady pincushions, brown felt sparrow calendars, windmills, plant pot holders, flannelette blouses (all tacking thread given back at Miss Antrobus's desk) pinafores, knitted pot-holders, cross-stitch handkerchief cases, hot-waterbottle covers, clothes-peg baskets, covered hangers in ruched silk, cards for Mother's Day, Easter, Christmas and most holy days. Any important school messages were written out on the blackboard and they copied them on slips of paper to take home.

"Christmas holidays will be from the 18th December to 10th January. Please remember dinner-money will be 1/8p." The free dinner people smelled and had rats tails hair. They wore plimsolls all summer and wellies all winter, even indoors. Their socks had holes in the heels. When the nit nurse came, they had to go home, sent away that afternoon with a note. There were other things happening to them, too; sometimes all their hair was shaved off and strange purple or orange dye was painted on odd parts. They usually had warts too, all over their hands. Nothing could be done, they had to live like that.

At home, Celi helped her to make a Christmas grotto from a Shredded Wheat box covered with brown paper, dimpled here and there to imitate rocks. Each year they went across to Mr Green's woodyard for some wood shavings to imitate the original stable's straw. Outside the workshop long planks leant against Blake's wall, half-sheltered under a corrugated iron roof that rattled in any strong wind. Inside, the long workshop with its three blurred windows was always, whatever the season, a warm fug of wood-dust, shavings and pure white chamfered pieces of wood. Parts of chairs and chests of drawers were being worked on, scattered along the workbenches. Sawdust littered the floor in a haphazard carpet. A carpenter and an apprentice using handsaws and sandpaper without much use of machinery - this would have been what Jesus was brought up in.

Celi and Mary were here to ask for a bag of wood shavings, the same as every year. Jimmy, the carpenter, swept a handful or so off the bench-top into a paper bag. One year he also made a complete doll's house, although it was not a patch on the one Lucy was given, which also had running water from a concealed tank in its attic. However, this one did have an interesting exterior, where sawdust had been glued all over the walls and then painted, a fair imitation of a pebble-dashed suburban detached house. It matched the felt tea-cosy in its fairytale truth of a house with a central door, windows with window boxes either side and a cascade of roses painted round the door.

They distributed the shavings inside the little grotto, then the Holy Family was deposited with the donkey and cow, along with the two shepherds and two sheep. The three kings were usually kept back until they arrived at Epiphany in January; it made it more exciting. The Child Jesus, however, was from another set of figures and was unfortunately at least three times larger than his parents. He was also made of plaster as opposed to their papier-maché. The plaster round his neck had fallen away, which made it possible to turn his head from side to side most realistically. It looked as though he was smiling at everybody as he lay on the straw. As a final point, bits of cotton wool were deposited over the rocky roof to show it was wintertime.

When Mary was older, the added sophistication was a small torch pushed in at the back, with red cellophane stretched over the bulb, which gave an unearthly glow to the nativity scene. The miniature figures were transformed into a striking theatrical performance , placed on the centre of the sideboard.

When they moved on to sitting at desks for two, the class were told to leave a space on their benches so that their Guardian Angel could sit beside them. The Angel accompanied them everywhere and sat beside their bed all through the night. Other angels had wings and could do messages for God, but Guardian Angels were either sent from heaven specially or volunteered to stay earthbound in order to care for us mortals and stay beside each one of us until our moment of death.

After that they probably returned for further duty, but that point was never covered. Meanwhile, God himself, accompanied by Jesus and Our Lady (and probably as many saints who could crowd in) were looking at you from any ceiling, watching your every move. This was both protective and witnessing. Jesus and Our Lady were always there at the front, but God was somewhere in the background, being busy with other duties and of course, having no exact shape. He was invisible, which meant he could be anywhere. He made everything. There was also the Holy Ghost who could fly around anywhere, just as He liked and give you all sorts of bright ideas, a wild tropical bird darting about, like a parrot let loose.

Flickers

She helped Nannie to scrape off the brown paper crosses from the window-panes with Nannie and the big wooden stepladder that creaked wildly. It was a happy mixture of hot water and scissors and kitchen knives. The upstairs living room was flooded with light, something that had been missing all through the war. It reached the back wall. Some windows round town were left with traces still on for years after.

For a long time, Nannie had prefaced many a comment with "In peacetime, " or "Before the war," and now perhaps it would all return again, like after a thunderstorm when the air is clear.

Mary was sitting on the floor in number eleven, cutting out pictures from the Liverpool Echo. This week it was dogs, not royalty, she was searching for, to stick in a scrapbook. Often, in fact most times, this did not happen, the cut-out scraps merely grew into a stack of slithering paper bits, to fall to the floor from the little imitation school desk in the corner of the living room at home, downstairs. The grown-ups were talking adult talk. This would not make sense. Sentences were not finished, the talk came and went in bits and they often left out all the important parts. It was impossible to make up the missing bits sometimes, but usually she could guess quite well.

If it were Mummy and Aunty Kay they would go into French for the secret parts, with smiles and linking of eyes, the conversation swooping above the children. One day she would learn French too and then they would have to invent some other secret way of communicating. But here she was at Grandpa and Nannie's and they did not speak French, no one did. There were several people in this living room – Grandpa and Auntie Julie and two of the neighbours, people Mary had not seen before here in the house. The words went to and fro, just as usual, nothing interesting. She was not paying attention.

And suddenly something terrible happened in the room. It all went red. Their voices changed. Words staggered out, slowly. Forced. Then their voices seemed to go back into their throats, as though they were trying to swallow what they had just been saying. Then it all stopped and there was a shocked silence. The only bit that she caught was 'Black and Tans,' which made no sense. It sounded like a shoe polish. Someone they all knew, someone round another street, he had been a Black and Tan. Something horrible, to affect five adults like this. Mary went on cutting out any old picture now, hoping they would not notice her. What was it? How could it come into the room like that? Why did adults not explain, even to themselves? What was this about?

The neighbours had strange names. The previous tenants in Mary's house had been called Concannons, there was also something to eat called colcannon, and there were posh priests called canons. The words whirled around, not making any sense again. Mr and Mrs Nugent stayed for another cup of tea and then clattered down the lino-covered stairs to the front door and off to their own house down Maryland Street in the dark.

There were still places at the end of streets where houses had been cut away in a shelling; the ground where a house had been was scattered with cut glass diamonds in the soil, showing the remains of windows. Mary thought that all soil had glass diamonds in it. Other houses had been ripped open and the wallpapers of all their rooms, or even worse dark distemper paint, showed the complete layout from top floor to bottom. In a few cases, the upstairs floors had bedsteads left embarrassingly marooned on fractured floorboards, with half a staircase remaining, stranded steps leading to the sky.

Across end-walls were still the happy big white writing: *"Welcome Home, Bill,* or *Welcome Back, Paul, Jim, Bert and Pete."* A whole streetfull of names, still up there in bright white. How had anyone got up there to paint it?

In other parts by Brownlow Hill there were more recent paintings in white and yellow, the papal colours - "God Bless Our-

27

Pope." Along Clarence Street, in little pockets here and there they had even painted the kerbstones in yellow and white, about a foot of each colour alternating. It wore off all by itself, never officially removed. Other places had "God Save King Billy" and red white and blue stripes. It all looked so merry, as if the street itself became art, all knitted together, for those who did not have paths or steps, the pavement outside their front door itself became part of the home - scoured with soapstone into a breadboard cream colour. But not for the Martineaus the circular demarcation of scrubbed doorway area, or painted window edges; only common people did that. Of course they were too posh to do such things – their pavement door-front was merely subtly a little more clean than the surrounding paving stones.

They also had no one to welcome back, as Uncle Alban Sinnott, taken prisoner, had died on the Burma Railroad; Father was in a reserved occupation, had a weak heart, so served as a special constable and fire watcher, with a whistle and chain. Uncle Tom must have come back - but there was no big whitewashed welcome for him along St James's Road as the cream-plastered houses were too posh, unlike the brick-built terrace streets.

As the war and its rules and ordinances receded, the Morrison shelter was dismantled and its massive iron sheets lay in the yard. Lucy and Mary played at dancing on the pieces and as they danced and jumped, it sounded like thunder, which they enjoyed, but the dog did not understand and ran about barking madly. The shelter had taken up most of the living room and was, again, something that the children and dog enjoyed playing in.

The mattress underneath and the low iron ceiling turned it, ironically, into a perfect play-house. They would lay there, looking at the grown-ups' knees and giggling. As the family had not been evacuated, the government had distributed them from March 1941. Men came to install the Shelter, bolting the girders together at the corners. They were free to families that earned less than £350 a year, so Vin qualified. His mother claimed a place in the convent shelter, so her house did not receive a Morrison shelter and her rooms were not disfigured at all by the war. The downstairs parlour was too small to accommodate it and so the room kept its Victorian state. Two wedding photographs hung above the piano, one a family group and one of the married couple. Beside them hung a photo of baby George who, unlike his twin Christina, had lived long enough to be photographed, looking pale and serious, six months old.

On the opposite wall between the two windows was an oil painting of George Martineau, done from a photo by a friend. He stood with his back to the convent, a real paterfamilias, young and serious too. As his own parents had died, George and his younger brother Hubert had been placed in Beacon Lane Orphanage and Industrial school. There he had learned a trade and stayed on (with the 'butterfly nuns') as the establishment's plumber until his marriage to Rosa at the age of 30. His parents dead, his first children dead; it was no wonder he looked serious.

6

Tommy Ball stopped her in the corridor outside the big hall.

"I've got something to tell you. We're moving away, I think it's New Brighton, I don't really know. I'll have to leave school." His eyes looked deep into hers. They clasped hands. It was all going to be impossible now. Tommy Ball and herself were going to get married, they only had to wait until they were grown-up, they had decided, or perhaps it had been decided for them by fate. It was an absolute. It had arrived from outer space and hit them both.

Mary's heart was breaking, just as Miss Gill passed by in her pastel-lilac dress. Adults could not understand. They stood there, small, waist high to an average adult.

"Come on now, you two, don't be blocking the corridor," Miss Gill remarked, although in a kindly way. Mary knew it was the end. Tommy and herself could hardly write to each other, not the thoughts and feelings like right now; there were all the complications of envelopes and addresses and getting the right stamps and going off to the pillarbox. Adults would interfere and mess it up and ruin their private compact. Mary could see that Tommy felt helpless too;

they were trapped. They limped into the big hall for singing lesson, where Miss Grownie thumped at the piano, with

> 'And brown-leaved fruit's a-turning red,
> In cloudless sunshine, overhead,
> With fruit for me, the apple tree
> do lean down low in Linden Lee.'

followed by

> 'D' y' ken Elsie Marley, honey,
> The girl who sells the barley, honey,
> Elsie Marley's grown so fine
> She won't get up to feed the swine
> But lies in bed till half-past nine,
> Lazy Elsie Marley,

and other remnants of the rustic past that still existed in Our National Song Book. Some of their grandparents would have lived out in the edge of the city and worked on farms and known the truth behind these songs; but their parents were now in factories and offices and the docks. Or at sea. Every Liverpool family had someone at sea, always someone away, expected back from the ether. The River Mersey pulled at each street, enticing menfolk away.

Items labelled 'White Star Line' furnished many a house with sheets, bed covers, glass-cloths, towels, pillowcases, cutlery and crockery all labelled with the same name. It was never disclosed how these items appeared throughout Liverpool, either through disposal sales or gradual pilfering.

In January 1946 Grandpa died. He had coughed seriously, loudly for several years and eventually gave up. Each time he came in from work at the convent, his coughing could be heard all the way up the lino-covered stairs and he would come into the upstairs living room and almost collapse on the first chair by the door in a fit of coughing, unable to speak.

As he grew worse, he was taken to the Hahnemann Hospital along Hope Street, it was near and convenient for visiting. There was more fuss about his dressing gown being burnt, something about it hanging on the back of a door and falling down, than his death. There were central fires in each of the wards, but this was exceptionally strange and Nannie and Julie expressed their grief by venting anger at the hospital. It was as if a new dressing gown, delivered to number eleven and wrapped in tissue paper would have solved all sorrows. The fuss Nannie, Julie and Vin made about this overshadowed his escape from life. Grandpa just disappeared.

His dedication to his wife was summed up in his humble will, written on two scraps of paper, full of love.

Important. 9/3/45

I am just recording here a few items of information in case of The Death of Rosa or Self.

In the hands of Mr T. Hurst, Solicitor, Dale Street, Liverpool are the deeds of a grave in Anfield R.C. Section, it is in the name of Mrs Barlow and Trevor Barlow, there are only Mrs Barlow and Trevor Barlow buried in it, so there should be room for four more.

Also there should in the event of my death a £10 benefit to come from the Plumbers' Operative Union, in the case of Rosa's death, £5. There are also the insurances which would become due from the Royal Liver Friendly Society. There is also a grant from the Knights of Saint Columba of £25 if I am in good standing.

If anything happens that I, George James Martineau should be called to God first, I wish all I have, and own in money, valuables and furniture should pass into the hands of my wife Rosa Maria Martineau for her use during her lifetime and for her to dispose of to her wishes. George James Martineau., 11 South Hunter Street.

Details of bank accounts and his Post Office savings bank followed. It was a touching document, showing the care and frugality he had followed to keep his family safe, trying to protect them for long after his death. The date showed the last ditch of the war – but he was not to know that. He was buried in Anfield, as he had wished, in the Roman Catholic Section 4, no 2014.

A swirl of adults, like a hurricane, appeared instead and Mary was lost somewhere in the midst of the hubub.

Nannie stomped around saying

"The convent killed your Grandfather. Too conscientious by half he was, too good by far." How the nuns had managed this was a mystery. She said it as though the nuns had all ganged up together and knifed him.

"Here," Daddy said, " Grandpa left you these." A ring of keys, all strange shapes and fitting no locks on any of the doors. There were some coins, the stub of a carpenter's pencil and a minute wooden box. It was a puzzle why he had left her these unconnected things and often she used to lay them out and look at them and try to guess why he had sent her these things. They were unlike Grandpa and yet they summed up his life. Al she could remember now was the way he used to kiss her, his moustache gritting into her skin and his kisses that tasted of salt. When no one was looking she used to wipe it away but she did not like to hurt him. That, she remembered, and his coughing. Nothing else. Sometimes he had given her lumps of putty to play with, to make small sculptures, but they always dried out and crumbled away a few days later. His plumber's certificates stayed hung up on the staircase walls, the family's pride in his qualifications even greater after his death.

Nannie went on as usual. Mary caught her crying once in the scullery. She had not known that old people could still cry, surely they had no feelings to spare, having experienced everything? She thought they did not mind things any more. And Nannie was such a good cook and was always so clean and her hair always in a neat coil -how could she cry?

"Nannie's crying in the kitchen," a puzzled Mary told Auntie Julie, who dashed into the little scullery and comforted her Mother.

"It would have been our ruby wedding anniversary this May if he had lived," she cried into a lavender-scented handkerchief. She said it didn't seem right without Dad, she just couldn't help it. He had let her down grievously. Auntie Julie was stern with her, then gentle and they were all very kind about Nannie for quite awhile. She went on making gorgeous soft yellow chips on the range in the living room corner where the fat was splattered all up the wallpaper. The only difference was that now she had a little less to do and could sit in the rocking chair earlier in the evenings by the fire with her big coral shawl round her. Her hands would be scrubbed white from the washing, wedding ring rubbed bright with wear into an almost white-gold, next to its plaited gold keeper-ring.

Nannie always kept her pinafore on except for Sunday afternoons and going out, which was rare these days, weekly Mass being the only time. There was a small ritual called *Letting the light go,* which paid respect to the remnants of the day. As she sat by the fire before lighting up the gaslight, her hands would twitch, or move on the arms of the chair as though she was still working. There had been so much to do all he life that there was little time to relax; because of this she had no training in rest, only in work. All the family was like that. They were proud of the way they worked, proud of their jobs. They did not seem too happy when there was nothing to do. Daddy would spend hours polishing his shoes or playing solitaire rather than do nothing.

The other Grandmother, Nana Sinnott, had meanwhile moved from a flat at the corner of Catherine Street and now lived at 3 St James's Road, almost directly opposite the Anglican Cathedral. It was like Buckingham Palace with all its rooms and the number of people living there was unclear. A large tiled vestibule held a carved coat-stand and there was a separate brass umbrella stand. Thick brown lino covered the long hall floor and the sitting-room had folded-back partition doors leading into the dining room. These two rooms were so big that couches and deep armchairs were easily scattered all round the space. The dining area had a walnut Victorian table and matching sideboard. Being less holy than Nannie, a tarantula stood proudly on the sideboard next to the mealtime-gong, with its three decanters and their silver labels of whisky, sherry and port.

Across from the St James's Road house was a little Greek temple right out of a history book, except, being in the centre of Liverpool, it was now ebony black with the soot from coal fires. From the house they could hear the clanking of chains from the hoists in the workyard behind the cathedral. When the wind rose it was like a ship's rigging being whipped, and the men could still be heard working on Saturday mornings.

"It's going to go on for years yet, they'll never get it finished while we're alive," Nana said. Some houses further along, nearer to the cathedral entrance, the two Misses Dornan ran a second-hand book business from their house. Stalls of books led along the approach to their front door and what had once been a front parlour was crammed with musty books from floor to ceiling. Ancient hard-backed novels were stacked on the shelves -

The Seven Streams by Warwick Deeping, Miss Fallowfield's Fortune by Ellen Thompson Fowler, Under the Iron Flail by John Oxenham, Poultry and Profit by William W. Broomhead, A Human Face by Silas K.Hocking – the absolutely necessary nestled against outdated fictional fripperies. Most were two pence and smelled of damp wood, mould and spice. Expensive books of engravings with tissue paper inserts were kept indoors – whenever it rained, one of the Misses Dornan had to dash out and hurl a tarpaulin over the tables until the shower stopped as abruptly as it started.

Mary was often invited to stay the weekend with her cousin, Lucy, who was also an only child. This Sunday they were both invited to Glynis's birthday party further along St James's Road. Mary had seen Glynis before as she wheeled a snotty baby in a smelly pram, doing the messages for her mum; Glynis had rat-tails' hair. She wore a dirty cream cardigan and the hem of her dress drooped here and there.

"You've got to go." Kay told Lucy."It will hurt her feelings if you don't. You've got Mary to take with you, you can come back early. I'll have to give you both a bath afterwards and check you for nits, though. Poor Glynis, we have to feel sorry for her." At the party in the dismal downstairs flat they sat and tried politely to eat a bit of what was offered, but both felt uncomfortable. The baby cried most of the time and little Jimmy, two years old had warts all over his hands. Glynis's mother shushed and hushed the baby until it all got out of hand and the two cousins said they had to go, almost running away, leaving their present of a doll's dress and pram coverlet, embroidered by Kay.

Back at number three, it was tea time, Kay brought a plate of bread and butter interleaved down the plate, with either square bottoms or rounded tops.

"Which side will you have, Catholic or Protestant?" Grown-up women could do clever things like cut these perfect slices of bread from any loaf. They could also do that juggler-like trick of drying saucers or plates by shuffling them front-to-back. They stood in the long narrow kitchen in St James' Road gossiping about private matters, women's talk, having to resort to schoolgirl French if Lucy or Mary were hanging about, listening. But later, when Mary won the scholarship to the High School and started to learn French, the system obviously broke down. Right now, however, Lucy was always ahead with social accomplishments, although she was a year younger, being able to strike matches and use the telephone, as though someone was giving her secret lessons. Mary was outfoxed completely.

This side of the family was intricate and never fully explained. Aunty Cappy, Nana's sister-in-law, white-haired, dentist's receptionist along Rodney Street, lived in the half-empty top floor. It was a proper flat, but had an eerily empty bedroom and a living room still semi-furnished Someone had died here, the adults never said who, perhaps it was Alice's husband, never mentioned or explained. Some binoculars had been left on the heavy Victorian table of the unused living room. Lucy and Mary looked out over the bombsite at the streets below and further towards the skyline. They thought it was a view of the Welsh Mountains through these high windows but later Mary found out it was really Birkenhead. Another room had a large circular mahogany table and set of chairs, like a museum. Aunty Cappy's part of this floor was locked and they never went there.

On the middle floor, Nana's youngest child, Tommy had a bedroom kept for him although he was usually on duty aboard the liners to New York as a steward. Jack Waller, part time taxi driver, wife Kay, barmaid, and their daughter Lucy all shared one bedroom. Other rooms on this floor were the gigantic square bathroom which

35

took up a great space. The separate mahogany-seated toilet along the landing was so grand that it had a reproduction of the Mona Lisa on the wall.

When Lucy stayed for a weekend she was both fascinated and wary of the big bath. Set like a drinking fountain in the wall, a lion's head brass tap gushed furiously and delivered unbelievably hot water. The two girls were tingling after getting out of the bath into the clear cold of the high-ceilinged room as Kay clasped a towel round them. It was so cold at times that their teeth could be chattering while their skin was still scalded with the hot water.

The youngest daughter Marie, a civil servant, probably used the box-room right over the front door and Alice Sinnott, Nana's widowed sister-in-law, had a large front bedroom. On the ground floor Nana herself had a bedroom in what had once been another large front sitting room.

Down in the front basement room was Alice's aged mother, Mrs McKenna, who had a small shop in Crump Street. As a treat, Lucy and Mary were taken there to visit and even to serve behind the counter. A special implement cut ice cream into the proper shape, and slapping a wafer top and bottom, and charging tuppence, they felt really grown-up, able to sell cigarettes too. Mrs McKenna sat in the shabby back room behind a curtain, like many small shopkeepers. Too old to keep her balance, she fell down the outside stone steps one night coming back from the pub. No one talked about it, but Mary was terrified looking through the railings and seeing splotches of blood on the steps. They never mentioned her again in front of the children. She was sent away somewhere, or perhaps had died, they never spoke of what had happened again. The next downpour washed away the traces of blood spatters. Adults kept too many secrets.

There was even a special wood room in the cellar, just for cutting wood. It was always locked. Mary's cousin Lucy showed her through the large keyhole. Benches, saws, nails in jars, a window. Only the men went in there - Uncle Jack, Uncle Tommy. Lucy never knew quite what they did in there. It seemed too big for firewood. On the other side of the long cellar hallway was the washing room, with its gigantic sink, two draining boards and drying racks hung from

36

the ceiling. Lucy and Mary would drive about on the toy car or a bicycle around the grey flagged floors while Aunty Kay worked at the sink and mangle.

From there, a steep flight of steps led down to the back garden which had a six-foot high wall. This side looked out onto overgrown dark privet bushes, always with their sick-sweet stink, the flowers to be avoided. Beyond them was the original outside toilet, built like a little temple. It looked foreign, as if dropped from a plane from Greece. Beside the rank hedge, steps downwards to the doorway into the back street, which did not strictly exist any more, now merely a cobbled line threading along a bomb site.

The Council had put a children's playground on the cinders – swings and a heavy wooden roundabout. Sparkles from broken glass, bombed-out houses, traces of old windows, shone in the gravel. In the night, drunks from the pub went on the swings. The laughter of the men and women playing around in the night carried up to the bedrooms,

"Gerroff. Gerroff der, lah!"

"Oh, oh, oh, go on then, gis us a push. Ha! Ha! Gerroff!"
Adults being children in the night. Mary used to lie awake, top to toe in Lucy's bed, staying over the weekend, listening in the dark.

"Tara, der."

"Tara."

"G'night." When they had gone, corrugated iron in the garage workshops further along flapped desolately now and then in the wind and an uneasy guard dog barked at infinitesimal sounds. The mounds of scrap cars creaked from time to time.

The bedroom curtains had a pattern of Tudor hunting groups, which, as they moved in summer evenings when the window was open , gave the impression of the hunters going off on the chase. Mary lay in bed watching these changes, before drifting to sleep. Later she was woken by Jack and Kay coming in and putting on the light. She could see Kay wore a glamorous black nightdress and hear Jack laughing as they got into bed.

Then she fell into a deep sleep, but about this time, Lucy would always wet the bed. At first it was warm and Mary could shift her legs out of the way. Then, in the small hours it got icy cold and she had no sleep. Sometimes, deep in dreams, she missed the first warm part and woke to find herself stranded in icy water. The middle of the mattress formed a valley and she clung to the firmer edges, but kept falling back into the gully. The mattress had blue stains, widening through the year. The middle went brown. Then they must have thrown it away because the next one did not have the valley in the middle where the puddle had always collected.

These weekends, Mary enjoyed exploring the house. As well as the large print of Mona Lisa alongside the mahogany toilet bench, Beatrice d' Este, delicate and supercilious, was halfway up the stairs. Each part of the three-storey house was a subtle mix of the opulent and the shabby.

It was absolutely Liberty Hall. The girls played trains, sitting on the bottom shelf of the food trolley, and slid down the bannister or tobogganed down the stairs on trays with cousin Tom who was a year younger. Their ages went down in steps too. No one stopped them. They made rude phone calls on Saturday mornings. Lucy had found an unfortunate man's phone number. She taught Mary how to dial a number. Mary dutifully phoned,

"Are you Smellie? Then what are you going to do about it?" He would start to splutter, to protest, but they had had their reward and gulped suffocating laughter, running away down the brown-lino hall. They also rang up the Chinese laundry in Berry Street and complained about their Father's shirts not being ready yet, all five of them. When the poor man tried to make sense of it, searching dockets and labels, they chanted,

"Wishee washee Chinaman, washed his mother's shirt" and giggled merrily at the perplexed laundryman. Once, an operator came on the line, telling them off, thrilling them with the danger. A hand coming out of the sky. It was the first phone number Mary knew - *Royal 3089.* The adults in the house did not notice or mind all these goings-on. Things were different here. They also played at Post Offices, using the fireguard as the counter barrier, and imitation money from Christmas games.

Uncle Jack came and went in irregular snatches. Handsome as a film star, he seemed to have strayed off a dance-hall into everyday life.

"He gets a lot of money now and then. But it's not regular, like your Father's," explained Mummy. "That's why Aunty Kay has to go out to work at *The Swan.*" It looked like an extremely good arrangement – a tall-dark-and-handsome easygoing man could be got by Kay working as a barmaid. Mary looked at her Mother and realised it could not work in their house. She could not do it. Father would not allow it. Uncle Jack had a matey, conspiratorial air. The deep black eyes treated Mary as an equal. She saw him, one evening very drunk, climbing up the stairs on all fours. He looked back at her over his shoulder. Beatrice d' Este looked on from her frame.

"Best way, I highly recommend it." Mary agreed. There was something in him she understood. He was not a real adult. One weekend there was a fuss, the women dashing from room to room. When things were important, they spoke pidgin French in front of the children. Whatever it was, was frightening. Uncle Jack was suddenly at home and not going out at all, nor answering the door. His hand was bandaged. Don't ask. A touch of the flu.

Mary wandered into the long narrow kitchen. No one else around. It was such a big house that the public and the secret mixed, lived aside, blending or hiding in other rooms. Him and her together. He was bathing his left hand, peeling off yards of stained bandages over a little bowl of water, a blue Dettol bottle nearby. He looked at her and smiled. The two smallest fingers were mashed red, held together awkwardly.

"I've shot myself. The gun just went off when I didn't mean it to. Butterfingers." They had tried so hard to keep it secret, and here he was, telling it all to her alone. He grinned at her again, then gave a slight wince as the Dettol stung his hand. It might have been the truth. Or he could have caught his fingers in a taxi door. She would not tell anyone she knew. Not even Lucy. This was a privilege, that he should be confiding in her like this. She also realised that he would probably be the secret to how Lucy knew how to do mischievous things.

The two grandmothers, Martineau and Sinnott, were like bookends at opposite ends of the family. Although there had never been any battle declared, Mary could not remember ever seeing them in the same room together. It was as if they would have had nothing to say to each other; such a conversation was impossible to imagine They did not visit each other but worked through intermediaries. They must have combined in the past when they both had to look after her as a youngster. Nana Sinnott was always smartly dressed in black, usually a black skirt and cardigan, giving the impression of a suit, with a cream blouse. Her white hair was set in a neat roll round her head, and she always wore pearl drop earrings and usually smelt faintly of 4711 eau de cologne.

Nannie Martineau was likely to have a similar outfit, but favoured navy blue, with a wrap-around flowered apron and a coral-coloured fringed shawl in the cold weather. She always wore a three-stone amethyst brooch at her throat and wedding ring with a massive plaited gold keeper ring with it. No earrings, just sleepers which hardly counted as jewellery. Her grey hair was in a bun at the nape of her neck and she was smaller and fatter than Nana Sinnott.

They both had rocking chairs; Nannie's was dark and bulky and creaked, while Nana's was more stylish, black carved wood and dark tapestry upholstery. Mary could work up a dashing speed on Nannie's one, but Nana's rocking chair was both more elegant and usually occupied

Both grandmothers had taken care of her at different times.

"Nannie couldn't cope with washing the nappies after a while, they had to be done by hand and took ages to dry, after all, in that house, so you were sent to Nana instead," Aunty Kay told Mary years later.

She did have a distinct memory of a brown lino floor in an upstairs flat at the corner of Catherine Street. A big, lumpy chintz sofa and Aunty Julie sitting in an easy chair talking to Nana and handing her over - for how long? No one said. She was concentrating on playing with a toy at the edge of the carpet while the adults talked, Nana sitting on the sofa and Aunty Julie explaining something. Mary would be staying here for a time.

There was no trace of any of this and she could not drag it up now, they would not want to talk about it.

As a remnant of the war, Vin still had an allotment, shared with Andy Parkes from the office. It was conveniently at the side of Greenbank Park, on the 73 bus route and until the emergency was over, they had a spread of vegetables and fruit to eke out the week's Rations. On a Saturday afternoon it made a cheap day out, with sandwiches and a flask of tea and sometimes a bottle of Tizer for Mary and Lucy if she was joining in. An afternoon picking redcurrant or raspberries was a child's heaven.

"Careful, you'll be getting the collywobbles if you eat too much of those raspberries," Celi warned. They collected carrots, potatoes, beetroot, cabbage, all a way of stretching out the Rations. Uncle Jack would collect Lucy, but they always got the73 bus back home,laden with the heaps of vegetables and fruit.

Upstairs on the crowded early Saturday evening bus, Vin, Celi and Mary collapsed on the seats, bits of veg and soil falling out of their over-stuffed bags. The rest of the passengers were young people setting out for a glamorous Saturday night, dancing at Reece's or going to the pictures at the Forum, the Scala or the Futurist. Girls wore their newest dresses, hair coaxed out of curlers at last (some, still worried something would get out of place, had a chiffon scarf protecting the arrangement until the last minute.) Perfumes battled against each other and against the smell of the lads' brilliantine. Clean shirt, polished shoes, best suits, they matched the girls in hope and smartness.

The family sat in the midst of all this glamour, their hands covered in soil and with black fingernails, wisps of roots spilling out onto the floor. They had strayed into a romantic world where they did not belong.

Back home the dog greeted them wildly and they could wash the imitation countryside off their hands.

Exploring the cupboards in the St James's Road house, Mary found a statue of Our Lady that was the same as the one which was crownedin St Philip Neri's each May. It was like hugging an altar.

"I wonder if they would let me have this," Mary asked.

Lucy was not interested,

"Ask Nana."

"Nana, could I have the statue, you know, the Our Lady of Lourdes. She's up in the box-room cupboard."

"Oh, that." Nana considered implications Mary was not aware of. Then she shrugged and patted her hand, "Well, if it makes you happy. It's doing nothing up there. We 'll have to see what your mother says, though."

Celi was not too enthusiastic, but seeing how eager Mary was, said it was OK as long as they could return it if the idea did not work out. It was heavy and her arms began to hurt, Mary hugged it for as long as she could along Rodney Street, with Celi taking over when they crossed the main road. It was so important, it was fun and exciting and right. It was also rather large. Father snorted at the rubbish it represented. Any moment soon, it could be taken back to St James's Road. It wouldn't last long.

Nana's side were no longer really proper Catholics who went to weekly Mass. It was something to do with a row at a christening. They were always kindly, tolerant and, rather like Labradors, would have been good to breed from. Nana had the gift of blending people and of accepting more and more relations into her house. While three St James's Road had several spare rooms and floors and the residents were happily scattered about , it functioned well.

Each May the church erupted into a feast of flowers with the Crowning of Our Lady as a centrepiece. The life-sized posh statue of Our Lady in St. Phillip Neri's was dressed in pure white with just a hint of light blue in the sash round the waist, which fell in two folds down to the bare feet. Here and there it was picked out in gold – the edges of the veil, the hem of the dress and the rosary which hung from the hands folded in prayer. This side altar was decked out in as many flowers as could be crowded around it, all the flowers of May, as the hymn went,

Bring flowers of the rarest, bring flowers of the fairest,
From garden and woodland and hillside and dale ...
O Mary we crown thee with blossoms today,
Queen of the Angels and Queen of the May.
The statue of the Sacred Heart on the opposite side of the church
was neglected in comparison, but he (they were, in spite of being
apparently a matching pair of thirty-year olds supposed to be a
Mother and Son) would have his turn in June, when the church
exploded with a wall of flowers in the Exposition and Perpetual
Adoration. The monstrance, containing a consecrated host would
be placed centre of the altar and prayers would be said for three days
and nights, with parishioners volunteering to watch throughout each
hour. Luckily Father Garvin knew someone who worked for the
Parks and Gardens Committee and a lavish arrangement of
hydrangeas and ferns mixed with roses and gladioli would make an
absolute cascade of flowers right across the sanctuary.

The best-behaved and prettiest schoolgirl, who also usually
had parents who were well-off, was chosen by the school to crown
Our Lady in May. The school crowded into church, all in white
dresses and veils – even the boys were wearing short white trousers.

The chosen girl wore a long dress and blue cloak, plus a
crown herself; and wearing all this finery she would have to climb
a special set of stairs set behind Our Lady's altar and place a circlet
of gold on the statue.

Last year the family did not have enough money or
clothing coupons to get proper white material for Mary's home-
made dress and it had to be made from surplus curtain material.
That was bad enough, except that there were small polka dots of
blue embroidered all over it, which the girls sitting in the same
bench giggled about all through the sermon.

All this came back vividly from the previous year. Now
she had her own Our Lady and could crown her whenever she
wanted to. On Saturday afternoon when Father was in the pub and
Mother had gone round the corner for the potatoes and the week's
joint, Mary rushed up to the bathroom.

Luckily there was still some warm water left in the taps. Mary
stood the dirty statue in the bath. Little bubbles spurted out as the

chalk rapidly soaked in the water. With the nail-brush and Imperial Leather soap, Mary began to wash the statue. The dirt streamed down, the colours coming slowly out of the mist.

Touches of gold appeared at the edges of veil and gown. How could they have neglected her like this? Nana must be really rich to have such things as this in cupboards. She kept a trunk full of unsold brand-new toys in her bedroom after all, the remains of her last husband, Pop Sinnott's business deals.

The three foot high Our Lady looked out at her over the side of the bath, her feet in a swirl of muddy water. Mary could be as near as this, much nearer than the girls chosen each year to mount the little ladder and place a golden crown on her head. They only saw her head; Mary was face to face with her now. Dirt was encrusted in the dimples by her mouth, in the folds of the cloth. Here and there the paint flaked off and an audible *dot dot dot dot* showed where the water was entering the plaster and the air was still bubbling out. Back from the shopping, Mother brought out some old cloths to dry the statue, not very enthusiastic but supporting Mary's mood.

Lugging her down to the yard, to the amazement of the dog, Mary stood the statue in the sunshine to dry. It had to be admitted that she was going to remain a blue-grey colour and her gold had faded to a light brown in places. Further washing would only encourage more paint to flake off. More ominous bubbling sounds came from fissures in the chalk as the water and sunshine conflicted. The dog sniffed cautiously.

But this was definitely the same statue that was crowned with the gold and diamanté crown each May, and she carried it up the steep back stairs to her bedroom altar, made from Nannie's trousseau trunk, which still had the carrier's label from Barnet. She moved the Holy Child of Prague, who was much smaller, onto the mantelpiece next to the pottery rabbits and squirrels.

Out in the streets, the month of May affected other children too. Children dressed up in long clothes, girls in veils and carrying bunches of flowers walked through the streets just before sunset. They used old curtains as cloaks and wearing their mother's tottery high heels, they clattered along South Hunter Street. Young boys acted as train-bearers and other attendants had a collecting tin for pennies. These haphazard mini -processions came from past Hardman Street, probably from Pilgrim Street, as they were complete strangers and were never seen the rest of the year.

7

They were being prepared in Religious lessons for their First Holy Communion, which of course had to be preceded by a First Confession, which was a profound moment for her. The class had been instructed to go through their entire life so far, all seven years of it.

"Think of everything you do at home or at school,anything naughty, have you ever told lies or not said your prayers or been disobedient, answering back, anything that meant you had turned away from God. This is your chance to confess anything bad you have done." Mary went through her limited options. There were no sins to tell, only a vague grey mist with nothing special. No sins that had a shape. She would have to make something up in order to qualify, a proper sin.

So in the dark little confessional booth in St Philip Neri's, going in after Billy Grogan, who came out giggling, she knelt in the special place and told the priest

"This is my first confession. I stole a sixpence." The priest lifted up the little curtain that separated them. Now she could see his grumpy face clearly through the wire mesh between them, complete with its curtain on his side. This was a complete breaking of the rules as they had learned them. The confessional was secret; that was its basic worth, you were confessing to God through the agency of his priest, they had been told this time after time for at least the last six months.

Adults did not obey the rules, however keenly a child tried to keep doing the right thing. They wanted sins; she had supplied a reasonable one and now he was cross and was looking right at her with his lumpy face. He looked angry and told her off, this was no way to carry on and she had to pay the money back immediately, or save it out of her pocket money week by week.

"One Hail Mary and never do it again. Now, the Act of Contrition." Weeks of careful preparation gave the words up easily. Jesus on the crucifix beside her looked on in his kindly way even though he was left there, dying in agony for all their sins. He might have been her friend and stopped all this.

The class walked back in twos along Blackburne Place past the presbytery and along Hope Street to school, ready for First Holy Communion. Their souls were glowing with cleanliness inside them, perfect and new.

First Holy Communion. The happiest day of your life. The front room is the largest room with all shades of green, the carpet and the Bergère suite almost a matching light green. They've brought a mirror in here and the dress is almost finished. There's extra material lying on the side of the armchair and the sewing machine has been brought in from next door. It's always kept on the other sideboard on Nannie's landing next-door, between the two antique tea-caddies and the red collection box for the African Missionaries.

The dog has come in to nuzzle against me, just to join in and reassure me. They are talking about picot edging and how much it is a yard. The cars outside in the street bang about as the garage boys mend them on the cobbles. Blakes Garage uses the street as its work yard, Father's always angry about it.

Very strange to be wearing all white, it'll get dirty in no time. The room smells a bit stale, it's only used at Christmas and the furniture's all heavy and dark. I hate that big oak table with the Jacobean bulbous legs. The sideboard Mummy bought is much nicer with Queen Anne legs, much more graceful, like the little chest of drawers over there, full of secrets. The bell's going for the Angelus, so it's time for dinner, they'll put the radio on soon for the dinnertime news. It's rabbit stew because it's Tuesday, the smell doesn't reach here, it's too far from the back kitchen.

Everything is suddenly important, standing in the sitting room dressed in white, the tacking stitches still in. Picot edging for the frill, bits of material had to be sent away to be done specially. Auntie Julie has been fussing about for days, as our authority on needlework. Although Mummy is the mainstay, she talks less, it is her sister-in -law who fusses and discusses and wonders.

Should it be George Henry Lee's or Blacklers? She has bought some good thread from T.J.Hughes and the best mother-of-pearl buttons are provided from Nannie's dressing-table drawer. By putting lots of bitty questions she has obliquely taken over. Mummy always has cooking and shopping and washing and dusting to do. The soot motes are everywhere, every day. They are on every window ledge. I can tell Mummy and Auntie are both happy, though . I have to turn away from some of Auntie Julie's questions and try to restore some say-so to my mother. Nannie wanders through, approving, disapproving. I am like a building being made by them, they discuss the outside and I am the inside.

Saturday morning and it is the great day at last. Mummy put a blackboard at the end of my bed last night with a NO EATS message chalked on it, to remind me not to eat anything. You can swallow a bit of water while brushing your teeth, but the consecrated Host needs a pure and empty stomach. You should be fasting from midnight onwards if you want to go to communion.

Just walking into here and looking at it all,everything is white, except for the black patent leather shoes, clothes laid out on the settee, the dress, petticoat, vest, socks, pants, white gloves, veil and even a new white plastic covered prayerbook. I've never had new clothes all together at once before. Perhaps all of life is going to be like this from now on, apart from having to give the buttons back to Auntie Julie. I can't work out why she is so important, why Mummy is just that bit further in the background, always worried and always just that bit not there. Auntie Julie is kind, they always say that, but sometimes like now, she is too near, like a fire that's too hot , and I wonder why.

I don't mind that they all gather round me, but why does she make so much fuss about the veiling and the belt? Why are these things important to her, but not to me nor my mother? If Nannie asks me one more question I shall start not answering at all. I can't tell lies so near to Holy Communion and it's wrong to be feeling this angry , but I do wish Auntie Julie would stop fussing around and go off and do something else. She's always changing things slightly and then changing them back again.

"Now let me see, no,no, now perhaps...Now turn around." Mummy and I make a face behind her back. I wonder if that is a sin. She used to put the pins in her mouth like a proper dressmaker. That was very brave and very silly. What would we have done if someone knocked on the front door and startled her and she swallowed them all in one gulp? She wanted the dress ironing again and the fire's not hot enough yet. We've got to be careful because the sides of the iron can shed rust on things. What will this dress be used for afterwards? I don't go to parties. It'll do for the May procession, we can let the hem down too. At least she won't be able to carry on like this next year.

The wreath, of course, to keep the veil from blowing away, it's over on the sideboard. Lots of white flowers and even white leaves. I wonder where they got it from. White ribbons for my hair. Mummy is brushing it specially now and tying it in two bunches. Perhaps I'll wear the ribbons to school. Auntie Julie has started some long rigmarole about her planned summer holiday this year. Mummy is fed up. I can hear it in her voice. We know that Auntie Julie can't be stopped – she has to come to a natural end.

Mummy is peeling carrots and I am standing in the big dark-green kitchen and I shouldn't be, all dressed in white like this. Auntie Julie should go home and get ready for the service, leaving us together. We talk together without talking and we need time alone to do that. That is why Mummy is in the background and Auntie Julie is at the front, gassing, as Father calls it.

She is always giving things to us, every week something, she must be well off, not like Mummy, who is wearing a grey cardigan and a pinny, not in her proper clothes yet for going to church. They have made me different, all white like this, it doesn't seem to have anything to do with carrots or housework. Auntie Julie doesn't seem to do any cooking really, Nannie does it. Perhaps that is the difference. They both love me, but in different ways. It is nearly time to go now. I am beginning to feel hungry and excited. She will walk up to St Philip Neri's later with Nannie. I don't know where Daddy will be. He is always somewhere else. At work.

48

The consecrated Hosts were the true Body of Christ. The children knelt at the marble altar rails and the priest, with practised ease, dispensed the small papery wafers right onto their tongues from the heaped wafers kept in the gold chalice. An altar-boy held a gold paten under their chin, in case anyone dropped a sacred Host. The priest repeated the same words for each one "The Body of Christ, The Body of Christ," all along the row. Jesus was in them and with them now, inside their very bodily fabric. Now they had been accepted into the sacrament they could come here to morning Mass every day if they wanted to and receive the Body of Christ, becoming more and more near to God.

After a drink of milk and a biscuit in the church house next-door, to break heir fast, they walked down to the convent grounds for a group photograph to be taken with Father Garvin, who inexplicably gave each communicant a lucky threepennny bit. They did not need luck, surely, they had God right now.

The worst winter ever. Going down Leece Street to Thompson's with Mother where they were registered for the rations, it was difficult to see over the mounds of snow that the clearing-men had dug off the pavements. Here and there they had left a gap in the piled-up white walls, so that people could cross the road. At the top, Hardman Street was almost cleared by now, though it was slippery walking down the hill.

All night the sound of spades scraping the pavements and roads carried up the streets. Mary could hear them as she lay in bed, hot-water bottle not helping the itching chilblains. The men, rounded up from Leece Street employment exchange, wore thick dirty greatcoats with mittens or mismatched gloves. Some had string round the waist in place of a belt. They all looked fierce and old, unlike the men who loitered outside Windsor Street Library coughing and spitting, who were also unemployed or perhaps old-age pensioners. When possible, they went into the reference section and read the day's papers for nothing, but the librarian kept an eye on them and did not let them sleep or stay indoors all day. Old women stayed at home, except for doing the shopping.

Auntie Julie came in with a recipe from *Home Notes* magazine for making coal briquettes to eke out the fuel. It was a mixture of four parts of coal dust and one part of cement powder rolled in the hand to an egg-shape and left to dry out.

"You have to put them on top of a burning fire, as they burn very slowly. They don't do much, but they'll keep it going." That was as much as they hoped for, to keep any sign of fire alive. The day's cinders were raked over too and any unused bits made the basis for the next day's fire. The criss-cross of firewood sticks were arranged in a wigwam shape over the screwed-up bunches of newspaper; it was a skill. Mother's hands were hard and crackled as if an invisible layer had coarsened with all this housework. The textures and dirt made the back of her hands chapped every winter, with Easter as the demarcation line of healing. No creams could cure it; like chilblains, the raw-red effects magically disappeared about the time of Holy Week, to reappear in November.

They set-to with a bucket and shovel in the back yard and produced a dark mixture, but Celi drew the line at hand-rolling cement and coal-dust and poured the mixture instead into a collection of tins saved from the rubbish. It was a month before the next coal delivery could be ordered. Mary did not know how these things were arranged; occasionally they walked up to the depot in Crown Street, a small office surrounded by heaps of coal and lorries backing into the yards. It was near the railway lines for deliveries and was the equivalent of the edge of the known world, past Myrtle Gardens. Looking up at that barrack-like frontage, some windows glowed with a red geranium set in a polished brass pot proudly on their window cill between ice-white net curtains. Others hid from the light with neglected dirty and torn curtains and in one case, a broken pane stuffed with brown paper.

Once, from the docks, Father brought home some 'knock-off', a couple of tins of ham in their distinctive oval-shaped tins. Celi and he were scared stiff of being found out and prosecuted or fined. The tins were prised apart with a tin-opener, then those pieces bashed with a hammer and then carefully put into the fire for several days, until all identifying marks were burnt off. Then Celi dropped one piece into the rubbish each week, carefully messing it up with remains of sloppy cabbage or mouldy potatoes. The salvage men could easily see what each family's rubbish contained as they lifted the stuff into the cart and tipped it out.

The salvage men were benevolent giants, and often Mother would take Mary out to feed the carthorse with the crust of a loaf. One of the men would lift her up and show her how to spread her fingers out of the way as the horse, with impeccable delicacy, managed to eat all the bread without chewing her fingers. Both man and beast were larger than life, yet both had this grace and underlying gentleness. He lifted her back onto the ground and became the ordinary rubbish-man again, wrapped in a thick dirty overcoat covered with a sacking apron.

At other times, Celi would throw mouldy blue-mottled bread scraps onto the fire with the plaint,

"God bless the bread," and she always added "There's starving Europe to think of, some poor children would have been glad even of that." Mary could not see the connection and thought it more likely that the bread would have poisoned the starving children. That was what war did; it messed ideas up completely.

There were many economies to make that women swapped tips about. These were housekeeping matters of life and death. Mary went with her Mother up to Aunty Frances on the tram to Penny Lane to exchange some more magazines and recipes. This time the two sisters discussed how to make pillowcases out of old flour bags. They were in the back kitchen in Berbice Road.

"It's all right, you know," Frances stretched it out, with obvious distaste, trying to encourage Celi, "The worst of the label washes out about the second time." The imprint *McDougall's plain Flour, One Stone, New Mills, Hartington Street* showed up clearly. Mother still looked at it doubtfully; things were this bad. She still had the wedding-present bedlinen from nine years ago, perhaps they would last out a bit longer. They swapped recipes for fish cakes – main ingredient, mashed potatoes.

With any luck there would be some knitting wool or American magazines to take home. These would be, via Nana's, off the ships, fresh from America itself, unlike the supply from Killip's fishmongers or Rosie's antique shop. Uncle Tommy was a steward on board liners between New York, where he gleaned Saturday Evening Post, Life, McCalls and the odd New Yorker magazine. Tanned people opened fridges as large as wardrobes and stood, smiling, leaning triumphantly against the open door. Not only did they possess the fridge, an achievement in itself, but they also owned all the piled-up food inside. Even the doors had to have little shelves to carry all the extra bottles, eggs and butter.

Other photos showed white colonnaded Southern mansions, styled on *Gone with the Wind,* black maids in starched caps and aprons, cars which stretched across two pages and salads larger and brighter than real life. Everyone, in every picture, had perfect white teeth. The black men holding open car doors or sometimes driving as chauffeurs also had perfect teeth. They stood in front of double garages and beside private swimming pools. People ate ice creams as big as their face and drank either whisky or orange juice without care. These magazines and the films at the Rialto told us clearly how good America was. We in Europe had failed miserably. If there had been no war, First or Second, we might have achieved the same milk-and-honey glamour. The Americans went on smiling, in glossy full-colour three-page spreads.

Celi and Mary went to the pictures on Friday or Saturday nights. As they went to Confession and the library roughly every fortnight, they went to the pictures fortnightly too. The marble steps of the Rialto were apron shaped, curving round the side of Upper Parliament Street. However early they went there was always a queue. They were ruled by a commissionaire dressed in a maroon uniform, with frogging and tassels and a peaked cap. Some even carried folded white gloves stuck through their epaulettes, a throwback to their army career. They herded the queue against the wall. It was usually raining. Just to get as far as the lowest curved step began the experience of luxury. The posters outside that they had been crammed up against, were crude painted images from the week's film; inside, large framed sepia photographs of the stars, sincerely autographed, smiled at them all seductively.

After being allowed to buy tickets from the tiny box-office, they were handed on to one of the usherettes, also in a maroon outfit. The hold-up outside might well have been caused by the cashier's knitting; they all knitted – in the Forum, the Scala, the Palais de Luxe, the Futurist – even at the Abbey and here in the Rialto. Cashiers were all elderly women with bright dyed hair, were all slightly peeved, as though it was not their proper job; they had been trapped in the little kiosk by accident and locked in like a fairytale princess; and they had to knit jumpers and thick woolly socks for an entire family as well as deal with tickets.

The foyer walls were maroon too, thick flock wallpaper, with panelling tricked out in gold. The carpet had whorls of red, crimson, magenta, maroon. Chandeliers hung everywhere, of all sizes, down to the smallest possible. An usherette beckoned and led them to specific seats, pointing them out with her massive torch. For the next two hours or so the audience was rapt in the coloured diversions fed to them, though the Pathé News was black and white. By the time they had sunk into a stupor, it was time for the King and most people stood to attention for the National Anthem before everyone straggled out from the warmth and luxury into the black wet streets. Real life. If Celi and Mary had gone as far as the Smithdown Road Picture Playhouse, they would huddle in the bad weather waiting for the tram back into town, minds still in Arizona or Chicago, men whistling bits of the tunes.

Looking at her reflection in the tram windows, with the rain varnishing the black pavements it seemed that all the fun in the world, all the sunlight, had been collected into the films. As they both got off the tram at the Philharmonic, two women in fur coats turned to look at the descending passengers. The light from the tram hit their earrings, scintillating in the dark as they sheltered in a doorway.

"Rhinestones," explained Mother. "And they're not interested in classical music. They're prostitutes," – said mildly. From wide reading of the Echo and Nannie's Sunday Dispatch, Mary knew what prostitutes were. As they were both on the same shift, as it were, they became on nodding terms.

"Night, dearie," in their professional voice -

"Good night," acknowledged by Mother. Whiff of their scent, powerful, and their chatting, one going further out of the pavement to look out for a man. Glamorous, confident women. Mother broke rules. She was also on nodding terms with a peroxide blonde they called Mrs Darling. Either a retired prostitute or now on part-time, she wore loud colours, a leopardskin coat and extra-red lipstick.

"Hello darling!" she would yell across Rodney Street. It was easier to be friendly with her than to ignore her, with her high-heeled swagger,the waft of cigarette smoke and the gravelly voice.

Another boundary crossed was after Mass at the Pro-Cathedral on Hawke Street, when they trooped across after the Last Gospel and right into the Jewish bakery on Brownlow Hill. Even some of the shawlies,with their sovereign earrings, rosary beads rattling, the most devout of women, went in, on the lookout for stale rolls. It was a subtle blend of shifts and balances; the bakery was really open for the rich Jews who were supposed to motor in from the suburbs, like Childwall. Now and again it did happen and a blonde-dyed woman with real diamonds and an expensive camel-hair coat would be standing, embarrassed, in the queue. They exchanged news.

The Jewish men were better-looking than their disdainful womenfolk. Mary stared and stared at them. The golden, sallow skin, the dark contemplating eyes. Proud, unstupid, they brought a dignity to making bread. Scrubbed wooden plank floor, trays of buns fresh from the bakery at the back, floury dust over all. Spice smell and strange goods on the shelves. One of the sons, bored, entered the shop with a large wooden tray of fresh bagels. His cheekbones formed carved sides to his face. He glanced at her. He was the image of Jesus. The bakers knew where the queue had come from, prayer-books in hand. A couple of bagels or poppy bread for their breakfast, totally unnecessary as they lived so near to Kirkland's –Mother went there for something else.

Co-op number thirteen twenty-three double oh, chanted every week at the Co-op butchers and the Co-op store up in Myrtle Street. The divi paid for pyjamas and nightdresses each year. Then Celi continued up to the Maypole Dairy, the International Stores and

M & Bs, - Myrtle Street was scattered with these competing grocery stores. The black-painted Post Office at the corner of Chatham Street sold blocks of paint set in bottle-caps in the window, a sign of how the economy was still at risk and Mary always tried to steer her mother towards it. Magic painting books also were a temptation.

After school, the children trooped into Kirkland Jennings *(Vienna Baker)* and bought yesterday's cobs for a ha'penny. There were stale cakes too that had been reduced in price. There was still rationing and bread was still on Bread Units. One day there was a notice in the cake-shop window saying "No BUS" meaning that the bread was no longer on coupons and everyone thought there was no buses, though luckily there were trams to choose from. The three schools all came out at four o'clock and crowded onto buses on both Mount Pleasant and Hardman Street, going off to the suburbs. The poorer girls walked back home into town or thereabouts.

On fine spring evenings the year's playing-out started with twirling round a lamppost outside the school gate with a rope. It was spontaneous, no one organised it; it just happened. The gardener's boys took it home with them, or the Morans. In the winter, the gardener's children could get them into the playground, to play in undisturbed snow over a weekend.

8

Mary had to continue sleeping in her parents' bedroom until age eight – the wallpaper in her own bedroom was peeling off with damp, it was too cold to sleep in. Anything left in the cupboard set into the fireplace alcove went mouldy and had to be dusted off now and then. Moths appeared too. All the books hidden inside the wooden trunk (Grandpa's building books, especially one giving all the steps needed to build a nineteenth century house) had little white mites running through them. Our Lady's statue reigned alone there until springtime, meanwhile Mary's bed was stuck between the tallboy and a cupboard door in her parents' room.

When they came to bed later, the gaslight was put on, which woke Mary up. The greenish light forced its way into her sleep and sounds were louder than in the day. He went on talking and talking. It was total nonsense. The light went on, grinding into her eyes while she pretended to stay asleep.

Mary felt sick. Terrible. She had to call out. Mummy got out of bed. The lino was covered with bits of raw onion rings as she hawked it up. There was always a bowl of onion rings in vinegar left in the sideboard. They did not stop her eating them, she did not understand why. The light was dancing round and she was strapped to a big wheel that fell downwards. The rattle of the mop and the mop bucket. It is all over. He is cross,

"Let's get some sleep!"

There were also hunger pains, gurgling and weaving round the innards. Growing pains came later - long narrow pains down the leg bones.

Sore throat. That far away feeling again. Doctor Bligh's eyes are brightest blue, like something in a jeweller's window. He is big and lumbering, he fills up the bedroom doorway. I could hug him, but he does not know this. He is more posh than we are; he is a justice of the peace. When he calls, he is given a bowl of warm water and a small huckaback towel, a visitor's towel, to dry his hands. They pay him money, it's larger silver coins, probably five or eight shillings, and talk to him down in the hall. He blames all illnesses on tinned food and the Government in equal proportions. Quite deaf, he looks far into you and smiles, crinkles round his eyes.

In one of these illnesses I tell him why I am crying. I am depressed, he says,

"Why?"

"Because of my Father. I am frightened of him." He writes this down in my notes and seventeen years later, left in a London waiting room with my medical notes, I read his careful Victorian writing, recording that precise instant. Help would have been that near; a hairsbreadth. The date is 1947.

An ambulance appeared. Cheerful stocky men lifted me down the stairs. Nice fluffy red blanket. Mother worried, collecting

things. Driving through the Liverpool streets, really close to people and their not being able to see through the black glass windows. Smiling at them as they stood to cross the road, but they were not able to see me. Magic. I am invisible AND sick. Mother is worried, I cannot tell her not to worry, because I am very busy here and I have things to do. Lots of red sparks and a large, loud tune playing beneath.

Netherfield Road. Isolation Hospital. Nurses in white aprons, iron bedsteads, large fire in a green-tiled central pillar. Something yellow and gritty to eat. Brimstone and treacle? Wasn't that for wicked people in the Bible? Probably to make us go to the toilet. Eleven other girls. They are all rough.

The nurses do our hair every morning and put new bows on. Grapes appear, sent by my Mother, I can't eat them. Colouring books. Fruit. Coloured pencils. Never see her. See no one. Days, three days. Now it is a week. They have visitors. No one here, everything is gone. I have slipped through space. A nurse is explaining, as if I am very stupid, that the coloured ribbons and the toys meant for me have been given out to all the other girls on the ward.

"You have been sent too many things, you see, and they don't have as much." I cry and look with hatred round the ward. Why don't their parents bother? Every girl is wearing ribbons that my Mother had sent, they had torn apart her love that was for me, and they were playing with toys and puzzles that were really my belongings. A great sadness. Everything taken away and spread out without trace.

Each day she had taken two different trams to get to Netherfield Road and had left the little parcels at the patients' entrance. Not allowed in. All that useless travelling to and fro, taking up all her time in the cold weather. Love. But it was not able to get through the walls nor stop the nurses interfering, as though Celi could not arrange it properly. Flowers. Letters from classmates, they liked me. Cards.

The tough girls got up at night and played hide and seek in the ward, under beds, behind curtains. They kept the rest of us awake. Amazed at their devil-may-care fooling about, I sat up and

57

laughed for the first time. The night-duty nurse stormed in and took away the pillows of all those taking part, including those merely sitting up in bed.

"Then we shall know in the morning exactly who you are and what things you get up to. You are all deeply in trouble." This was unfair in a hospital - it was also difficult to sleep without a pillow, very hard, the mattress creaked. We were supposed to be ill, how could she take away our pillows? A veiled hostility was the main method of running the hospital. Every morning we were woken early, to be sat up for Matron's rounds. A stern woman with black wire-framed spectacles, wearing a navy cloak even though it was warm, she reviewed us all as though we were soldiers. Unless you were extremely ill you had to be awake and clean and sitting right up. Lots of medical people came round with her and usually one of them darted back later and stuck a needle in an arm or buttock. It hurt badly, whichever place they chose.

Days and days. I learned to count all the panes on the six windows opposite. In the quieter nights, the fall of the coals in the grate made crunchy sounds. The firelight shot moving shadows up on the walls and the dark corners of the gigantic ward. Looking out of the windows in the daytime, the houses opposite were grim and tall; like looking at prisons from a prison.

I learnt to cry without crying, so that there were no loud give-away gulps or sobs at the end, that went on as you came down the other side of the mountain and the power of the sadness subsides. The nurses disapproved of crying.

It had taken only a fortnight, but it had been an abyss of time. Back home there was a hot water bottle in the bed, the dog licked me happily and the library had burned my books. The Contagious Diseases Act meant that the three books, unfinished, had been incinerated. I blamed Windsor Street Library and Doctor Bligh. The books had leather bindings, I could remember them clearly, but not their endings. Probably other things had gone as well but I was strangely apathetic and did not really care. A weird feeling, floating and soaring, growing. Mother was vaguely sad. Father came into my bedroom straight after work each day. You could hear his shoes yards away. He came up the front stairs so extremely deliberately, one-creak-and-two-creak-and-three-creak, his shoes making the same slow sound on each step.(Other people's feet had a far lighter tune, in fact their progress was unnoticeable.) Then, tread, tread, tread across their bedroom into mine. I already had my smile on.

Then I would have to find something suitable to say. He would stand awkwardly and ask how I was then, "How are you, then?" Then he might sit on the bed, as there was only a broken chair otherwise. "Have you managed to eat anything today? Taken your medicine? What did the old Doc say?" I moved across the bed, to leave him room to sit. Then, having run out of conversation, he would tap the side of the sheet as if it was tin, in a half-hearted attempt to tuck me in, and go off downstairs to the beginning of the six 'clock news. I relaxed. He might come up again to kiss me goodnight, but he might not. It was two hours to go yet.

The large brown and chrome tray kept behind the radio was used now, Mother did it up with a crisp white tray-cloth, sometimes even flowers or a card, with two boiled eggs beaten in a cup. Pepper and salt speckled the golden mixture, butter glued it together. Buttered bread laid on a small plate. Warm milk to drink.

Measles, chickenpox, flues and colds followed. Cousin Lucy got scarlet fever, which was just as important as diphtheria and went to Fazackerly, other cousins got polio and rheumatic fever; each illness moved us forward, with penalties like a game of snakes and ladders. There was a ritual to a day's illness. At nine o'clock in the morning I would be removed to my parents' large high bed, with its pillows and bolster, and sat high up, reading books all day.

Ordinary illnesses meant going round to Dr Bligh's house in Mount Pleasant. He had a proper maid to open the door with a flourish. She was far more stylish than the convent's young girl, with a white apron and a starched white cap. Patients were shown into the dining room, where a long mahogany table had a spread of The Illustrated London News, Punch, Country Life and Tatler. Celi and Mary were usualy the only women; the room was full of old men who coughed and spluttered and had a pungent smell if they sat too near. They sat reading about who had been presented at court and the latest country houses for sale while hoping they were not catching something else. A large silver soup tureen stood on the sideboard ready for Sunday dinner. The mix of public and private life was unsettling.

"Oh, it's Saturday evening," Dr Bligh said, sitting at his monumental desk, "They haven't anywhere else to go. I have to give them something, of course, and then they go home quite happy." His cure for everything, and Mary was often prescribed it, was Parrish's Food, a bright red iron tonic. It tasted of iron railings, she always thought, boiled up with cochineal colouring added. They went on to Mr Harriman's Chemists at the corner where the shop smelled of soap and talcum powder and went home in the rain clutching the magic red liquid.

Being ill over the years - flu, chickenpox, also meant being moved into their big bed for the daytime and having the photo albums and postcard albums to look at. Grandpa's cousin, Aunt Mary Dignan, had been a governess to the family of a Spanish banker from Barcelona. For business reasons, he took the entire family all round the world and Aunt Dignan kept sending postcards as they travelled. Peasants from the Middle East stood by dusty roads or in sweltering marketplaces blinking against the sunlight, captured on film. Ruins of a Moorish fortress, La Alcázaba, Málaga January 13th 1901. Then, to Tafira, Gran Canaria from the 18th to the end of the month. By February they were in Cádiz and Tanger where a water seller sold water by the mug. The heat and dust were almost tangible in the sepia images. Consequently, each illness became a trip round the world as far as possible, from before the First World War. By 1925 Miss Dignan was back at Barcelona, and the flow of postcards almost stopped.

There was also an album of postcards of the Royal Family, with one aristocratic lady, a princess or duchess always looking sad, wanting to be rescued from the photograph, her eyes screaming.

From this bedroom, the street-sounds were different - high voices at playtimes sounded clearly but better than that was home-time, with the shouts of the schoolchildren as they passed the yard wall as all the schools came out at four o'clock and flooded South Hunter Street. Over the wall she could see the chattering crowd as they went past. Three schools -the Dem, the Central and the High

60

School all appeared at once. Three sisters stood out amongst the others - Faith, Hope and Charity, tall, with long golden plaits, they walked by each day from the High School in their green uniforms. At half-past five Mary was returned to her own bedroom. With three outside walls, it could be icy. One time, Celi lit a fire in the grate and the room was cosy and believable in, just like a fairytale. Then, when the fire had died down, a mouse hopped out of the fireplace and Mary saw it in the half-light and life was never the same again. She became sick with fear.

Auntie Julie cemented the fear completely.

"It's all right, I understand exactly how you feel. It happened to me when I was a little girl, when a mouse ran across my pillow." The fear ratcheted even higher. Mary heard noises all night – they always had been there, running across the ceiling, dashing behind the skirting board – but now she realised they had other motives: to get out at us. The many mice she had seen half-dead in traps in the kitchen, others hanging already limp and grey, others already in a bucket of water at the back door, showed how many were about. She went to stay in Nannie and Auntie Julie's for a night as a treat and strangely they had no mice at all.

At some time they had a black cat, which Whiskey got on with very well, probably because of the cold nights when cat and dog slept together on some old coats in the back kitchen. Mary missed the births of the many kittens which must also have happened at night. Several times, she saw a bulging sack of kittens that had been pushed into a bucket of water outside by the coal bunker. The secret cruelty of Celi, it made her wonder about what really happened, the controlled dramas of a household. The cat disappeared without any trace, perhaps it found the convent grounds a better hunting ground.

On Saturday night bathtimes, her Mother told her all about babies and how they were born. Babies came out of the same place as wee-wee and the daddy put the seed that started it all off in there, in bed with the mummy-to-be. They had to take all their clothes off to do this.

Mary was happy to be told about this, to have the real facts. She knew women got very fat, the baby was inside them and then they went off to the maternity hospital. But she thought it was a religious ceremony, that in the labour room the doctors and midwife prayed and the baby magically rose up through the woman's skin, fully-formed and everyone was happy. No one talked about the pain, the messy blood.

Celi was more forthcoming about the creation of Adam and Eve.

"Well, they were the first two that God chose. Before that there were just monkeys and over the centuries they changed more and more into humans. And then God took two out of the crowd and said they were going to be special and we are all descended from them. That explains how Cain and Abel got wives, as there were spare humans around then but they were not written about in the Bible." That made sense, but it meant Celi was a heretic.

For Christmas they gave her a doll's pram from the Blind School at the corner of Hope Street. Going to Mass they always looked in the windows at the new woven furnishing and toys. Magazine racks, cots, Moses baskets, shopping baskets and trolleys, garden trugs, they all shone with golden raffia or brown cane-work.

The pram was woven from some golden raffia, so it was obviously not weatherproof, any rain would easily fall onto any doll under its small canopy. The wheels were made from four solid rounds of wood, each about an inch thick, attached to a cross tie and so the pram made a rattling noise when Mary pushed it proudly round the streets. However, the wheels moved askew on their wooden axles, thumping loudly and also picked up much of the dog-shit that was freely spread on the pavements. Trying to avoid the mess was not always easy and so when Mary got back into the hall there was a rank smell clinging to the wheels. And when she proudly showed the pram to Lucy, her cousin pronounced it was not a proper pram as it was all like a piece of knitting and might dissolve in the rain. They went for a rattling walk down Maryland Street, with Mary already experiencing misgivings and hoping that they would not meet the gardener's boys who would be quite rightly tempted to laugh at her.

About this time Princess Elizabeth became her obsession. The papers issued souvenir editions to mark the Royal Wedding on November the 20th 1947. She sat carefully cutting out the treasure-trove of Royal Wedding photos from the stash of Daily Express, Daily Mail and The People at 3 St James's Road. Nana and Aunty Marie were bemused at Mary's delight at finding the papers, but humoured her, giving her scissors to cut out the photographs which she clutched all the way home along Rodney Street.

The previous April, the Royal Tour of South Africa, provided a glut of coloured photos from *Illustrated* magazine.

Cutting right round the outlines exactly, following shoulders, arms, hips, legs, down to the high-heels - it was as close as she could reach Princess Elizabeth, her heroine, and Princess Margaret, the alternative. Wartime photos of the two sisters in a pony-trap in Windsor Great Park were merely a glamorous version of herself and Lucy; in Mary's imagination she too was in that carriage with them.

Until teenage arrived, pocket money of 6d each from Daddy, Mummy, Nannie and Auntie Julie mostly went on Royal Family postcards and glossy books from Pickering and Inglis, bought from the shop at the top of Bold Street. At one time Mary could have drawn - and did draw - a layout of all the rooms of Buckingham Palace and knew far more about their family genealogy than her own.

It was about the same time as she hit the wall of St Thomas Aquinas's *Proofs of the Existence of God* that Mary lost interest and the books and postcards of the Royal Family remained, neglected, among newer items.

In 1948 Nana moved, with Jack, Kay and Lucy to a terrace house near Penny Lane. This house was much smaller but it still had a servant-summoning bell in the front room inset beside the slate fireplace. Mary had learnt that all these marble fireplaces were in fact slate. Real marble was for rich houses. Lucy showed her round the terrace house but no one mentioned what had happened to all the other residents of number three St James's Road who had disappeared.

Bit by bit, Mary worked out that Marie and Tommy had both got married and moved off with their spouses, Cappy got a flat in Rodney Street and Alice became a hotel housekeeper in Scotland. Front room, dining room, kitchen, with three bedrooms and a bathroom upstairs, it was like a doll's house in comparison to St James's Road.

Nana kept a teapot on her bedroom mantelpiece.

"I save every three-penny piece in that and that goes towards the mortgage" she announced. But later Kay could not resist saying,

"Don't believe her. If I didn't go out to work, how would the mortgage really get paid, and how would we eat? Thrippeny bits can't pay for much." For years Kay had been a barmaid as it fitted in with school times, 10.30 am to 3pm and then 7.30pm to 11pm. It also had been her only way of seeing her husband, Jack, as he used pubs as his office for whatever he was up to at the time.

A fair-haired boy loitered by the railings at the bottom of Maryland Street.

"You live at the top of the street, don't you?" he asked.

"Yes. What school do you go to?"

"St James's Road." Church of England. A Protestant. But he had a pet tortoise and Mary could come back and see it, if she asked her mother to talk to Mrs Elias. The mothers had a conference during the week in the street and it was agreed they could be friends. The difference had to be acknowledged and permission given. (By whom? From where? How was it done?) Lucy, after all, was now living up in Penny Lane and a tram or bus ride away and a new friend was a lucky benefit.

This led to an invitation to tea. It was a boarding house, run by his mother. Their back basement had a large rush-matted room – the dining room for the veterinary students, which was also David's playroom. Toys lived in a tea chest, a deep well of assorted games

64

and little figures. They tipped it all out onto the matting, parts of trains and farmyard figures, arms and legs, had fallen to the bottom. He had some musical instruments, a xylophone, a toy piano and a recorder that he could already play quite well.

"I'm going to be a musician," he announced, which impressed her.

There was also a television. Michela and Armand Denis were always going through jungles and finding new and dangerous animals. Totally ridiculous, Mary thought, it did not fit in with life at all. A film about the docks, or the inside of the flour mills, now, that would be interesting. Tigers were not necessary, but Michela and Armand went on, searching for more wild animals week after week, pointless and extremely small on the eight-inch screen. Other weeks, Hans and Lotte Haas took over, swimming endlessly underwater for no apparent reason. In the black and white film they often looked like tadpoles writhing about.

The tortoise munched lettuce leaves stolidly. He was not that interesting at all, quite ugly in fact. Each time they tried to talk to him he retracted his head back into his shell. It was no use poking a finger, he might bite.

Their basement kitchen, facing the area, however, was exciting. If anyone went into the kitchen quietly and switched on the light (it was always dark,) mice dashed across the shelf up alongside the wall, stacked with saucepans and jugs. Mary could see them actually jump over the handles of the pans. At home it frightened her; here it was a game.

The vet students were merry, hearty, always in the middle of some complex of jokes, like a shuffling pack of cards. Brogue shoes and pullovers, each in a different Fair Isle pattern, each student was a variation of fawns and browns. They already wore their life's uniform, the walking colours of rich dun earth.
They smoked pipes,and wore horn-rimmed spectacles, hoping it made them look wise and much older. A Mr Birt , who worked for the BBC had the front room, Mrs Elias showed it to Mary – his own gas fire and a tan candlewick bedcover, really sophisticated, she thought.

Outside, in the back garden, David let her dig new places for the nasturtiums and marigolds which the tortoise would perhaps eat in the future. Here in the middle of town all soil was deepest black, the nearest colour to coal. Nothing grew in their own garden, no marigolds at all. Along the path was the original outside toilet, a lesser version of the small black temple that was in the St James's Road back garden.

She was invited to Sunday tea. Progress. David, however, was going to Sunday School, which meant Mary had to go too. It was not polite to refuse and too complicated to explain. To explain at all would be rude in the extreme. She trotted along with him to St Bride's in Catherine Street.

"It's all right, I'll wait out here. You go in." David hesitated, guessing something was wrong. Tactfully, he asked no questions and went into the church. She stayed outside, staring at the blue-painted walls. An adult hand scooped her in, bringing her to sit in the front bench and she risked eternal damnation. It would be better to confess to God direct right now. Probably a mortal sin to be in here attending a service. The children were told a story from the Gospel and were given little coloured stamps of Jesus to stick on a special Bible Stories card. They even gave her a spare card. Then they prayed for the King, who did not seem to need it. With a sense of unease she went back to David's to tea at number six and left the card there. Secrets. Life was much better if adults were kept out of it.

Sheila's Cottage won the Grand National in 1948. It was the first mare to win since Shannon Lass and Celi had luckily put a bet on it. Vin had to go off round the pubs and find a bookie's and lay the bet – she could not have done it. With her surprise winnings, Celi paid for a holiday staying in a farmhouse at Hope, near Wrexham. The Welsh family was right out of a picture-book.

Kindly Blanche, their grown-up daughter with long black hair carried Mary when she was too tired to walk any further. Farm pond, chickens, geese, ducks and sides of pork hanging from beams

66

across the large farm kitchen - it was all the things that existed in Enid Blyton's *Sunny Stories* or *Sunnybrook Farm*. There really were geese wandering round a pond in front of the farmhouse and hens clucked from all directions. Blanche took a basket to collect the eggs and showed Mary under the hedges where the hens laid their eggs and also showed her a china egg.

"It's for a broody hen, it encourages her to lay proper eggs." It was a perfect imitation. Mary rolled it round in her hands. At breakfast they sat beneath the meat hanging above them from the rafters, the entire place devoted to producing food, eating thick home-made marmalade on generously buttered toast. Blanche took Mary into the cowshed and showed her how to milk a cow, the clutching and tugging of the swollen teats.

"Here, you can try." Mary tried to hold the pink udders but could not manage to squeeze them as tight as needed. Blanche laughed and started again; milk splattered into a bucket and Blanche reached for a metal jug and gave a sample of the milk to Mary right there and then. It was warm, with globules of gold fat floating on the surface like bits of straw.

Father was bored until he found a pub in Hope village and the farmer's wife said it was easy, they would babysit. One day they went off to Wrexham to an auction and Celi bid for a mirror that they had to have delivered back to Liverpool, which Vin said did not make it a bargain after all. But hung above the carved chair in the hall, it gave a dignified appearance if anyone caught a glance into the house while passing by.

Other holidays were always spent at Heswall, over the water, facing Wales. Uncle Jack's taxi gave them a lift, all packed in, with Whiskey the dog looking out of the window, already excited.

They bowled along lanes that had never been tarred and were in fact made by the locals throwing out cinders to patch the potholed surfaces.

Each year they knew it was getting nearer when they reached a field with a white horse at the turn of the road. And each year the children dashed out of the taxi and went across to the horse, who seemed to have been waiting for them an entire year. It was as if the white horse was giving them his blessing each time.

These holidays were always spent in bungalows leading down to the shore, a series of Nissen huts left over from the war. White picket fences disguised their original army use, and owners had transformed them with rambling roses and mixed cottage-garden flowers, hollyhocks, sweet peas, marigolds, lavender and carnations. It was like a story-book illustration. People had bought them up and rented them out each summer, having filled the rooms with discarded Victorian furniture and installed bunk beds for any children. There was no electricity, lighting was via oil-lamps which gave a soft glow. Cooking was done by a Calor gas canister in a tiny lean-to kitchen. The children washed in the sea most of the time, brushing off sand all over the floors.

No indoor sanitation either, only an outside Elsan toilet and on the last day the men of the family lugged it to the back hedge and tipped it over, covering the sewage with topsoil. Blackberries grew richly as a result, although during the fortnight, the container gradually filled up and it became awkward to use. Going back to Liverpool became a relief then, as well as a disappointment.

Lucy and their other cousin, Tom were included too and sometimes his parents also rented a bungalow further along. Then all the Spanish in-laws appeared and played card games late into the night. Uncle Paco, Aunty Isobel, Hortensia, Sef, Frances and cousins sat with bottles of beer and stout at the tables in the large living room with its massive curved ceiling. When it rained, the roof rattled dramatically with each pit of rain.

They were far away from all shops. The richness was in the family complexities like the cast of a play that changed slightly each day.

No one asked the children where they went all day. There were a couple of accidents, however, one where Mary, having read that dogs could swim, and wanting to show Lucy it was true, took Whiskey up in her arms and, walking into the sea until she was waist-high in the water, dropped the trusting dog right into it. Whiskey fell below the waves and there was silence. Mary had killed the best friend she had ever had. She froze. The water gave no sign, until a gasping Whiskey's nose appeared and a very determined dog swam accurately and rapidly towards the shore.

Another day she fell against one of the concrete blocks littering the shore, placed to stop German tanks from landing. Here and there were still dangerous lengths of rusting barbed wire scattered about in the sand.

"Oh yes," Nana had told them, "the seashores were forbidden places for people like us until a few years ago, they haven't cleaned them up properly yet." Lucy, Tom and Mary were happily jumping from one concrete block to another when Mary fell, bashing her shin against a sharp side. Blood flowed, the cut was almost right to the bone as there was not much flesh there and for years afterwards there was this reminder of Heswall holidays etched into her left leg.

They watched the cockle-pickers go off across the River Dee almost as far as the Welsh coast. It was a dangerous thing to do, as the tide would race into the central channel and they could be marooned on a sandbank if they did not keep to the strict timetable of the tides. One gatherer even had a pony and trap, to get further across and perhaps pick up more cockles.

"You know, that song," Celi said, " *'Oh Mary go and call the cattle home across the sands of Dee,'* well, that's what you are looking at right now. It ends with *'the tide crept up along the sand'* and she gets drowned." They walked along to Parkgate for a proper cockle and mussel tea. Here, too, the war was still in evidence as there was a deserted empty swimming pool waiting for its future to arrive.

"It used to be very popular," Nana said as they sat down to tea, "People used to come from all around and have parties here too." Right now though, they were the only customers at the gingham-covered tables and the empty swimming pool outside the windows was just as historic as any Roman ruin.

The children rapidly became sunburnt, playing out with other kids along the shore. In the evening they were a mass of itchy burnt skin, and spent the time before bedtime happily peeling lengths of raw skin off each other's backs. They also got heat-spots, which

Kay cooled down with calamine lotion, leaving them with daft white spots all over their bodies.

A boy their age lived at the last bungalow all the year, right next to the tide. He had a massive aquarium sited in a conservatory at the side of the house and was only too pleased to show them all the tropical fishes. His mother invited them in for lemonade and biscuits and so they were settled as belonging here immediately. The only other resident was an elderly lady who appeared each midday, bathing suit, bathing cap, large towel, the same every time and who went for a short brisk swim before walking home to her own nearby trim Nissen hut.

On Sundays they walked up to the Top Village to Mass, coming back laughing, sliding down the gigantic brown clay sewer pipe that led from the upper to lower villages. In the lower village was Matthais's General Stores. Not much larger than a wooden shed, it sold everything from frivolous buckets and spades to genuine fishing nets and wellington boots. The two glamorous Matthias brothers were Mary's first crush, as they strode around dressed in fishermen's gear either coming back from the early tide or hurrying out to launch their boat. They belonged to something dangerous and exclusive, the world of men. She bought a colouring book to hide her embarrassment while Lucy and Tom searched for new sweets.

One day on the way back, caught in a quick summer shower, the women and children dashed into a church for shelter from a thunderstorm. It was a Protestant church, as, set in the middle aisle was a large framed prayer for the King, Queen and the Princesses. It was puzzling that they should need praying for at all. It showed they were in the wrong church. Get out, you don't belong here, they might catch you, Mary thought. Various flags hung from the arches making it look like a silent indoors war, standard set against brightly coloured standard.

Outside, they meandered past large 1930s houses set far back from the road. At the corner of Telegraph Road a large copper beech shimmered in the after-shower sunlight, its sheer beauty causing them to stop for a moment. Above it a sharp rainbow gave the usual reassurance, right from Noah's time, God's promise written in seven colours, a physical sign of a spiritual bond.

One holiday they hired a wooden bungalow nearer to the lane. Boys from the Boys Brigade had a holiday camp in a field nearby, they could be heard laughing and screaming as they dived into their outside pool behind the thick hedge. Other times they could be heard marching along the lane in formation, singing loudly,
"*Left, left, I had a good job and I left, left*" followed by
"*Browned off, one two, browned off, three four,*
Browned off one two, one two, - three four!"
It was actually supposed to be 'Sound off' but they had changed it to a more comical meaning. Other afternoons a lorry carrying German prisoners of war trundled along, taking the men back to their camp after their day's work out in nearby farms. They waved happily at the children, but Nana, Celi and Kay looked the other way, ignoring them. It was bizarre, in this summer sunshine, to be still caught in these last coils of the world war.

Some evenings, they went for a walk after a summer shower, to find frogs from the ditches either side determined to cross over from one side of the lane to the other. At times they all had to stand and wait as the little figures jumped across from puddle to puddle. The air was damp and sweet with the refreshed plants in the hedges. One year Celi had come across with Mary by train and bus to book a different bungalow and pay the deposit. Mary, fascinated with the heaped white and red blossom from the hedges, wanted to take some home and though Celi said it would bring bad luck, you did not bring hawthorn into the house, it was special, Mary insisted and her mother gave in. The strange result was that, apparently for family reasons, the landlady said she had to cancel the agreement and returned the deposit in a letter. But she did know someone nearby who they could approach.

"See? I told you it would bring bad luck!" Celi said and they started the search again, this time for a cheaper one. They found a small black-painted wooden bungalow off the lane opposite the boys' camp. This time most of the family stayed back in Liverpool and came over at the weekend as there were only two bedrooms, one for Nana and Kay, one for Mary and Lucy. The other side of the family never visited; Nannie and Julie remained back in Liverpool.

One August holiday in the black bungalow, after a languid sultry afternoon, a dramatic thunderstorm erupted, and Nana sat on the back step watching it all. There was little else to do, but even so she seemed to enjoy the storm. Kay stayed inside, peeling potatoes or washing the blackcurrants they had already collected from the roadways nearby.

"There's a belief about the lightning that it's needed to ripen the crops. When you think about it, they're getting a massive dose of something stronger than sunlight, it must hurry them up." They sat together and waited until the rumbling died down. "It sounds like Beethoven's music, you'll find that out later when you grow up," she added. The sounds bounced away over the scattered huts and sheds.

There was no real pathway between these bungalows, anyone cut through all manner of back gardens, lane-ways and tracks on the way to the shore. Mary loved exploring here on her own, without any fear. Now and again a dog kicked up a noise, but usually it was a totally peaceful backwater.

A man was sitting astride a brightly-painted kitchen chair near one of the grass pathways that ran between the scattered bungalows, his back a red-bronze colour and shockingly beautiful. He was reading a newspaper and did not notice her. She did not know men could be as beautiful as this. Mary stopped, transfixed and stared, then stole past him silently.

Snapshots
9

Summer evenings meant all the street came out to play. Nannie sat at her open upstairs window and looked out. Once the evening Angelus had rung it was the sign for all the children to come out of their houses. The four gardener's girls and boys, little Barry from up by Mrs Cook's, Gerald Moran opposite and Mary. Whiskey joined in, as near to a child as possible. It was quiet enough to hear the odd car approaching and plenty of time enough to scatter as it came into view. Hopeful pigeons pecked in between the cobbles outside the garage but only turned up small screws and bits of metal.

One evening they managed to knot two skipping ropes together, and though skipping was a girls' game, the boys joined in too, and soon they were all leaping up and down while Marie and Bernard kept turning the ends. Whiskey barked happily at the edge, not realising what was really going on but eager to join and scampering up and down. Then Mrs Moran herself joined in and even Mrs Van came out and sat on her step and watched.

At such times it was like being in a village totally cut off from the city. Once the day's clatter and garage work had stopped they were playing out as if waiting to reclaim the street and make it more human.

Nannie was hungry, isolated in her eagle's eyrie. She sat draped in her coral shawl, its long fringed edges swirling round, not like the shawlies, who always wore black. Any time Mary went in to visit her the stream of questions began.

"Did you see anyone to speak to? Did you see anyone you know by sight? Did you see anyone you know by sight to speak to?" They were arranged in order of nearness.

"Can you fetch me? Can you make this out?" Young legs, young eyes could read easier. Anything mentioned as being in the future was always qualified with "If God spares us." He was ready to pounce at any time and yet he also had our lives in his hand, powerfully protected. He was too hard to make out.

Once Grandpa was dead, Nannie became frightened of lightning, and when a thunderstorm approached on summer days, she came down, through the sitting room and into their living room to sit until the worst passed over. Perhaps it was also a throwback to all she had been through in the war, which was never spoken of now. Perhaps he had somehow provided the necessary personal reassurance, merely by being around sitting reading the paper.

"I locked the sitting room door at her side when we first moved in here," Celi said, "but it caused such an almighty row that I could never do it again. She rattled that door like billyo, demanding to know what was going on!"

73

Uncle Joe was usually away with the airforce but now he decided to emigrate to New Zealand, the very same year the Maori song *Now is the Hour* became a hit. Nannie stood on the Pier Head, past the landing stage, crying into a lavender scented handkerchief. Her favourite child was going to the other side of the world, further away than America. Aunty Julie held her arm supporting her but looking upset too. Vin took an hour off work from Cammell Laird's the other side of the Mersey and stood with Celi and Mary to wave goodbye to his brother. The band played rousing music as the gangway was lifted and the passengers lined up at the rails to wave goodbye. He had decided he was joining the Royal New Zealand Air Force and was off to a new life. They might never see him again. Joe stood waving from the top deck's railing, they could see him smiling at his entire family and waving until he was merely a blur and then they could not make him out at all as the liner moved stately along the Mersey and away to the world beyond.

Miss Grownie's classroom was across the corridor and it was time to explain things to the class properly in the religious lessons. Our real existence was spiritual; we just happened to be trapped in these strange bodies. Inside each of us was an immortal soul, our absolute essence. Our main relationship was with God, a secret arrangement. It became clear what adults were doing and why they were so smug. If you made the Morning Offertory on getting out of bed, each action after that earned you grace. Grace was never fully described, but Mary envisaged it as a mixture of Mother-of-pearl sequins. For each one good (or average good) action = one sequin. By the end of a day or better, one week, you would have a growing collection. A well-lived life accumulated a hoard of grace. It built up, sequin by sequin. You became lit-up from within.

"For instance," Miss Grownie said, "If you have made the Morning Offering, even picking up this pin can earn you grace." She held up a pin from the top of the teacher's desk and earned a sliver of immortal grace.

74

However, Miss Grownie said, if you committed a venial sin, that broke the laying-up of this treasure and a black mark went on your soul and a bit of grace (one sequin?) was deducted. There was then, lurking, a major snag - big sins. One mortal sin brought the entire system to a halt. No more sequins were allowed to be accumulated until that mortal sin was confessed, penance given and some kind of restitution was made. If you had killed someone or done a big robbery for instance, they were mortal sins; stealing a penny was venial. There were also special sins that only adults could commit, called adultery. It was all waiting for them when they grew up.

But once the mortal sin had been confessed and penance made and restitution made (though how a murder could be restored was a mystery) the entire system cranked back into life again and the sequins shot down from the skies. A more adult theme was that you had fallen out of the friendship with God, your soul was black and you were in an outer darkness. There was something even worse to come, though.

If you died in a state of mortal sin, you went to hell straight away. That nice Jesus turned into the bad-tempered tyrant from the painting of The Last Judgement in the Vatican, hurling bad people into hell.

The venial sins added up like black sequins and could easily be effaced by weekly confession, penance, usually three Hail Marys and restitution. You paid the penny back to the person you stole it from, or put it into any of the church collection boxes, *St Anthony's Bread, The Poor of the Parish, Peter's Pence* – there was a wide selection.

All authority came from God, then it filtered down via the King and the government, priests, policemen, teachers and parents. Children were at the bottom of the pile and had to obey all those above them; a crushing weight.

They also learnt that if a woman was ever at risk of dying in childbirth, the doctors had to make more effort to save the child than the mother. It was all about bringing a new life into existence, another soul. Sitting there, eight years old, Mary could feel the sadness and puzzlement of a young wifeless man being presented

75

with a new motherless baby and his feeling lonely and bereft. It did not make sense. When they were also told that a worker had no right to steal his employer's time, however, Mary had to put up her hand and object.

"But why does the employer get to own the worker's time, then? It does not sound fair."

Miss Grownie explained that the employer gave wages in return for work, so had rights to a week's work from all employees. She added that strikes were almost the work of the devil and destroyed communities. Workers worked, that was their life's destiny and the employers were kind to give them the opportunities. Anything else was communism, which was dangerous, as they also did not believe in God. Communism was all over Russia and might spread if they were not careful.

Cathy died of leukaemia, the first death anyone in the class knew about of anyone as young as themselves dying. The nature table and the statue of Our Lady was smothered in flowers and Cathy's desk was emptied of any of her books. Leukaemia was all they were told; it could be anything, the adults could not tell the children any more because it was a brand-new mystery illness that no one knew about.

They all signed a card and said extra prayers but it still seemed unreal. Yet her place was there, waiting to be taken up by a new girl. She had long black hair and always wore a pastel pink cardigan and a nice dress, no school uniform. Black and pink; a clear image of someone who had disappeared. She was prayed for at every Angelus along with all the other dead people. It would be lonely for her in heaven, there would not be many other children to talk to there. And of course she was right up there in heaven, not having had enough time to commit many sins.

To cheer the children up, Miss McGinty took them out to the lower playground with a gramophone. To play music outside like this was almost a crime, it blared out under the one alder tree with its black woody husks. The class danced about in the space, enjoying the sunshine and the unusual experience. The Valeta, the Dashing White Sergeant and country dances – they galloped through them merrily. A few days later, Mary was stopped by the stately Miss Etherington, who lived halfway up Maryland Street.

"I was watching you dancing, from the upstairs window, and I have to say that you were most graceful, most graceful indeed." And with that, she gave a small smile and went up her steps into the house that no one ever entered. A real lady, Nannie said, she had lived with her mother, never married and once that mother died, she started wearing the clothes left in the wardrobe. The result was that she looked like Queen Mary, broad-brimmed hats with black feathers, long-gowns and black coats, button boots and always black gloves and a black umbrella. It was the only time they ever spoke. She had eyes the colour of water.

Summer evenings and the street came to life. Just like the children in Enid Blyton, their gang had an attendant dog, Whiskey, who functioned as an honorary child. They went exploring and even managed to get into the Unitarian Church next to the Philharmonic Hall, by opening the small door that led into the boiler-room and just walking up from there.

The same method got them all into the St Andrew's Church on Rodney Street, where they wandered round the inside and ended up on the roof. Even better was their exploration of the Demonstration School, where they found the attics and rooftop littered with broken desks, chairs, discarded stage curtains and old textbooks. It was finding how things worked, this going into places where adults did not bother to look and finding out that so much was forgotten. The dog sniffed around appreciatively, while they felt like proper explorers in foreign lands. They stood on the flat roof and surveyed their new kingdoms. Not a word about this was ever said to their families; it was not necessary. They would not understand.

Other summer evenings, they got out the old pram base that made a sled and raced down Maryland Street, also taking the dog on their knees, barking merrily. The skill was in managing a circular swirl at the bottom of the street and not letting yourself drift into Rodney Street traffic. The slope was so perfect that gangs would come from other streets and ask if they could have a go, sometimes bringing their own sledges. A quick negotiation, sometimes involving pennies as payment, was gone through at the top of the street and the newcomers then welcomed to join the game. As they came form boring flat streets or ones with more traffic, they had nothing to barter with and so were looked down on and pitied. They were always polite and, just as in tribal life, it was handy to have some nearby allies if necessary.

Later on summer evenings, Mary lay in bed, the blind not really keeping out the light, listening to the sounds of the street. When it was really dark, she could hear Jimmy Moran singing as he came home from courting a girl who lived along Pilgrim Street. She could hear his voice as he rounded the corner of South Hunter Street, the sound of a young man in love on a summer night. It had hope in it, confidence and dreaming, all combined as if he lived in a far better place than here. She entered his mood, knowing no one else could hear him or pay any attention to his song.

10

First being punished –Miss Melvin of the next-door classroom took the class as Miss Antrobus was off sick. Mary was the only one who owned up to laughing as the chalk screeched along the blackboard. Miss Melvin came to the back row and brought her up to the high teacher's desk and rampaged that she would be reading about Mary in the Liverpool Echo in the future as she was obviously going to be a criminal, being so dishonest, while the others who had not owned up sat and watched. Mary knew a major disparity was going on here and that Miss Melvin was stupid and exceptionally vehement. Her dark eyes and dark hair bobbed up and down as she ranted on. How could anyone be so stupid?

But the network of spiritual life was thriving in other quarters. Having to go to Mrs Clark's tobacconists, Mary was sent to ask for ten Craven A and ten Park Drive. At first Mrs Clark had been in a proper shop on Hardman Street next to Mr Ingham's Dairy and Greengrocer's. Then she had moved to a little shop at the corner of their own street but now had ended up in a minute booth in Hope Street along from the back doorway of Blake's garage. There was just enough room for one customer at a time and Mrs Clark was trapped behind a packed counter, as if she was playing at shop.

"Can you do me a favour?" she asked Mary. "Can you say a prayer for my niece, Sally Payne? She needs another operation. God always listens to the prayers of children, He pays them more attention." Mary felt this responsibility but also wanted to say that surely if Sally changed her name from Pain, then all these illnesses would stop. Mrs Clark smiled at her above the banked display of cigarettes and sweets and chocolate. Her hair was always tightly waved and she looked like a worried version of the Queen with her dark Marcel waves. Mary went home with this responsibility yet again – she was often asked to pray like this. The unseen Sally was part of their spiritual network, twined in with cigarettes, matches and pipe-cleaners.

Mother prayed at the side of the very bed that was the cause of her problems. Kneeling on the empty-fireplace side, she leant on the colourless bedspread and the oily-edged eiderdown, her hands entwined with her rosary.

Sharp-eyed Pius XII looked down from over the brown-painted mantelpiece where Celi kept her rosary beads and prayerbook and a box of matches for the gas-light. The framed Papal Blessing seemed to do no use. Pinched nose, high cheekbones, glasses balanced, he looked uncomfortable, suffocating in lace and silk. The war was on when the photo had been taken. Either Father, on his trip to Rome with the Young Catholic Men's Society – or Auntie Julie - had brought it here already in its cheap frame. His cold stare made the bedroom that bit more chill, as he stared out through his little wire-framed glasses. He looked as though he fasted for more than Lent and Advent. His right arm was lifted in permanent blessing across the bedroom.

The eiderdown had been something magnificent, once. It would have fitted into a sepia Hollywood film with its ruched ribbon edges and silken valleys. It lay upon a cover of some silky material, also in the same faded tan-grey. The colour of loss, beyond subtle beige. Yet another fixed monument to a richly-promising past, it all looked down at heel, slummy. Once they had been at the height of luxury. Unable to afford dry-cleaning and too proper to consider sewing a patchwork cover, Celi left it to fester above their bodies' problems, which might also have been beige.

Celi subscribed to the Carmelite News and the Little Messenger and as a special gift had received a miniature keepsake. A used eggshell, cleaned out and set with slivers of balsa wood and a few strands of cloth made a perfect replica of a Carmelite nun's cell. The little window, a bed, a little chair and table and a minute crucifix on its curving wall - it was a complete work of art.

There was also the mother-of-pearl rosary case, shaped as two parts of a moon-coloured egg set in a brass edging and hinge. And, from Lourdes, there was a carved and pierced rosary case shaped like a shrine, with a tiny spyhole in the spire, with Our Lady of Lourdes set inside, an infinitesimal eighth of an inch high. But over the years the image had decomposed and she was merely a blur, which made it even more significant.

The year had distinct markings, with Holy Week one of the high points. On Maundy Thursday it was the custom to do The Seven Churches and Mary went across town with her Mother from one church to another. It took all day, with the shopping mixed in with it. They knelt and prayed, with the strong smell of onions drifting up from the shopping-basket. They started at St Philip Neris' and going upwards, to St Anne's in Overbury Street, past Myrtle Gardens,then they called back home, going downtown to St Peter's Seel Street, with a clear run to St Patrick's, St Vincent's, then a dart back to the middle of town to St Nicholas's Pro-Cathedral in Hawke Street,with the lucky addition of the convent chapel to make up the entire seven.

Father balanced this with his seven-plus pubs, The Crack, the Phil, The Vines opposite the Adelphi, Ma Edgerton's, the Roscoe

Head, the Lord Nelson, Ma Threlkeld's, the Grapes. Men got pulled away all the time by football, the races, cricket and drink; they had no time to visit churches which were on a different timetable. After all, the churches closed their doors at nine o'clock, which Mary thought was against Jesus's teaching. Surely he would have kept them open all the night for anyone needing to pray?

On summer evenings the light managed to come through little pinpoint holes in the bedroom blind. The open window made it billow slightly in a breeze. Mary was led through the night prayers by her Mother, who knelt at the bedside,

Matthew, Mark, Luke and John,
Bless the bed that I lie on
And if I die before I wake,
Pray to God my soul to take.

This was her favourite one, before the prayers for the Holy Souls or the family. Then she was left with her Guardian Angel to look after her through the night. The golden-haired angel sat at the end of the bed, its long wings trailing into the fluff that gathered on the cracked lino, its white gown luminous and an air of tranquillity as it sat there. By morning, and morning prayers however, it became invisible.

11

Miss Antrobus had the scholarship class upstairs. For some reason, which seemed unfair, they went into her class before the age of ten, which gave them nearly two years to repeat the jumping through hoops that the exam demanded. There were over fifty pupils in the class, with an entire section of a dozen who were already hopeless cases.

Those girls sat along on the window side and spent their days trying to get through the class reading-book, still learning laboriously how to add, multiply and subtract and, when all that failed, continued with endless needlework. From kettle holders up to flannelette blouses they all worked slowly, even learning how to do inset buttonholes. Then the brighter girls started the exclusive puzzles that would make up the scholarship papers.

Endless carthorses hauled leaking baths up steep hills on hot days and the class had to calculate how much water (gallons, gills, pints) would have dripped away before the tired horses reached the summit (feet, furlongs, chains, miles.)

Other puzzles were about if oranges were equal to pears, then what was a pineapple equal to? And which of these strange shapes was the odd one out? Did adults not realise how silly these questions were and how had they got themselves into such a muddle with the poor horses and the leaking baths? Why? Were adults really that stupid? What was the real use of all this?

Outside, the Virginia creeper crept all up the side of the Central School, turning more crimson day by day through the end of the autumn. The girls over there, who wore navy blue uniforms, learned shorthand typing and went straight off to work in offices down town. They also learned cookery in the downstairs of the gardener's house round the corner from Nannie's. The two kitchen rooms at the back of the house smelled of scoured wood and flour, the epitome of cleanliness.

Here in the Demonstration School girls could end up scattered anywhere. Meanwhile, the clever pre-scholarship girls battled on with their pairs of horses dragging leaking baths up mountainsides and flour dribbling out of sacks weighing a hundredweight across fields. They became adept in recognising at once that if six of green apples equalled four of oranges, how many bananas three boys would have needed. It was a surreal world where no one set out having a clue to what the repercussions would be of their slipshod preparations and yet these ten-year-old girls had to solve their incessant problems.

While they tried to solve these crazy adult difficulties, the less bright girls were given books to read, easy exercises to complete and their sewing to do. It was the only way a teacher could cope with a class of fifty-two. Luckily there was always a couple of girls off sick, which made it easier.

At the front of the class was a gigantic Victorian wardrobe of figured maple. Its glass panels were curtained with green material, but inside were all the materials to keep the class occupied. Precious sheets of paper or bolts of cloth were kept   locked in there. Everything had to be saved - any unused pages in any exercise book were ripped out to be used as rough paper and even tacking stitches, once pulled out, had to have the cotton thread given up to Miss Antrobus. They were like long white worms. Rationing was drawing to an end, but shortages were still likely.

One day there was much excitement. The class had been told already that children in Canada felt sorry for them and so their government was sending over crates of apples for each school. A crate of red apples appeared on teacher's desk and each girl went up and chose one apple. It seemed a lot of fuss about nothing and Mary did wonder about how much it would have cost to post these apples across the world. Disappointingly they did not taste as sweet as they looked with their bright red peel. They were told to take them home and not eat them at playtime, but some girls did try a bite, which caused grimaces of disgust.

There was a innovation, however, in the scholarship class. Monday mornings after taking the register there was an interrogation about their Sunday Mass-going. Girls had to stand up on their bench if they had not gone to Mass on Sunday. Miss Antrobus strode up and down the aisles of desks, questioning them about attendance at Mass, communion and confession and preferably benediction and entered it all in a separate register. Girls were told to take non-Catholic friends to benediction if they were at their house for Sunday tea.

"And tell your parents. Do not take holidays or spend weekends in remote Welsh villages if there is no Catholic church nearby." You would have to take bus rides when on holiday with non-Catholics. It was testimony to their innate honesty that none of the girls lied and stood, blushing while Miss Antrobus teased out each excruciating detail of their misdemeanours. They stood, up there in space, while Miss Antrobus roamed about, making angry remarks while they tried not to cry. It was a personal crusade that no other teacher carried on, she had taken this as her personal duty. Miss Antrobus lived at home with her Mother in Blundellsands, past Crosby and had to take a train and a bus to get to school and back, an unstinting routine. Perhaps that was part of the problem that led to this hard-line attitude.

After Mass, very hungry, it was omelettes and bacon with lashings of sugary tea listening to the new radio programme, The Archers, all about countryside life and shutting farm gates. Any real country was so far away, perhaps a bus-ride past Hale, that it was easily filtered through the radio and made into drama.

Celi's network of magazines had gone full circle now, as she collected a few to take down to Ashwell Street to Stella's, her newest sister-in-law. Once Tommy was married, Stella wanted him on shore, no more trips to New York, which meant no more magazines. Tommy became a docker. The family was quietly shocked. It was the quickest job to get at the time, but was fraught with risks.

"You see the hiring-man and he chooses who he wants for the job and you see the older men puffing their chests out and trying to look strong and worthwhile. And then he chooses his favourites and the rejected men mooch off. It can change in a day." With life so precarious, they had taken this condemned house as they had three children now. They had turned up at Nana's with the first baby and were taken in to live in the front room. A wooden double bed was squashed between the fireplace and the piano and a small cot was set on top of the sofa. Clothes hung from the picture rail all round the room.

Nana adjusted yet again. Vin said,

"It's statutory overcrowding, five adults, one child and a baby, Nana could be taken to court."

"And what would that achieve?" said Celi, almost daring him to make so much trouble for the family. "They're on the housing list and it shouldn't be too long now."

"It's a bit awkward, you could say that all right, baths and so on," Uncle Jack said, "But when you find someone's been using your razor, you have to draw the line." Tommy and Stella had agreed to take any house at all and ended up in Ashwell Street, a small condemned house, which would lead to them being rehoused. Front door right off the pavement, and right into the living room. Back kitchen, small backyard with an outside toilet. In no time Tommy had whitewashed the yard and blackened the living room range.

Celi and Mary arrived on Saturday evening to a small warm room bestrewn with drying clothes, children's and adults' Hanging from the ceiling drying rack , they also hung all over the long fireguard and over the backs of chairs. Stella was by the fire, reading a library book, the radio on quietly as the children were upstairs in bed.

"He's out. Well, a man has to have his Saturday night drink, doesn't he - it's all he's got and it's not much, we can't afford much. Sammy? Oh, he's in hospital, he fell off the table last week, it was a real flap, but he's on the mend now, thank goodness." She also told Celi that she was pregnant again with their fourth child.

As they left, Mary looked back at the little house and noticed its doorstep; it was beaten gold, shining out the evening twilight. A house with love and life in it . They walked up past The Blackie and up the hill to home. When Vin was told about Stella's pregnancy he made a comment about them "squashed in that place and breeding like rabbits" but Mary remembered the vision of the golden doorstep and knew the new baby was going to be welcomed and loved.

Mrs Allen was their cleaner, she walked up from near China-town every Monday morning. Although they were poor, this cleaning arrangement was necessary because Celi was not strong after her attacks of TB. There had been a scare when she was only sixteen, but the main episode arrived after the marriage, and of course, giving birth. On Sunday afternoons she would disappear upstairs for a rest, emerging well after five o'clock after Mary had set the table.

Mrs Allen looked even weaker, she was about six feet and made of sticks, like a chimney-sweep's interlocking set. Her legs were so thin that her woollen stockings, summer and winter, constantly fell down or wrinkled; no garters were made small enough to encompass her skimpy legs. To see her kneeling scrubbing the red and black tiled floors was to wonder if she would ever be able to stand upright again. She unfolded like a deckchair. Her nose dripped even in summer. Yet after she had done their house at number nine, Mrs Allen would go through the sitting-room to Nannie's house and work through the afternoon, after a silent, miserable lunch with Mary and her Mother, sniffing through the usual meat pie and chutney and cups of tea they gave her.

Mrs Allen suddenly said she was leaving, having to look after her grandchildren as her daughter had got a job at Tate and Lyles, but she could send a friend, a widow-woman, Sara, spelt without an 'h.' Already, Sara sounded an improvement.

Sara Deakin bustled into the house, eager to work as if turning it into technicolour. She brought a brightly coloured crossover apron, a towel and soap, indoor shoes to change into and a constant cheerfulness, plus her own packet of thick doorstep cheese and pickle sandwiches.

Strong as a horse, brave and generous, she was plump and cheerful. The only time Sara was ever crestfallen was during one winter fog which was so bad that it had got into the house and into the two bedrooms. Each room was pale grey-blue with mist. She came downstairs almost in tears,

"Mrs Martineau, I've tried and tried, but I can't get that wardrobe door up to a good polish. There's a thick blue bloom on it that I can't shift at all." Celi said not to worry about it. The house was so damp and cold that the wardrobe door would stay blue, on and off, until spring; the clothes in Mary's bedroom cupboard would grow mould (which she scraped off) and her bedroom wallpaper would curl off the walls gently, to be pushed back and re-glued with a flour and water paste when the good weather returned.

There was a bit of diplomatic work to be done before that first morning, though. Mother had to go through into Nannie's house and have a confab about the new cleaner, for apparently Sara was an

86

Orange-woman and both houses were knee-deep in holy-water stoups at each upstairs doorway, the framed Pope's Blessing in the big bedroom, shrines to the Holy Child of Prague and the Sacred Heart on fretwork brackets in the corners of bedrooms and halls, with red votive-glasses holding night-lights.

The altar at the foot of Mary's bed must have been a bit of a shock too. The news came back that Nannie "would see how it goes" and Sara was welcome.

Soon, everything shone. The living room and back-kitchen floors looked new; brass sparkled; windows gleamed, all wooden surfaces were larded with polish and buffed to a shine; and all the time Sara told us about what it was like being an Orange-woman.

"The parades? Well, we save up all year, money every week into a club, most of the women make their own, you're told what material to get, and we have proper tailoresses too, and we all get the same outfits." In fact, they all looked like air hostesses for their summer parades. "We have the Bible and a certificate of authority for the parade, we have to get proper permission from the Corporation. Oh yes, it's all organised and very holy It's the Bible is in those glass caskets, on that silken pillow. And the other one's the Remembrance Book of the Dead. Oh, it's all done proper, like."

The King Billy and Queen Mary, whoever it was, looked very like the glamorous Prince and Princess from Christmas pantos – long crimped wigs, hats trailing ostrich feathers, pale blue silken jacket and trousers and white stockings and shoes for the King and long silk pale peach dress and train for the Queen. Some Sundays there were more than one couple of the King and Queen placed along the procession, which was rather un-nerving. A brass and pipe band accompanied them. The big drum that kept it all together was borrowed from St Vinnie's band down town near the tenements where Sara and Mrs Allen came from. Droves of men with proper suits, waistcoats and wearing displays of medallions and ribbons like Lord Mayors marched past. A working class transformed.

Sara also told us tales from the wash-house, where she went to do her week's wash and have a good gossip with the neighbours from round Windsor Street. She managed to move the lot in an old battered pram.

"You can't beat them for carrying a week's wash! And we do have good laugh, too!"

Years later Mary went to the Liverpool Museum of Labour and, right there was a photo of the old wash-house. Among the women stooped in the little washing cubicles was one young woman, standing proudly, with long red hair - obviously red, it showed even in the sepia photograph. A proud young woman, it could well be a photo of the young Sara, newly married, the strength and vitality blazing out through the years, the laughter and the warmth.

But religious matters were not always as balanced as this. Often on Sundays in summer, just as Sunday lunch hit the table, the booming thrum, thrum of the borrowed Lambeg drum drew them out into the street. Leaving the dinner-table (a crime at other times) Vin, Celi, Mary and Whiskey would dash to the end of South Hunter Street to see the procession. The well-drilled men and women paraded past, transformed by new clothes and strident music. One day now and then like this, they could show how they really wanted to be, smart and confident before the return to daily life in the tenements and terrace houses in the slums. Brass bands were interspersed between these formations of marching people.

"You notice, they always play loudest as they pass the convent or any church," Father pronounced, "They do it to annoy the Catholics." The convent however, was over on the side of Mount Pleasant, so he was being exceptionally suspicious. The merry parade disappeared down the hill, apparently getting a train for a trip to Southport. The afternoon, in contrast, was even quieter now as they returned to the house and the deserted plates, sometimes with the Sunday dinner having to be warmed up again.

Then, with the parade's return, at sunset, there came another transformation. Men and women limped past, spruce clothes awry, flowers wilted and shoes pinching. The band had completely stopped playing, with only the thump, thump of the drums left holding it together. In their triumphant day out they had also collected a motley band of drunks and street urchins. Slatternly women pushed prams with bawling babies up the hill, worn-out toddlers holding onto the pram, and dragging them back all the time. Behind them a wide selection of stray dogs, who marched triumphantly at the rear, were happily wagging their tails and hopefully following the limping parade wherever it would lead to, while half-heartedly yapping and fighting each other now and again. They progressed, worn out, up the hill and disappeared towards the Children's Hospital along Catherine Street.

On other summer Sundays the circus would arrive, going up Hardman Street and along to Princes Park. This time it was a troubling collection of lions and tigers in cages wheeling past. Saddest and most bizarre were the elephants lumbering up the hill, trudging just like the exhausted weekday workers going home. But these large grey lumps looked out of place and whatever their entertainment value later on, right now they were pathetic and humiliated animals.

The year's pattern ended with the Scottish Church of St Andrews celebrating his feast-day on 30th November and the beginning of Advent. Christmas was in sight. The kilted soldiers paraded along Rodney Street with a skirl of pipes and drums. They stood, a block of wild colour, tartans and white gaiters, outside the church and brightened up the grey late-autumn street, falling leaves at their feet.

It looked as though the more sound and ceremony a religion had, the less its centre was important. Winter Mass in the old workhouse chapel up Mount Pleasant with little Father Byrne had a transcendence that could lift the congregation out of the physical sphere without any help from music or colours. The Little Chapel was so cold that their breath made clouds in the damp building and bits of plaster fell down each Sunday. But at the consecration, Jesus Himself zoomed into that drab building and they, for a moment, were back at that Last Supper instant when Jesus promised them his continuing presence in the bread and wine. It did not matter that it was a slum church serving people from the slums around, the consecration was the same in any church or cathedral.

It was a tense performance to get Father to make his yearly Easter Duties, which were the least spiritual essentials needed to be part of the church. One confession and one communion had to be made around Eastertime; it was a conspiracy that Celi and Mary had to carry out effectively. Talking about times of church services and how they had both completed their duty at mealtimes, they dropped heavy hints daily but could not actually take him to the confession booth or the altar and had to take it on trust that he had complied. It was as if he belonged only out of some primitive fear, not from any actual belief, but of course none of this could be discussed.

Every now and again Father decided to cut his toenails. He sat in the fireside chair snipping away. The dog eagerly ate his toe-clippings. They set-to together, Whiskey snapping up the trimmings. He took it as a rite of adoration. Mary watched from the other chair, doing her Latin homework. It was repulsive. How could Whiskey behave in such an abject way? Perhaps, if science lessons were easier, she could prove that it was necessary protein for the dog,

12

Winning the scholarship brought changes that no one could have foreseen. The gang playing out in the evenings disintegrated. Their street-life was broken by having two hours homework to do most evenings, with double at the weekends and an awkwardness grew between them. The easy camaraderie was gone, replaced by the awkwardness of advancing adolescence.

Nannie and Aunty Julie took her to George Henry Lee's, where the Notre Dame High School bottle-green uniforms were kept in a large glass showcase. Woollen dress, dark green cardigan, blazer, (plus badge on pocket), Gabardine mac, beret, lisle stockings, sandals, proper shoes, navy knickers, (green was not available, but they did have pockets) and, in spring, two light green linen dresses. A Greek-style gym outfit was also needed, that could be made by a dressmaker; it was a completely new life, but not paid for by her parents. A gap somewhere. The list also demanded a Hymn Book of over a hundred hymns that spanned a year's changes and feast-days.

The High School had a large green weathered notice-board outside the front door proclaiming in faded gold "*Notre Dame High*

School for the Daughters of Gentlemen." It was only by the grace of the scholarship that Mary was able to attend the same school as her Mother and all aunts. Soon afterwards the board disappeared and was never replaced.

Up the steps, through the large carved door and straight into the presence of Sister Veronica, rotund stalwart portress and guardian, with her companion, the minute Sister Pauline. They vetted visitors, received guests and parcels and inspected girls leaving, whether they had changed from indoor sandals to outside shoes and were wearing their berets with the school's silver brooch, its motto *Suavitor in Modo, Fortiter in Re.* That translated into 'Gentle in manner, Strong in deed,' or as some said, an iron fist in a velvet glove. It was strange to have an entire school crammed into a couple of words.

The High School had an impressive imitation ELucyabethan staircase of polished wood, long corridors and the intricate network of gardens alongside the Convent grounds.

Morning Assembly was a new experience in the hall beneath the convent's chapel. Sister Joseph of the Incarnation sailed majestically into the Lower Hall with a sheaf of papers which held the daily pronouncements. A sixth-form girl would play the piano for the hymns. Throughout the year they worked through a mixture of the agricultural calendar and the progress of Jesus through his life and death, the two intertwining via the hymn book of over a hundred hymns.

There was the haunting Holy Week hymn about his crucifixion,

Man of Sorrows, wrapped in grief,
bow thy head to our relief,
Thou the cup of fire hast drained
'till its light alone remained.

Or the gentler one petitioning Our Lady -
Mother of mercy, day by day
thy gifts are strewn along life's way

or the rumbustious

91

Around that rock resounding, the angry foeman raves,
Upon that craggy headland beat high the sullen waves.
The entire year was compressed into these songs, with a certainty in their yearly repetition.

After-dinner assembly, on the other hand, was calming, almost hypnotising. They said the Litany of Our Lady in the lower hall, under the convent chapel, kneeling in class lines. In summertime the room was bright, green leaves swishing outside. It was a five-penny bus ride to see trees like that otherwise.

Mystical Rose, pray for us,
Tower of David, pray for us
Tower of Ivory, pray for us,
House of Gold, pray for us,
Ark of the Covenant, pray for us
Gate of Heaven, Morning Star, Health of the Weak...Mother Most Amiable...Mother Inviolate, Mother Undefiled, Queen of Angels... Queen of Apostles...Queen of Prophets... gently it continued like a dream, each image replacing another like a necklace of different jewels. Then at the end, it crashed into real music, a torrent of words that made an insistent rhythm:

Hail Holy Queen, Mother of mercy, hail our Life, our Sweetness, and our Hope. To thee do we cry, poor banished children of Eve. To thee do we send up our sighs, mourning and weeping in this vale of tears.

Turn, then, most gracious Advocate, thine eyes of mercy towards us; and after this our exile, show unto us the blessed fruit of thy womb, Jesus. O clement, O loving, O sweet Virgin Mary.

Said at a gallop, this sent them off reassured and calmed as teachers filed in to collect their own class for afternoon lessons. They walked in almost-silence along the cool lower corridor with its cream-tiled floor and arched ceiling to scatter among their various classrooms.

Several evenings, the policeman slowly checked every door on Roberts Woodyard and Blakes Garage, and went on down town, flashing his torch through jewellers' little slits in their shutters. He tried front doors here and there and once found their own front door unlocked one night and woke Father up to tell him.

"We used to use the Convent shelter" Mother told her. That would have been better than the shelter in Back Maryland Street, a low building with a flat cement roof. In the night, screams and shouts could be heard coming from it as drunks capered round inside. Once Mary went in with the dog and found it dark, windowless and stinking of pee. A few wooden benches remained fixed to the walls but most had been ripped off. And there was no door. A few air-bricks let in even more cold air. Then the Corporation workers pulled down the entire building and the street looked wide and clear. It did not make sense that such a small building would have saved their lives -if that thick cement roof was hit, it would have crushed everyone immediately. Better to stay at home and die surrounded with your own furniture.

There were afternoon school visits to the Convent Chapel to mark various feasts throughout the year.Sister Austin, the chapel sacristan, glided around with a lighting taper as if on wheels, with a glazed smile. Everything in the Chapel was cream and gold, the pale parquet floor polished to a glowing cream too. She lit the candles either side of the altar with practised gracefulness and tweaked the flowers into perfect arrangements as if on stage.

The classes wore white veils which transformed them into misty beings groomed for prayer. They had spent music lessons learning motets to sing at important feasts like the Ascension or Candlemas. They learnt Gregorian chant, its plangent simplicity striking right to the core, giving each note a sharp power with its plainly-marked notes.

Tota pulchra es, Maria
Et macula originalis non est in te
Tu gloria Jerusalem,
Tu laetitia Israel,
Tu honorificentia populi nostri,
Tu tota pulchra es Maria
Tu tota puchra es Maria,

93

Oh Maria,
Maria, ora pro nobis.

It ended with the heartfelt cry of *Oh Maria*, as if she was in the next room, asking her to pray for them. Most of the hymns to Mary were about asking for a mother-like intercession, a go-between working for them with an all-powerful God, just like a clever wife or mother or grandmother tackling an awkward man.

Other music lessons consisted of preparing for the end-of -term concert. It was Benjamin Britten's Christmas Carol one year, with school and parents holding their breath, hoping that the youngest two a and two alpha classes could manage to reach the top notes. One year however, almost all the music lessons were spent learning the Belgian national anthem in readiness for the visit of Reverend Mother Provincial from Namur. She arrived, plump, little black-button eyes and two haughty companions, and sat while the entire school staunchly performed it. In heavily accented English she thanked them and everyone received a holy picture to mark the occasion. It was all a great disappointment.

Noble Belgique ô mère chérie
À toi nos cœrs, à toi nos bras,
À toi notre sang ô Patrie!
Nous le jourons tous, tu vivras!

Strangely, once it was performed, it completely dropped out of anyone's memory and a year later no pupil would have been able to sing any line of it. Miss Sullivan was then able to revert to her first love and spent the rest of the time playing them records of Mozart operas interspersed with their own haphazard orchestra which was not much different from an infant's triangle and tambourine band. Anyone who could play the piano was already proficient via private lessons at home; they were not taught anything so useful at school.

The girls who played the piano for morning assembly were all privately taught, bringing a false sense of proficiency to the school's curriculum.

Their dual language Latin/English prayer-books locked up a year's celebration, with lists of saints' days at the back of the gold-edged pages. At their christening, each girl had been baptised with a saint's name as a way of making sure that there would always be a saint looking after them. It was obvious that anyone called Opal, Ruby or Beryl would be a Protestant girl, as there were no saints with those names and so no one would be looking after them. On November the 2nd , however, there was a special day, All Souls' Day , devoted to the many unknown saints, where they huddled in after the proper publicly-canonised saints of November the 1st. Everyone was counted in as a saint-in-waiting who had died in a state of grace; their names covered all the countries of the world.

On Sunday evenings, Celi would take Mary up to Nana's in Cassville Road to find her alone, Lucy and Kay gone into town. She was often found washing her feet in a bowl, using lavender soap or in extreme bad weather, some mustard. It was a private indulgence. She sat in her rocking chair, drying her feet,
"Now, any news this week?" But this week the news was totally dramatic, never to be rivalled. Kay had thrown Jack out as he had not ... well, the details were not gone into in front of Mary. Celi was aghast. Marriage was sacred and couples promised to be together through to death. Getting rid of a disappointing spouse was not allowed.
When they turned up a fortnight later, Kay was still in the house and Celi refused to speak to her. Being polite and perceptive, Kay knew Mary would react differently and they smiled and greeted each other as normal, but in the circumstances it was easier for Kay to leave for work early as a way of escape. Sunday pubs opened at 7.30pm. Celi could not cope with her own sister breaking away from an unsatisfactory marriage, when she herself was plodding along unhappily with Vin. Mary was also jealous as Lucy said she met her father, Jack, in town and he took her out to a café for a meal and gave her pocket money.
Further developments were worse. Jack started to appear at number nine at dinnertime, obviously in need of something to eat. He looked dirty, with greasy hair, and his collar was edged with black, his fingernails were dirty too and he quickly wolfed down the meat pie and chutney that they usually had, followed by three cups of tea.

When it was time for Celi to go to work at half-past one and for Mary to go back to school, he left; there was an awkward pause as she saw him out.

"I think he was going to ask me for some money, but luckily he thought better of it at the last moment," Celi said. It was an example of her practising her religion, giving kindness to the sinner while disapproving of the entire situation.

He turned up a few times in this dejected state and then one day he appeared clean, well dressed and obviously settled in a new place, probably he had got his share of a taxi-driving job again. One dinner-time he tried to warn Celi about Vin and some woman.

"She's quite a looker, you'd be surprised, that's all I'm saying." He tapped his nose. Celi cut him off, not wanting the talk to continue in front of Mary, or not wanting to hear it herself. Anything not put into words could be controlled, kept out of sight. He turned to Mary, smiling his usual devilish smile,

"What can you do round here?" Now he had managed to re-establish himself he never called round again. News about town was that he had moved in with some woman who was a young widow with some money of her own. His dark good looks would guarantee him success in no time at all, unlike other men.

There was worse. Sunday evening again at Nana's. Everything had to be spoken about in front of Mary. There must have been some contact through the week perhaps a phonecall or a visit to Aunty Frances's in the next road. Messages must have been sent in secret. Mary could not understand what was going on this time. Celi was now angry with her own mother.

"Mum, how *could* you!" How could you let this go on in your own house!" Nana looked quite composed, not ashamed at all.

"But Kay pays most of the mortgage, you know, so what could I do? Lucy did not object, I suppose she was asked about it. Kay wouldn't have just turned up with him out of the blue, " she said mildly as though nothing had happened. The news was that Kay had now installed a lover, a blond Polishman called Jurgens, obviously from the Polish Club. It was as if Nana was always going to be attracting extra people, her good nature letting more and more into the house. This time, when Kay appeared, Celi turned her head away and the atmosphere was tense indeed. Kay just said

"Goodbye, Celi, Mary, goodnight, Mum, I won't be late," and went off to work, Lucy being at the pictures at the Abbey with friends from Plattsville Road and expected back later.

Each summer, Julie was able to go off with her friend Ann Derham and choose somewhere in Europe for a fortnight's holiday. Tossa da Mar, Oberammergau, Marbella, Lucerne – she disappeared and returned with presents, photos, fatter and deeply tanned. For a couple of weeks Julie became like an exotic bird, telling never-ending tales of these distant places while Celi went about various tasks in the dark back kitchen.

"Oh really, Julie. Just a minute now, I need to reach that saucepan over there." She was stuck with Julie, as Vin, sitting in the warm living room was doing his stamps and almost snarled if Julie came anywhere near him.

One year as a treat, Nannie and Auntie Julie took Mary to Blackpool, staying in The Grand Hotel. They went to the Opera House for "*Hobson's Choice*" and the next day went up the Tower, where a sad lion lay in a white-tiled cell, part of the zoo. It looked tired and moth-eaten, not exotic or educational, lying there like a discarded floor-cloth. There was no way of stopping this, (Nannie and Auntie Julie did not see the point) but Mary was dumbfounded that such treatment was allowed. The attendant said he merely sold admission tickets, there was no one to approach to protest about the scandal of such bad treatment of the shabby lion, however, and she had to forget about it.

As Nannie was left behind alone in the gigantic house for the summer fortnight, Mary was asked to stay and sleep each night with her. The high double bed crunched, as if the mattress was stuffed with bits of horsehair or even straw. She did not really want to know either way. The bedstead was quite modern, an almost Scandinavian design in light wood, strange in the circumstances since they must have bought it early in the century.

But there were little luxuries like the glow of the bedside oil-lamp, runners of richly-coloured Axminster carpet each side of the bed, the gas fire with its little trivet for making a pot of tea and the view of the school playgrounds from the two ceiling to floor windows. The trees wafted about in the night and the sound of the convent bell was that bit clearer here across the grounds.

There was an atmosphere of peacefulness and contentment here. As Nannie undressed or dressed in the morning, her rotund body showed a mass of rich flesh. Five children, including the dead twins, had come out of that body, an entire difference from her own Mother's stark single one. Her nightdresses were made of something called nun's veiling, a warm slightly flannelette material. It was ordered specially from somewhere and a dressmaker had to run them up from a pattern.

Because the bathroom was so far away up two flights of stairs and along the top corridor, Nannie kept a chamber pot under the bed, for any need in the night. The smell of her gushing pee was animal-rich and strangely reassuring. Mary could hear every drop and the farmyard smell quickly reached across. Nannie kept a piece of old sheeting to wipe her behind and in the morning would take the potty along to the deep Belfast kitchen sink to empty it. With the sheeting draped over it, she carried it across the hallway as if it was some important offering. If it was solid matter, though, she had to walk right up the stairway and dispose of the contents properly in the far-off upstairs bathroom along the top corridor.

Mary preferred to go upstairs and a torch was kept on the table at her side of the bed. It made wild patterns on the walls and she enjoyed frightening herself on the climb past the high echoing walls. The shadows danced and swirled and made the walls dissolve.

Also in the bedroom was a large trunk, another of the remnants of her trousseau, sent up from Barnet still with the tattered browning label to the original address at number 14 South Hunter Street. It was twin to the other one in Mary's bedroom, used as an altar and full of old books with small mites dashing through them, It stood beside the wardrobe, next to a smart black hatbox that Mary had always coveted.

"The street used to stretch further along before they built the Demonstration School and they renumbered the houses" she said. It was unclear how they had managed to move so easily and conveniently, just a few houses away. Adults kept these mysteries as if they did not care about the changes.

Mary sat up in the high bed and watched Nannie get ready for the night, the full raining-down of her grey-white hair, the stash of hairpins left on the little china finger-ring with its white saucer on the dressing table between the two windows.

On Nannie's side of the bed was the bedside table with her complete night-set – a large crucifix, a tall candle in a silver candlestick, her prayer book, and a small art-nouveau photo frame with a young George Martineau looking out hopefully, moustache twirled at the ends. Beside him coiled at the foot of the crucifix were her rosary beads and a small tin of Imp cough sweets, minute black liquorice squares, which did domestic miracles on sore throats. Everything was in its ordained place. A large wooden Crucifix stood as if holding it all together. A loud ticking alarm clock stood waiting to be wound up. Nannie still said 'five and twenty' past any hour in the old style of speaking.

In the morning, Nannie wound her night-time long silver plait back into its prim bun and resumed her usual uniform of navy skirt with purple cardigan and jumper. On hot days she wore a sprigged blouse with long sleeves, but kept the lisle stockings whatever the weather. An amethyst brooch, three little purple stones, was centre at her throat.

And Nannie was always an expert on weather. Her best item of prophecy was *cold-enough-for-snow,* which was far colder than real snow. She had also seen snow at Easter a couple of times, which was preposterous and showed what age could accumulate as strange experiences. Old people must live in a different layer of the present, always filtered through what they had seen long ago, like the saying:

If Christmas Day be crisp and clear,
there will be two winters in the year.

In the centre of the bedroom was a circular table with a writing set on it, an inlaid black box with china flowers inset here and there. It gave a dignity to the room. Next to it, between the two windows, the dressing table held silver-backed hairbrush and mirror with a small china hand to keep rings on. The minute white fingers pointed to the ceiling when they were off duty, waiting to guard her wedding ring, its keeper and engagement ring overnight

It was in the first term at the High School that one dinnertime the first issue of menstrual blood happened. Mary burst into tears at the shock of it, the danger and embarrassment. She was so lucky it had started now. What would have happened if she did not come home every day for dinner? Life was full of these canyons and you could fall down at any instant. How did other girls cope if it happened to them away from home? This luck was too precarious.

"Don't worry," Mother comforted her. "Now your spots will start to go away, it will all be different." She opened her side-drawer in the dressing table and brought out some pieces of old sheeting, already faintly stained from past usage. "Here, you fold it up like this and pin it each end to your knickers and it collects all the blood. I'll get some sanitary towels and a belt later on." As there was so little money, the shop-bought sanitary towels were really a luxury and so the secret life of having to cope began. Blood often oozed round the edges; you could hardly take wodges of sheeting into school or have anywhere to place the bloodied wads before taking them home to wash. They were steeped in pails of water to get the worst of the blood out, the pails hidden under the back kitchen stair-cupboard.

Blood did not wash out completely, the pattern imprinted on the folded cloth stayed. Faint print on faint print, monthly. It was obvious that tie-dying was invented by women; the unrolled cloths showed patterns rather like the Turin Shroud, each one different from the one before.

The blood-stained cloths were kept in secret places in the back kitchen and they had to wait until Father was out of the house, which was luckily quite often, to wash away the gushing reconstituted blood. So this was what Mother had been doing for years and years. It explained the strange rust-like smell that her dressing-table drawer had, and its duster-like cloths.

Games lessons became torture. Trying to climb a rope up to the ceiling of the gym, while worrying that cloth or pads would be shifted right out of place added to an already hazardous task. It was the fact that it all had to be hidden from other girls too – all females were keeping these embarrassing secrets from each other. Those who were brave enough to say that they were -er- not really feeling well today, were left to sit on the steps at the front of the stage, as if to display that this was some sort of punishment and they were cowards. The cleverer ones brought in notes from parents, which were only a small disguise.

Meanwhile the girls as small as shrimps, breastless, waistless, hipless and still pseudo-boys, gambolled about, hurtling over the box and horse like gunshots, plus landing gracefully and then dashing up and down the ropes like monkeys. It could be years before their periods arrived to disrupt their freedom and assurance. Mary clambered up to the horse or box (there was little difference except that the horse did have two handles to grab at the worst moment) bravely hurtling herself into space.

Often landing face-first onto the coconut mat, she had bruises and scorch marks for a few days after and felt she had learnt nothing at all.

If she had taken sciences instead of arts it would have been possible surely to prove that x weight of body by y speed of run by z effort of lift-off was an impossible experiment in gravity. What good any of theses exercises would be to any of them once they were thirty would be negligible. So far, games lessons merely developed her bravery, self-control and ability to endure public humiliation without showing any outer distress. They did not know that she usually spent the night before games lessons sleepless with apprehension and sick to the pit of her stomach in fear.

But the spots continued. Eventually, after various tears, Celi arranged to take her to a proper skin specialist. Dr Bligh had given a letter of introduction, as a favour. Surgical spirit had not cured them, in fact it was turning her skin to leather. Bright little yellow spots and abundant blackheads prospered all over Mary's face, with the occasional boil. Kaolin poultices were the home-cure, turning it into an almost mediaeval affliction.

The specialist had a big room to himself in the hospital and an air of authority, unlike the sympathetic avuncular air of Dr Bligh. He examined her face with distaste and prescribed a sulphur cream that would peel the top layer of skin and bring new skin to the surface. There was also sulphur soap to add to the treatment.

"And you will have to wash your face carefully, with hot water and the special soap and make certain that you rinse off all the soap so it does not clog the pores. That's the reason for the blackheads, then, a smut lands on the surface and forms a blockage, hence the spots." He sat being important while Mother murmured in obedience. Mary knew something was wrong here and was amazed at the man's mixture of ignorance and arrogance. She knew that the grease must be coming from the inside to the outside, and not the other way around. It did not make sense. Soap did not stay on her skin, it washed off. As she had not learnt enough General Science, she could not point out to him that oil emerging to the skin's surface would solidify and yellow on meeting the air. Even if she had, it was impossible to challenge such an important man.

But Mother was full of enthusiasm and even bought the expensive special soap which Mary imagined was something like fire and brimstone. It had a bitter smell and stung her face slightly. After a few applications of the strong cream, flakes of skin began to peel off. One morning Mary sat up in bed to a fall of skin-flakes but with all the merry spots still forming through the underlayers. She cried; it was hopeless and her thirteenth birthday was coming soon too. It was like bad sunburn without any of the enjoyment. No one thought of the fried bread, suet, dripping, lard, sausages, streaky bacon, chips, scallops, bread and butter, margarine, fried onions, cheese, biscuits, cakes. There was, as an occasional lucky treat, rich Jersey milk, real cream and all the fatty meals that caused the over-abundance of oil. Any salad had to be festooned with salad cream, which stopped it being healthy.

This usual diet was a prime provider of boils and the skin specialist did not seem to know anything about it. And when, in an effort to lose weight, Mother bought rock-hard special diet rolls, instead of ordinary bread from Kirkland Jennings, they were only made eatable by cramming them with butter, which only increased their weight-making possibilities. And then, of course, what was the use of any buttered roll without any jam?

At some time of the year the hot milk on Father's Shredded Wheat changed into cold milk. It was the subtle announcement of spring, more definite than the Annunciation. No more panic, running into the back kitchen, to the give-away swishing sound, "The pan! The pan! The milk's boiled over!" and the milk slurping down the sides of the pan and dripping down the sides of the fat black gas pipes and onto the white enamel tray. Along the little gutter at the front the hot milk ran, and cooled itself into a hard skin. Mother or herself would have to mop it out before tomorrow. Winter was a succession of these small panics, discomforts and extra duties; spring brought a quick cut of all these tensions.

"No wonder the mediaeval peasants went out and danced round a Maypole as soon as the good weather arrived!" Mother remarked, mopping the kitchen floor afterwards.

It was strange how Celi had so many friends who appeared at the house whereas Vin had no visitors whatsoever. While he went out Saturday night after Saturday night chasing after some dream, Celi held court. One of these visitors was young man who had no obvious connection with the family - perhaps their parents were friends, perhaps his Mother had worked in Celi's office. Paddy Gehogehan would call in on his way into town, checking his appearance at Father's shaving mirror over the needlework table.

"How do you think I look? All right?" His black hair, dark eyes, the swashbuckling grey mac with its cape and epaulettes – what was he, so glamorous, doing in their house – how had Mother got to know him?

"Sorry," he said, shrewd enough in the midst of his mercurial cavorting in front of the mirror, "You're too young for me and I can't wait until you grow up." He must have realised the hero-worship which Mary thought she had hidden so well. Cotton dress, white socks, sandals; years to go. He gave her a friendly hug, though, and strode out into the glamour of the Saturday night pubs.

Maisie, his girlfriend called round one evening-long red hair, a well-built woman who came round to ask Celi's advice. Should she marry Paddy or not?All this conversation had to be done in front of Mary as this was the only warm room in the house. Maisie accepted that Paddy was an alcoholic, as Celi pointed out, but was determined to marry him.

"I'll take the risk. I love him." Mary said nothing. But she knew that the sturdy body of Maisie was no defence against the stronger lure of the pubs. And soon they never saw him again, nor were they invited to the wedding.

Celi told her stories about Ireland, which was a rich place of fairy-stories. The three young sisters would be at a bonfire on the shore as the Liverpool mail-boat left.

"We were so close we could see the passengers and wave to them. Mum had to get back to the ship's chandler's yard over in Beaufort Street and we were left with Grandma and Cappy at Beech House for most of the summer." The death of James McGivern had cut right through the family, but his young widow was determined to carry on the business. "We spent a long time there, all the summers, really. There was a woman on the shore at Greencastle who made her own house on the shore, right from the stones there." That showed how magical a place it was, a woman doing just that and no one stopping her. But the war had intervened and destroyed it all, as Beech House was razed to the ground to make way for an American airbase, with old Mrs Mc Givern dying soon after.

"And, on top of it all," Aunty Kay said years later, "We lost out on everything. Old Mrs McGivern in Greencastle left us out of her will, she went and left the money for a stained glass window in St Vincent's instead. She disapproved about our Mum remarrying after James Mc Givern died so early. But Mum was young, with us three daughters, and Alban Sinnott came along. Totally unfair after all, because Mrs McGivern was Edward's third wife, so she really had no excuse!"

The High School was like walking into a dream. Corridors led everywhere, mostly with polished floorboards, though the Lower Corridor with its cream tiles beneath its arched ceiling was always cool. Unfortunately the science labs were along this corridor and occasionally a whiff of something like bad eggs drifted out of the rooms. The main staircase could have been ripped out of a Tudor building, a large ornate piece of woodcarving with shallow steps, that led to the first floor corridors and sixth form classes, with Sister Joseph of the Incarnation's office.

Reproductions of Raphael, Botticelli, Durer, Piero Della Francesca, Leonardo da Vinci hung along corridor walls gave a casual education in art history along the way. Prefects stood here and there to keep order and inflict silence on the passing classes.

The new girls were told not to talk to Sister Albania who drifted about along the upper corridor that led to the convent itself, needing conversation. She was supposed to be mad, but was also very important as she was the sister of Monsignor Atkins, Vicar-General of the Liverpool Archdiocese. She would grasp the hand of a second year child and ask if they were happy. It was as if Sister Albania really looked into them and was interested in their well-being. She often turned up outside the little prayer-room opposite the 2a and 2alpha classrooms. Further along that polished corridor was the way into the real centre of the convent itself and the chapel. Sometimes in the distance nuns could be seen placing clean laundry into cupboards.

"Oh yes," Nannie said, there's lay sisters too in the order, they're not all teachers and Headmistresses. You have to have some extra bodies to do the domestic work, you can't farm it all out." Green-overalled women came up from town to work in the convent laundry beside the lower playground at the Demonstration School, but that did not count as a religious duty and so could be a public job.

And then Mary walked into the Studio at the High School and life really began properly.

In English lessons especially they were taught that writing AMDG, Ad Majoram Dei Gloriam at the top of the page made it dedicated to God, from the Latin for 'To the greater glory of God.' So small, and yet they were looped up into the gigantic beauty of everything by small gestures like this. It was like writing on glass, with this presence shining behind.

Latin was wonderful, it stomped across the pages firmly, like its soldiers, neat in rows, especially on the back pages of their textbook *Latin for Today* where the verbs were laid out neatly. It was a sheer laboratory example of how language was constructed. English leant on this fabric, just as French did.

Miss Kelly taught them French although she seemed to be on her last legs. Every lesson was an effort. Frizzled red-dyed hair, chewing peppermints that did not exactly manage to disguise the blast of drink (always worse after dinnertime) she manoeuvred them through life with the Famille Dubois. They had a maid, Marie and a gardener, Jaques. Monsieur Dubois went off to his bureau every day in his moteur, while Madame Dubois arranged flowers and bought hats. Luckily, Mrs Aspinall who taught them Latin had provided the groundwork of grammar that French lessons could lean on.

Learning German was an effort. So soon after the war, it was almost a betrayal of all those who had been killed or maimed throughout Europe. It was also far more difficult than Latin or French, with no enjoyable rhythm. They learned the prepositions:

Mit, nach , von, zu, aus, bei, seit,

entgagen, gegenuber, über, ausser, *Mrs Pritchard.*

And those that took the accusative;

Durch, vor, gegen, ober, um, entlang, vieder, *Mrs Pritchard* The chant always included the teacher's name as though she was a preposition in her own right. She told them of being a student in Germany before the war and how it had been so cold that she had gone to bed wearing her coat. It served them right, the girls thought, they deserved to suffer, but the young Mrs Pritchard should not have had to go through that to learn proper German. She deserved to be included in their lists. The school, being adventurous had begun to teach Russian in the sixth form, as being somehow useful in the growing fight against communism.

Classes had the choice between following a Science or an Arts syllabus, which meant that often there were only fifteen in any classroom. Science was a mixture of the repulsive and the dangerous. Innocent white mice or specially bred rats were cut open and displayed on Open Day, their innards meticulously labelled. Bunsen burners flared erratically and obnoxious stinks could appear without warning. Small explosions were common: The chemistry and physics teachers wandered around dressed in thick white overalls as if wearing protective clothing. Jars of small dead animals cluttered the shelves like a warning.

Maths was even worse because Miss Harvey was a tyrant. She strode into the classroom, always on the edge of anger, rattled through any example of algebra or geometry, giving them several pages of the textbook to do as homework. Several lessons she totally wasted telling them about her driving lessons or her violin recitals. No one understood much of the gobble-de-gook, and the kinder, cleverer girls came in early and helped the bemused and lost girls through the previous night's homework. They stumbled through together like this; no one thought of complaining and no one would have known how to, girls and parents alike.

Him

Wilson, Keppel and Betty. Lord Haw Haw. This Jew merchant. Take, say, for instance. This dame. The fact of the matter is. Typical mentality. So I said to him, I said. All their shenanigans. You'll cut yourself on those scissors. How much did it cost, then? Gassing away. Jew boys. A tanner, a quid. Bung it here. Have a shifty. Blokes. Pie-eyed. Some merchant. What's this foreign muck? Shove us the salt. Those Braddocks are Commies. Down in the boozer. Have a dekko. Cronies. I've said it before and I'll say it again. Once and for all.

Smoke Gets in Your Eyes. He loved it. When it came on the radio, he looked up. Later, he would whistle snatches from it as he got the coal in. A clue. Love. When he had first loved Celi, or just a previous unidentified girlfriend?. Or no one? Just a general, wide longing? Not a question to ask. Deep in the dark pit of him and in the sketchy past. Photos of palm trees, a cruise mentioned. I haven't got time for all that. What about the paper bill, then and the insurance man? Put it in the drawer. A bit of a flap on.

Her

A little of what you fancy does you good. Gone, and never called me Mother! Tatti-fa-la-ta. Where the Mountains of Mourne sweep down to the sea. When Irish eyes are smiling. Oh, no, Sir Jasper! Saturday night theatre. Another cup of tea. Time to change our library books. Funny peculiar or funny ha ha. These bunions are killing me.

Eileen Ó, me heart is going grey. A Tree Grows in Brooklyn. Fame is the Spur. Little Lord Fontleroy. J.B. Priestley. Howard Spring. Kate O' Brien. A man on a galloping horse wouldn't see it. One nail drives out another. Bad luck to change the calendar until the new month starts. Fairies at the bottom of the garden. Never bring May blossom into the house. Starting another Novena. Worse things happen at sea. So-and-so says more than their prayers. A real peach. The Sun Is My Undoing. Three Little Maids From School Are We.

Before electricity was installed, walking through from one house to another meant passing through a pitch-black sitting room, through Nannie's hall, and up two flights of dark staircase, past *The Boyhood of Raleigh*, before reaching the upstairs living room in number 11 and the warmth of their fire. It could be frightening at times. Mary would play at being blind, holding her hands out in front to avoid cannonading into the sitting room furniture.

Once, going past the settee, towards the empty fireplace, Mary saw something new. In the cold black of the sitting room between the two houses, a figure stood waiting for her, a small woman with a type of lace cap and a soft shawl round her shoulders.

She stood perfectly still, waiting. It took an immeasurable time to keep crossing the room - the figure stayed, immobile. Mary could not manage to turn back, as if magnetised. She could see the furniture through the image as she came nearer, in classic ghost transparency. They were almost face to face. The woman did not exactly smile, but bowed her head slightly. As they drew level, the woman disappeared completely. The fear went too. Now, a feeling of gentleness and niceness remained, like a couple of words said over someone's shoulder.

Mentioning this to her Mother one lunchtime the next week, Celi calmly said yes, she had also seen the same ghost twice before.

"She must be one of the original owners, if the house was built in 1811, the costume is right. She must be just telling us she was here first, or there is something tying her to the building." That was all right then, the ghost lady was accepted as a quiet resident of the house, the rightful previous owner.

It was the week before one of those deep illnesses that shove the helpless child onto the next chess square on the life-board. She was lying in bed, bleached from flu, a February casualty. Barely in the everyday world, Mary hovered in the same grey land that the ghost inhabited. Mother came up to the bedroom and told her off for fiddling with the wallpaper. Such a damp room meant that the wall paper was only partly fixed; here and there, loose edges or bubbles asked to be peeled away. Mary had got through to the bare plaster and had got a fright. Hairs had started to fall out. Something living was sealed in behind the bed? All the surroundings began to seethe with possibilities. Mother made it worse, trying to soothe her.

"It's just horsehair. They mixed it into the plaster when they built this house." Then she said, " Really, I came up to tell you that the King has died," and burst into tears. The Liverpool Echo came out that evening with a complete front page photo of the King, surrounded by a black border. The radio played grim classical music all day and even by the time Mary was well enough to go out, shop windows round town were transformed into shrines, with his photo surrounded by black and purple drapery or crepe paper.

Another night, Mary awoke with a sudden desire to walk downstairs and out into the street. She got up and was halfway down their front stairs when Father opened the living-room door and shouted at her, What was she thinking of! What was she up to now! He broke through the compulsion and Mary was left puzzled, unable to explain why she was standing there in her nightdress at ten o'clock at night. His anger drove any explanation away and she was as puzzled as they were. A few days later Mother said it was probably sleepwalking, it was something girls of her age were likely to do.

Christmases entailed walking through the cold sitting room several times, with the bread sauce from Nannie's house, the gravy-boat, extra bowls and plates and all other necessities. Each year Father made a complaining performance of the carving, sharpening the long blade on the burnishing stave and then struggling with the poor chicken as though it was made of concrete. Each year he said,

"Where did you get this one from, for goodness' sake! How am I supposed to cut with this!" and the women would *tut, tut* and try to change the subject while he attempted his once-a-year duty. Each year it was either the Co-op or Mr Phillips butchers who were to blame. One year they went so far as to get a turkey and that was real trouble, as if he had been asked to saw through tree branches.

The table would be covered with bowls and plates of sauces and gravies while everyone waited for the entry of the pudding. Then there were the presents, always surprises from Nannie and Julie while Vin gave everyone cash. He gave Mary a new ten shilling note each year and she had to pretend to be both surprised and pleased.

"I couldn't go round the shops looking for something suitable, you never know what to get that way," he absolved himself from any Christmas shopping each year.

Their money situation was a mystery. Mary asked her Mother what was Father's job - you could not ask him direct.

"He's an accountant, he works in Cammell Laird's offices, he deals with the wages. He's often angry at how much the ship-labourers earn compare to himself. Don't be going asking him questions about it, will you." That was the end of that. Mary knew that real accountants had their own offices and did not work inside shipyards; also, she knew, from Celi's little housekeeping book kept in the sideboard cutlery drawer, that he gave her £3.00 housekeeping each week and that had to cover everything including the gas bill.

He paid for the coal delivery, though -which was why Mary or Celi had to stand in the yard, counting the bags as the coal-men carried the heavy sacks down the outside steps into the cellar and ended up tipping the last five hundredweight easily into the metal coal-bunker that stood outside the back door.

Then they had to go through the cellar to next-door's cellar and unhook the safety chain on the metal coal-hole cover to let the sacks be emptied from the pavement. It was humiliating on both sides, as the men thumped the empty sacks onto a pile near the back door to the street and Mary had to stand there counting each one.

Nannie's coal cover was right outside the front door of number 11. All up Maryland Street each house had its own coal cover with its metal design set into the paving stones. The coal men were larger than life, covered with grit and wearing two overcoats sometimes, with the same sacking apron that the bin-men wore. Heaving a sack of coal on their shoulders they navigated the yard steps bravely, wearing themselves out. They would live up in Myrtle Gardens or the Bullring, somewhere tough. She would not recognise them washed and wearing a suit.

Now and again there was a delivery of Welsh coal and everyone cheered up. Welsh coal, almost liquid black, was almost jewellery that burned with vivid rainbow gusts of gas. Small bursts of colour dashed out of the shiny jet coals. It was a shame to burn it, Mary thought.

Photos

13

An official letter arrived from Liverpool Corporation announcing that their house was historic and they were not to make any alterations without permission, not even putting up a shelf. This made no difference to Vin, who did not intend doing anything to the place. This letter gave him their official permission to do nothing whatever to the house. His hands were shiny from working with paper and he had a seg on his middle finger where a pen rested all day.

"What's the use? It's no use - if you're paying rent, it only goes to the Corporation then. No need to work for them as well!" He brought in a bucket of coal from the bunker outside the back door and scooped up the dog's business from the yard into the dustbin and that was the limit of his household duties. When he had his weekly bath, usually on a Friday night, he left a triumphant black ring round the bath for Mary or Celi to clean off.

Yet after the evening meal he would go round the living room floor picking up infinitesimal bits – crumbs, threads, scraps of paper, anything the dog had missed eating. But to go and get the brush and do it properly was unthinkable for a man to do and no one would ever have suggested it.

If anything was not immediately solved, he would proclaim "If you want anything doing in this house, you have to do it yourself!" but neither Celi nor Mary understood what he meant, and Mary definitely thought of the weekly ring of black round the bath that had to be cleaned off by her Mother or herself.

But once, when Celi had flu and Mary was quite young, Mary was astounded that he could produce a proper dinner. She marvelled to see his hands could actually peel potatoes and carrots and he managed to make a really tasty minced meat stew. They worked together in the back kitchen easily, with her trying not to stare. All these years and he had known how to cook! It had been an act, all that helplessness and apartness. They washed the dishes together amicably afterwards,Mary still staring suspiciously. The next day Julie came in with some shopping and a helping of rabbit stew for them and Celi got up on the Wednesday and started to get back to normal.

Meanwhile, he filled up the coal bucket from the bunker outside the back door and then scooped up the dogshit distributed around the yard by Whiskey, who somehow resented this fact and skittered round him, barking gently. The sound of the shovel grated across the gravelled surface. This evening ritual was marked by the Angelus bell from the convent chapel at a quarter to seven. On summer evenings it was like living in liquid gold. Later, seeing Johann Vermeer's painting of *A Street in Delft*, that glowing red brickwork of the seventeenth century buildings had the same quality of contented peacefulness that byways in a city, unbelievably, can hold when the day is done.

Late workmen at Blakes Garage could be heard joking as they brought down the shutter at the entrance to the car bay. Another shutter was across the wooden platform of the doorway where they clocked in and out and sheltered from the rain at lunchtimes. The girls who worked opposite at Berwick's Toy Factory came across mid-day and they stood together, smoking and flirting. Sometimes the girls even joined in the football games, giggling and skittering around, though usually they stayed apart, saving themselves to be glamorous, their hair in curlers under a chiffon scarf. Evening dances were the real stuff of their lives, the daytime merely a way of earning a living to support the romance.

In the daytime the clattering of the chains echoing across as cars were lifted up out of the pit made a cheap street-music as the men from Blakes garage finished a job. Other cars were scattered along the street and the men wriggled underneath them adjusting parts and getting covered in grease. In the evening random petrol rainbows spread along the gutters and between the cobblestones showing where they had been working.

The radio became a magical tool and Mary started to experiment with tuning the dial to other stations than the Home Service or the Light Programme. Listening to the Proms, with the *Enigma Variations* brought her to near-tears. She was playing round like this one Saturday afternoon in the empty living room when a man's voice came on, flickering, yet near,
"Rigor mortis has set in...South Hunter Street...Yes, here, attending now." It had to be from the houses opposite and Mary

raced into Nannie's for a better view. For once, Nannie was at the centre of the action with her upstairs living room.

They watched out of the window as the corpse of the Little Body was stretchered down the opposite steps into an ambulance. In life, he was a pitiful limping figure with shoes that always curled up, soles that clapped apart and let in the rain. Nannie had given him Grandpa's old vests and even underpants and pyjamas in the past.

Once, the Little Body had insisted on lending Celi a copy of Franz Werfel's *The Song of Bernadette* but it was so dirty she could not read it and had to get a copy out from the library to be able to say honestly that she had. In order to give it to her, the Little Body had taken Mary and Marie up to his room in Maggie Moran's house. It was stark, walls blue-washed with prewar distemper, bare boards, an iron bedstead, shakey wooden chair, a few hooks on the back of the door with a jacket and trousers hanging and a battered chest of drawers. There was not another thing in the poverty-stricken room. A few books lay on the window-cill that overlooked Nannie's house.

On the sixth of March in 1953 Nannie died. It took about a week for her to leave the world. After washing and then putting up the net curtains in the top corridor windows and the two grown sons' empty bedroom, Nannie got pneumonia and had to stay in bed.

The first Mary knew about the onset was when she went in next door on her usual Thursday tea-time visit at half-past four and found a strange nun, peeling potatoes at the living room table. No black veil; there was a white under-veil pinned back, and her sleeves were rolled up. She had a white apron on and was smiling broadly. This is not what sisters did. It was even worse. The radio was on. Light music was playing before the Children's Hour at five o'clock.

"Yes, I know you usually come for tea with your grandma, so you can just go in and say hello, she's not so bad today, but don't stay long. I'm Sister Monica and I'm just making some chips for when your Auntie Julie comes in." After such a shock, it was reassuring to see Nannie looking immaculate and sleepy in bed. It was a sign of how ill she was, however, that the gas fire was on in the middle of the afternoon.

A week later and it was getting serious. The Little Sisters of the Assumption were giving twenty-four hour care now. One of the night-nurses, Sister Joan, explained that she was not allowed to sleep or rest, but had to try and keep praying through the night, just allowed to sit down once an hour. The rest of the night was to be spent pacing up and down saying the rosary, keeping watch. Mary knew that a practised prayer-monger could rattle off an entire rosary in about an hour, so by morning the rosaries would be stacking up merrily.

Other people came to take watch too, daytime or night-time. Bridie McAneirny, a teacher friend of Julie's, was the most enthusiastic,

"I've never missed a death yet!" as she brandished her beads. The Little Sisters of the Assumption kept their professional cool, pacing up and down.

Nannie died on the sixth of March just as the weather picked up. The adults formed a defence system; the nuns disappeared and Father took charge. He had been crying. His face was ravaged and lopsided for a couple of days.

Mary needed to see the actual dead Nannie, while Father tried to keep her away. She managed to slip into the still bedroom while he was out and approached the bed. Staring at the person in the bed, she had to concentrate to catch either herself seeing the rise and fall of breathing, or an undead Nannie breathing steadily. It took a couple of minutes to admit that the body was totally still and not an optical illusion. The skin glowed with a golden light from within and she looked peaceful, clasping her rosary.

When he found Mary coming out of the bedroom Father was angry but Celi shushed him and said it couldn't be helped, it was probably all for the best. Celi was quiet but not weepy. She sewed a black armband to slip over his riding mac sleeve. Many men used armbands instead of expensive mourning wear, but the women of the family all cobbled together outfits of complete black. Every woman had a black outfit at the back of her wardrobe and a marcasite brooch on the lapel to finish it off.

There was a day or two gap and then Nannie's body was returned to the sitting-room downstairs in a silk-lined coffin, with discreet powdered cheeks and her hair drawn back. The undertakers had arranged her neatly, like real life. Large candles stood at the head of the coffin and flowers had already arrived. Uncle Joe sent a massive wreath of white flowers from New Zealand, so large that it had to be kept on the middle landing to be out of the way.

They were in the front benches now, with the coffin placed at the centre of the altar rails. But Mary's attention was drawn to the round windows that pierced the dome of St Philip's, and looking up she saw Nannie peeping through and smiling down at them all with pronounced glee. It was as if she was triumphant at getting to the other side of existence and was encouraging them too. But as no one else seemed to notice and Father was still visibly upset, Mary did not mention it to any of them.

When they got back to the house it was to an invasion by the neighbours. The sideboard was festooned with plates of sardine sandwiches and Jacob's cream crackers either side of the big radio set. A faint scent of vinegar came from the mashed sardines. Someone was brandishing the bread-knife and slicing through yet another fresh loaf. The butter dish was placed beside the fireplace to soften the butter and make it go further. The Willow-pattern plates were scattered along the second sideboard and the wide-bellied blue printed milk jug stood centre-stage ready for the teas.

There were different plates and cups and saucers, teaspoons and knives brought from other houses. The place was polite pandemonium and Nannie would not have liked to see all these visitors trooping through her house. A tin of rock salmon had been produced as a treat. The curtains upstairs and elsewhere were drawn and the blinds down so that all the rest of the house was in deep gloom although outside the March daylight was crisp and dry.

The kettle was kept permanently on the boil. Mrs Nugent, Mrs Evans and Bridie McAneirney did the honours. It was unsettling to have people who lived down the street and comparative strangers who had never set foot in the house, rooting through the cutlery drawer and washing dishes in the sink.

Nannie had left trouble in her wake, however. Vin expected, as the man of the family, to become the main tenant, but the rent

116

book that held the two houses had already been changed into Julie's name.

He never forgave her and his usual impatience with her changed to something deeper. He stopped going in each evening to take down the ashes and only called in briefly with his weekly half-rent of thirty shillings on Friday evenings, or sometimes sent it in via Mary. There was little other change; all the furniture stayed exactly as it was for a little time. And then Julie started a new regime.

Night after night the sound of Julie scrubbing the floor of the long narrow scullery carried clearly through the landing wall. The scubbing brush knocked all along the skirtingboard.

Then, something amazing. A new gas oven appeared, complete with a glass door for her to watch the cooking clearly. She had to scrub the lino floor yet again.

"You know what that means, don't you?" Celi asked Mary. "You know the saying 'a bun in the oven' means being pregnant, well an oven symbolises the woman's body, her childbearing and rearing. There she goes, night after night, trying to efface Nannie and assert her own life, but it's all far too late." Mary could not help comparing the gleaming cream oven, fresh from outer space, with the sparse machine they had in their own gloomy back kitchen. Julie did make some scones, but the astounding oven was only used for the weekly Sunday joint – beef, lamb pork – before she went off on the usual 3o'clock bus from Mount Pleasant to Widnes for the visit to her friend Anne Dereham. They had taught at the same school, St Bedes, for several years, but Julie had moved to Our Lady's Eldon Street when Nannie was ill some years ago.

Now the new cooker was installed in the narrow kitchen, it meant the quaint Aga-like range in the living room, with its light green tiles was ripped out. In place of all the ins and outs of the fireplace, oven, top-plate, gas rings and silver edging, a bland, cream- mottled fire surround was put in.

"It's an all night burner too, and I've got a gas poker to start the fire off better than using kindling and fire-lighters if you're in a hurry." She also moved downstairs into Nannie's big bedroom, which left all of the top floor unused apart from the bathroom. Everything was different.

Mary had lost her defender, the strong dependable Nannie, who used to notice things that her parents did not. There was a memorable instance at one of the weekly Thursday afternoon teas.

"You're sad about something, what is it?" Nannie had noticed the long silences through tea ,shredded lettuce,cress and egg salad on Willow pattern plates or, in winter, golden chips, butter become potato. Afters were jelly or banana with evaporated milk or a slice of apple pie and custard. " You can come here and tell me next time he starts on you and I'll have a word with him. I know he's got a real temper on him. We wanted him to become a teacher, but we realised he'd be no good with a class-full of boys, too much temptation to get into trouble there. Such a pity. And if it's because your watch got stolen, now, love, don't worry." She drew the crochet shawl round her and went off, creak, creak, across the parched lino to her bedroom across the landing, coming back with something clutched in her hand.

Uncle Joe had sent a wristwatch from New Zealand to congratulate Mary on passing the Scholarship and someone had stolen it at school. At games lessons they put any watches on top of the piano in the gym. Mary had forgotten to take it and at four o'clock went back to collect it. She stood and stared at the clear piano lid. Miss Holton knew nothing about it. Sister Joseph announced it at assembly the next morning. In a school of almost 300 pupils, everyone knew each other. This was a betrayal, she could not understand anyone making such a decision. It was not the disappearance of the watch that was the problem; it was the thinking of the thief that hurt.

"Now, come here by the light", they sat by the window and Nannie produced a little gold ring, a golden heart set on a band that could be extended. "This belonged to my Mother, Rosa Peverelli she was, and now it's yours, a little keepsake to make up for what you've lost."

Adolescence crept onwards, with some strange advice from Mother,

"If you're feeling upset about anything, why don't you just go into the kitchen and smash some of the spare saucers." Cups did get broken, leaving a mound of these unmatched saucers. They broke dramatically, smashing on the red and black tiles. Sweeping up the bits was also soothing. It was a way of deflecting any hint of rebellion from Mary, as Celi also said

"For goodness sake, don't upset him about anything, as he just takes it out on me." She did not say how or when; there was no clue, but it was a sure-fire way of keeping Mary in check, to think of her mother suffering because of her.

The Coronation approached and Mother had to make plans to watch it somehow at a friend's house. Other families, however poor, made efforts to scrape together a deposit and went out and bought television sets on hire purchase but Vin was not going to do anything like that.

"It's absolutely stupid to get into those sorts of arrangements. You have to pay extra, they charge you. It's just getting into debt. And if you don't keep up the payments they can take it off you." Celi and Mary listened to this lecture as they realised he was locking them outside what everyone else was doing. Over the next years other families got TVs, record players, vacuum cleaners, washing machines and cars, but he remained in lone Victorian splendour. As the Corporation had installed electricity the same year, he did go as far as getting an electric radio. The six o'clock news remained sacrosanct and no longer needed batteries to sustain it. He had made a scene last year about not being able to afford the six shillings for a battery for over a week.

But Celi had discovered Mrs Schofield and their own life had become a bit technicoloured too. They were going to see the Coronation at Mrs Schofield's in Falkner Square.They walked up through wet deserted streets with their offering of a box of chocolates and a Victoria sponge. There was no one about except one negro who stood at the open door of a large house in Chatham Street.

"Don't stare, " Celi said. "It's a shebeen, and he's on duty at the door. There'll be a crowd inside there drinking all day now, as everywhere else is closed." A lone empty bus went past along Catherine Street. Mary wondered where Father might be right now too.

Mrs Schofield was as merry and as smartly-dressed as ever, welcoming them into a splendid house, its deep rose-patterned carpets a real luxury after the cold wet pavements and puddles. There was also central heating; they were surrounded with comfort and warmth. This was another example of Celi's gift for making friends. This had all begun by her going into Mrs Schofield's habderdashery shop in Myrtle Street. It was a small emporium – curtains, shoes, tablecloths, skirts, trousers, all hung from the ceiling. The counter and shelves were crammed with household goods like china, pots and pans, cutlery, and rag rugs. The magic Mrs Schofield's had, which beat the Co-op and its dividend, was that everything could be paid for in weekly instalments. They called in so often that once when Mrs Schofiled had the flu she asked Celi to run the shop for a few hours per day and all a Saturday.

Black dyed hair, black beady eyes, vivid red lipstick and matching nail polish, she was a bright bird that had landed in their lives. Of course Celi and Mary could come and watch the Coronation, she'd make a trifle and don't worry about bringing anything, there would be something to drink; they could make a day of it. It was not clear if Father was included or not, or whether she already knew he would be elsewhere, wherever that would be.

It rained in Liverpool, it rained in London, it rained on television in clear black and white.They sank into the deep chintz-covered settees and armchairs as the proper ceremony began.

"Oh, just a sec, now, what about a little sherry to start with?" Mrs Schofiled opened the corner cocktail cabinet, a walnut edifice that lifted open to show peach-coloured mirrors inside, with a surprise light which made it even more glamorous. Mary stared at it, utterly bemused.

Here was the almost-Queen, being anointed with holy oil by the Arcbishop of Canterbury, making an oath to serve her subjects, carrying the orb and sceptre, the entire ceremony a public religious service. The rest was a circus of celebration and flagwaving; but the heart of it was sacred. They sat eating trifle and drinking sherry, transported into the glamour along with all the country and the Commonwealth and the rest of the world.

"We'll be needing a new rag rug soon,too, " Celi remarked near the end, coming back to the present.

"There's some new ones arriving, I'll keep them until you've chosen one, then," Mrs Schofield said.

At Christmas, Julie gave Celi an electric iron, which Vin looked at with distaste. The new shiny iron swished across any material with ease, but of course it added to the electricity bill. As there was only one electricity socket in the entire house though, it meant that they still used the old flat-iron as otherwise Saturday Night Theatre on the radio would be unobtainable. Going to the pictures was often out of the question, it had to be paid out of the housekeeping money.

The coming of electricity had upset the hierarchy of the house. The old gas lights had to be carefully lit with matches or long tapers. It was one of the small ceremonies of the house, the lighting of the living-room especially on winter afternoons. It marked Father's entry in the evenings and as the year changed, it eventually became silly to be waiting for him in the autumn gloom. At some time, probably in early October, Celi would have to light the gas mantles before six o'clock, standing on a chair, and he would enter the living room, standing at the door, looking at it, nonplussed to be upstaged like that.

However, with the new brown bakelite switches set at the door-frame of each room, putting the light on was now a democratic right. He was visibly startled as Mary put any light on, passing from the warm living room into the cold dark hall. It was as if she might break any of the new switches. But she could not be expected to ask permission to put any light on any more; things were getting out of hand.

The new brown switches also conflicted with the holy-water stoups that hung at the entrance to both bedrooms; water and electricity did not mix. Knocking a new nail in the wall placed them adjacent to each other, the past and the future knitted together.

The old days of having all the rest of the house in complete darkness apart from the living room were over. Light also chased away the ghost, as she was never seen again, although the switch was placed on the wrong side of the vast room and the years of skilfully walking through the blackness with outstretched arms still had to be kept up. Any change of the placing of the smaller furniture – the stool, the tall ashtray, meant a collision.

By this time, Celi was working as a typist at the Child Guidance Clinic and so was out in the afternoons and Saturday mornings. Sister Leo at the elementary school had asked her for secretarial help in the past and had recommended her. The convent knew everything.

Nannie, in her turn, had known just as much too.

"Sister Leo, well, she's Queenie Murphy in real life, you know, and her family sell those flowers on Clayton Square." The idea of a nun having a previous identity was an awkward truth to digest. Sister Leo was important, the headmistress of the Big Girls school upstairs. Small and stout, she waited on the concrete stairway and snatched any girl who was talking or laughing on the way up from playtime. Punishment was being hit by 'The Slipper' which was the remains of a plimsoll and was flipped over the miscreant's hand. It did not leave a mark and gave a loud thwack as it landed.

Mary remembered mild Sister Monica hitting a boy on the stage down in the infants department, as someone had informed the school he had been seen throwing a milk-bottle across the road nearby. The classes were lined up to watch it and all of them felt punished along with little Sammy, who managed not to cry even though the slap could clearly be heard all down the hall.

As a preparation for the new job, Nana Sinnott bought a second-hand typewriter for Celi to bring her speeds up-to-scratch. The gigantic machine stood on the sitting room table and Mary had a couple of tries on it tapping out the neat little signs until the bell rang prettily at the end of each line.

On winter evenings the calls of the newspaper-man carried up Leece Street through the fog.

"Exy-ec-owe, exy- ec-owe" he howled out in a strange language. She worked out that he was calling out about the Express and the Echo, but it still sounded chilling. The paper was shunted through the letter-box about five. Often her Mother and herself read the news and skipped through the pages, and then it all had to be reassembled neatly as if it had never been touched, and laid on Father's side plate. He would then read through the Echo after dinner, and announce the important bits and they would both sit there digesting these snippets as though they were brand new and also tempered through his opinion. They had to make up suitable responses and pretend to be surprised.

"Fancy that! A new factory out at Speke!"

"Another zebra crossing! Goodness me!"

A lucky chance came Celi's way as Notre Dame Child Guidance Clinic was now starting a Catholic Marriage Guidance Centre three evenings a week. It was obvious that she would agree to be the secretary as it was just down the street, no difficulty on rainy winter evenings. It meant extra money. Monday, Wednesday and Friday evenings from 6.30pm to 8.30pm, it gave her just enough time, coming in at 5pm, to cook the exact 6pm meal and then leave the clearing-up to Mary and Vin. He was not pleased.

This new job entailed the installation of a large telephone in the hall. It would cost them nothing and they would be allowed a number of free calls as a sweetener. It was a complicated contraption which could reach the extension, hold calls, transfer calls or revert to a private phone. Vin saw it as an interloper, as if it was a wicked genie sitting in his house, linked with the outside world. He never used it and answered any calls with brusque efficiency. Perplexed couples rang up for appointments and were met by his quick passing them along the system without comment.

While Celi was at work in the evenings, Vin sat opposite Mary who was doing her homework, sitting in a fireside chair. He would sit opposite in the other chair and stare at her. And stare and stare, slowly twirling his moustache like a pantomime villain but not as archly. Mary continued in the opposite chair with her Latin homework. The atmosphere was tense. She tried not to freeze.

Turn this page now and then you can put this book back on the pile. Try not to look up, don't catch his eye. Thank goodness the clock has just struck eight, I can suggest making a cup of cocoa and go off to the kitchen, that will fill in a bit of time and break the atmosphere.. Or perhaps he will give up staring and decide to go out. Only half an hour before Mummy gets home. Let her be early getting back, please. It's not as if I can complain about this, she won't understand, it's almost imaginary, can't be talked about and anyway, she needs the job.

By Wednesday nights he had always run out of money and played patience or Solitaire, flexing the pack of cards with a flourish, then fiddling decisively with the laid out stacks of cards after gaps for consideration. But his underlying impatience ironically showed through in the deliberate slam of the cards as they were dealt out one by one.

By Thursday night he was desperate and delaying any further caused worse irritation. Sometimes there was a stamp collectors' meeting, the Registration Label Society, the Czechoslovak Stamp Association, the Matchbox Label Collectors; they were several. There was also a course of management studies he went in for but passing them made no difference. No promotion, no new job.

One day he threw the sardine sandwiches at Celi, saying he often dropped them into the wastepaper basket at work. There was no way out for either of them. There was no trace of how the extra money made any difference; but now she had two jobs some better food appeared, real cakes from Kirkland Jennings, milk with thick cream on top, better joints of meat on Sunday. But somehow there was no change in the daily sandwiches – Sunny Spread, Shippam's chicken paste, cheese and pickle, the dreaded sardines on Fridays, ham and mustard, tomato and cheese spread; the days circled round each other.

Celi made the sandwiches on the end-leaf of the table behind the teapot in its felt cottage tea-cosy, as if it had nothing to do with the table-clothed part. He was at her elbow, shaving at the corner mirror above the little needlework table,the dog at his feet. It was a tense ballet, punctuated by the weather forecast and the eight o'clock news. Frequently the poor dog got her toes trodden on and her yelp of pain happened too often.

Magazines were passed round from woman to woman, a secret world of dreams in coloured photos. Rose at the antique-cum-junkshop at the corner of Clarence Street; Joan at Killip's fish shop in the middle of Myrtle Street were part of the conspiracy. Fish on the marble slope, open to the street, flies and bluebottles jazzing round and Joan's red-raw fingers reaching between the iced fish, the parsley and the chunks of fresh ice. Glamour circulated in these American magazines. This part of the circuit broke down dramatically when Joan and her two strapping brothers emigrated to Australia. And suddenly Celi did not call into Mrs Schofield's shop either, any more. Mary was puzzled why they did not get some new underclothes and the yearly rag rug this autumn.

"I suppose I'd better tell you, then. Mrs Schofield was sent to prison for keeping a brothel at Faulkner Square, right in that house where we watched the Coronation. It explains why she was so well off. Now don't go mentioning it to your Father now. It was in the paper, but he doesn't know we know her. There's Freeman's up past TJ Hughes, we can go there instead. And we can make our own rug, for a change." She bought a handicraft kit with all the supplies from a stall in St John's market.It took weeks to thread the pieces through the piece of sacking that was supplied and Vin was not pleased at the mess. Unable to tell him why they had this sudden urge to make a fireside rug, he just accepted it as one more proof of the madness of women.

The sermon was a hotchpotch when it came to the announcements. From the pulpit Father Garvey read out the results of the parish football sweep, the banns - three weeks' worth for each couple intent on marrying, anyone of the congregation could object on grounds *of consanguinity, affinity or spiritual relationship.*

125

He would also announce the places where the parish priests would call:

"During the week the clergy will visit, myself: Vine Street, Heath Street, Chestnut Street, Mulberry Street; Father Dempsy, Myrtle Street, Chatham Street and Huskisson Street." Over time this did not take place but he went on reading out street-names each Sunday and the whole parish sat there listening to a weekly rambling fabrication.

But when he did use to call, he came round in the evening, a quick chat in the fireside chair, an offer of a cup of tea and half a crown or more if they were doing well. Probably boring and with few returns, it died out as a process.

Occasionally he had to take the Blessed Sacrament to someone who was sick, and could be seen progressing along the street, ciborium covered with an embroidered cloth followed by an altar boy. To see the sacred host outside in the everyday streets was a shock, like an intrusion of the spiritual into everyday affairs.

With Nannie gone, the routine did not change. Thursday afternoon teas continued. Julie still went out every Sunday afternoon at three o'clock to get the bus to Widnes and returned about nine at night. Although she spent a fortnight each summer holiday with Ann, her friend never turned up at the house, the visits were one way only. Nannie must have not welcomed her in the past and so this weekly pattern had been set up.

As no one noticed her on Sunday afternoons, Mary started to wander into next-door's front room and play the piano, inventing wild tunes and riffling through the books in the gigantic glass-fronted bookcase. The room was so damp that the books had a chill feel to them. At some time in the early part of the century Grandpa had bought Arthur Mee's Children's Encyclopaedia in instalments. He had not been able to afford to get them bound and the staples of the thick fortnightly volumes had gone rusty in the years since.

Lovely noble knights did their brave deeds in sepia paintings, Joan of Arc stood at an engraved stake, the Children's Crusade set off in detailed print. It was an enthralling mixture of history, geography, art and a complete educational hotch-potch, *Things for Little People to Make and Do* at the end of chapters gave instructions on how to make egg-cosies and paper windmills.

On the top of the bookcase were two silver aeroplanes,the legacy of Uncle Joe. It was his boyhood left behind like a pupa. Their silvery wings mocked the seriousness of the rest of the room with all the hope and intensity of adolescence left behind.

Mary also explored upstairs in number eleven on weekday afternoons when no one was at home. Opening the sideboard drawers, it was obvious that Auntie Julie was always beginning handicrafts and then not finishing them. Drawers-full of half-knitted jumpers, gloves, scarves. Patterns still pinned to their cut-out materials. Half a life, all stacked away in drawers, an impossible alternative. The programme for the Olympic games in 1922, a souvenir of the Coronation in 1937; past excitements stuffed into these drawers. So much had happened and left no traces.

But upstairs were the empty bedrooms. The front bedroom looked down onto the tops of Maryland Street's trees and the sound of leaves being ruffled by the wind carried clearly. What had been the two boys' bedroom was totally empty apart from both iron bedsteads. The net curtain masked a kind of death, the air still with past images that had left no trace. Mary only went into it once; it frightened her. Its air was hungry. Along the corridor, there was a partitioned-off bedroom that had once been Joe's and then had been decorated cream for Julie to take over.

Past that was the water-tank room which was Julie's real bedroom over all the years, next to the little bathroom. A gigantic brown-painted water tank burbled and glugged quietly to itself, like a pet animal. A small window looked down on South Hunter Street, while the sparse furniture was a wooden bedstead, a chest of drawers, a small brown wardrobe; another room of stopped time. Above the bed was a sepia photo of Julie's dead boyfriend,Tom Higgins. She still wore his turquoise engagement ring. A final-year medic and a trainee schoolteacher, their match was perfect.

"They were at a New Year's students' dance at the University and he walked her home in the snow, then he walked on to the Pier Head for the last bus to Widnes. He caught pneumonia and was dead by February and Julie never recovered."

"She got jilted after that by some other man, and after that, well, she went to country dancing and upholstery evening classes, but there was never anyone after that, and of course, Nannie was only too quick to grasp her tight in case she escaped," Celi told Mary when she asked about the photo, "And you shouldn't really be wandering round the house like that," but she said it mildly, it was not a real rebuke, as though she understood Mary's constant need to ferret something out. There was no explanation for the amount of loose, broken jewellery that she found in the top drawer of Julie's dressing-table. How could so many rings become squashed, with stones fallen out? Whether proper gold or imitation, it looked as though they had been attacked with pincers. How could necklaces be in three broken lengths, with fasteners fallen off? How could so many earrings be twisted out of shape? Her Mother's pieces of jewellery, similarly left rattling loose in the dressing table drawer, were not in a state like this.

There was nothing else for Mary to do on Sundays with no money. She would go down to next-door's sitting room by the front door and play the piano, which no one seemed to mind her doing. Sitting there she made up fantastic musical performances but as they were invented, had no real way of repeating them. She was the only child in Liverpool asking for piano lessons, but the entire family, even when Nannie was alive, treated it as a strangely alien request. They had been similarly dismissive, almost afraid, when she had asked for long hair, for plaits.

"All your energy goes into your hair if you let it grow too long."

"What on earth do you want plaits for?"

"It's not a good idea to have too long hair, all your strength can go into your hair, it weakens you." A chorus of disapproval.

When she got back from school one day all her parents' bedroom furniture had magically been moved downstairs into the large front room. If ordinary workmen could do this, then the translation of Our Lady's House from Nazareth to Tara made total sense. Things were magic if you did not look at how they were done. The cracked ceilings in number nine were apparently war damage but, strangely, Nannie's much taller house next door was untouched. Mary had grown fond of the cracks running across the two bedroom ceilings and had made up stories and images from them.

The Corporation took away both the bedroom ceilings and it was amazing how much extra hidden space there was, sloping right up to the slates. A new white ceiling was installed and as they had to peel off much of the paper the Corporation sent an official wallpaper book for them to choose new patterns from.

It had several geometrical patterns and some flower-sprays and others that were discreet but her parents chose an almost porridge-like design which proved a torment whenever she was ill because so many different images could be conjured up from it. Giants and grimacing dwarves and monsters all tumbled about from top to skirting board.

14

"Are we really French, with our name?" Mary asked. They had been studying the French Revolution in history that afternoon. She always tried harder at French lessons too, thinking it would be expected of her to be fluent.

"We are descended from one of Napoleon's generals, Comte Jean Baptiste Martineau," said her Father stolidly. He was reading the Liverpool Echo as usual, but deigned to give this news from behind his paper screen. "Napoleon said he wished all his generals were as good as Martineau." He disappeared again into the news. She knew to obey the silence. Another time, asking him again, she wanted to know more.

"So what happened after Napoleon became Emperor? What happened to Comte Martineau after the revolution, then?"

"I don't know about that time, he probably got some reward of land. But when the monarchy was restored under Louis Phillipe, all these Napoleon supporters were not popular, it got dangerous for them, so they went off to America to avoid trouble. I think the family had something to do with investing in the railroad set-up there."

"So how did they end up in Liverpool?"

"They followed the rail boom and set up as hauliers outside the station at Southport. Then that fell through, and then they ran a little boarding house. That's the framed gold sign hanging up in your Nannie's hall, it used to hang over their door with the name, just *Martineau,* like that." He closed the subject and went out into the back yard to collect the coal. Celi hissed at her not to ask any more questions of him.

"Don't annoy him, now." Mary could see no sense in this at all. They knew no French people whatsoever; all family friends and relations were either Irish Catholics or Liverpool Jews. Aunty Frances had married into a Spanish family, but that did not count. The amount of running-about the Martineaus would have to have done, darting about from country to country and then century by century was far too disjointed to fit into any known historical pattern. Mary meant to make a proper graph, like the timelines at the back of their school history textbooks, but never got round to it. The 1812 Overture was about the retreat from Moscow; her great-whatever-grandfather was apparently there, being pushed back into Europe across the snow, to be given his only memorial in Tchaikovsky's music.

While this had been happening to Comte Jean Baptiste, their house here had just been built, its date 1811 proudly embossed on the top of the gutter at the corner of South Hunter Street and Maryland Street. Mother had pointed it out and had also said the plaster was not strong, large horses' hair stuck out where the plaster broke in the bedroom, because the horsehair needed to bind the plaster of the inside walls was scarce as most horses were off fighting in the Napoleonic Wars. That incongruously brought in Jane Austen whom they were studying for O levels, where various gorgeous young men were drafted from the Pump Rooms at Bath to fight this Comte Martineau and his cohorts.

Time could zoom in from nowhere. Down Back Maryland Street, electricity workers installing wires bringing electricity in 1953 found a newspaper from 1812, with the remains of a workman's cheese sandwich in it, embedded in the wall of what was going to become Atlantic House, a hostel for sailors.

In the Picton Library Mary found out that Maryland, Hunter, and Baltimore Streets were named in compliment to his trade by Mr Hunter, a tobacco dealer, who lived over in Mount Pleasant. The amount of tobacco and sugar imported into Liverpool grew rapidly during the 18th century, and from 600 tons of tobacco in 1704 and 760 tons of sugar,by 1810 it had risen to 8,400 tons of tobacco and 46,000 tons of sugar. It was at the top of this boom that the building of Maryland Street had begun, with the confidence of increasing trade.

Mother's side of the family came from Ireland. That was common and ordinary; nothing special in that. It was a fairy-tale place where she said an Annie Kenny, an old woman, had built her own house on the seashore out of stones. The three daughters used to go across to Greencastle to their grandmother's for holidays, looked after by Aunty Cappy.

"We could wave goodbye to the Liverpool mail-boat from the shore, we'd have a bonfire too and see them off." Nana, a young widow, had to get back to run the ship's chandlers in Beaufort street. Their Father, James McGivern had died one spring of flu, though underlying tuberculosis was the real cause. Celi had a small sepia photo of him in the bedroom, a handsome young man of twenty eight. Dark haired and with a moustache, he counteracted the large Pope Pius over the mantelpiece. It was sometimes as if Celi was really more in love with this good-looking man than her real live husband. Years later when Mary saw a photo of Proust there was a similarity in the far-off, considered aspect, combined with a restrained vitality. James McGivern remained on the tallboy for all the years with his quizzical gaze. It was as if, Mary sometimes thought, that Celi was really in love with him, the glamorous photograph and not the loud real-life Vin.

Great clattering on Sunday morning. Sound of mop bucket in their bedroom – Mother was mopping the bedroom lino floor and the landing. This was against the commandment about not doing servile work on the Sabbath. It did not make sense. Mary got up, leaving by the back stairs down into the back kitchen and went to church alone.

Midweek dinnertime, Celi cautiously asked if she had heard anything going on the other night. She said that her Father came home drunk on that Saturday night and had collapsed to sleep. Getting up later to pee later in the night, he had opened the wardrobe door and peed in there, in mistake for the bathroom which was round the corner. Having no one else she could trust to tell, such things being hidden from the rest of the family, she had to tell Mary. They sat and laughed about it, sworn to secrecy.

He was still paid his expected respect; in his own eyes it made no difference to his estimate of Celi. Beyond that, he hated the fact that it had not happened to her, he hated that the two of them did not make the same mistakes, inflict the same cruelties that he did, while denying them both any freedom to do so.

Of course it never occurred to him that his daughter would get to know or suspect. He kept inventing new rules.

"Dinner on this table" – thump, thump – "at six o'clock and no later. When I come through that door the dinner should be on this table." Another rule, never exactly stated in words was that the evening paper should not be read by anyone else before he touched it. If it was obvious that it had been opened –for it was difficult to refold it exactly – he would *hurrumph* and snort, shaking its pages as if to stave off any intruder. He read out bits to his wife, who was allowed to read it after he had finished, sometimes being given a page if she requested it. Deep silence until the end of the news at ten past six while the Northern Home Service rationed out its information. If he was in a bad mood the mealtime was extremely tense, Celi and Mary either silently forbidden to talk to each other as he brooded, or carrying on a falsely bright conversation to keep their spirits up.

"May I leave the table?"

"Yes, you may." Mary always asked as soon as possible, then went upstairs to the bathroom and promptly vomited up most of the meal. She had bolted the food in order to escape from the tension. Of course she was hungry later on and would have to finish off the stale jam tarts from Sunday and any bread and butter. After the evening meal the parents sat and had second and third cups of tea and a cigarette and settled piffling debts of pennies for his postage or Celi bought cigarettes from him at tuppence each.

Mealtimes were one of the best occasions for his performances. She learned to mistrust any friendly approach as anything said in a confiding way would be used later in a twisted way against her. He started off all pleasantly enough, but like a drum-roll, the drama would start.

"Do you remember last Thursday, Mary?" She cast about, but nothing special came to mind.

"I went into tea to Nannies, at five o'clock, like always and came back about seven to finish my homework." The crescendo came as he hit the table.

"There was a thunderstorm and I went upstairs and you had left your window open! I had to close it, the rain was coming in!" Mary knew that the window had not been open much at the top, not enough to cause any problem, but here it was, a scene in the making. He hit the table again.

"In future, you are only to open your window an inch at the top so this sort of thing doesn't happen again." Each scene he managed to construct like this was the opportunity to introduce another new rule. They should be framed and hung in the hall above the weekly milk bill and the paper-bill money. Celi went on reading the paper, as it was her turn, and lit another cigarette.

Yet she had not always been like this. She had told Mary of an incident at a dance at the Rialto, where there was a gigantic dance-floor above the cinema. A young man had asked Celi for a dance and she refused.

"And he went and complained to the Master of Ceremonies, who went and stopped the music and announced that a young lady had refused a man a dance and this was no way to behave and that it was not the policy of this establishment to encourage such bad behaviour and that the young woman in question ought to be ashamed of herself. And so I went off to the ladies and hid for while – I wasn't going to give in like that." The fine independent young woman had been tamed over the years.

"When Vin brought me round to introduce me to his family, it was a bit of an ordeal, Grandpa was a very serious person indeed, never a barrel of laughs, but a good Father, I'll say that for him. They started later, picking on me, about the red nail polish, what was that for and about me smoking, surely it wasn't ladylike, not for a young woman, no." But she had been modified over the years.

"He had me crying soon after we got married and when we had our flat at East Prescot Road. I don't know what came over him, it was quite a shock." But she did not go into details what had happened to make him change so soon. So proud of being married, Celi had ordered visiting cards printed with her brand-new name, *Mrs V.R. Martineau, 315 East Prescot Road, Knotty Ash, Liverpool 14.* The original ones of her single life were discarded, the Celi Mc Givern of 43 Huskinson Street, Liverpool 8, with its proud 'Tel. Royal 6292' phone number, obviously one of the few houses in Liverpool with a telephone in the 1930s.

It was only much later that Mary realised that Celi must have become pregnant immediately; married on Boxing Day 1938 and with childbirth in October 1939 meant, counting on fingers, that there had only been time for one period before pregnancy setting in. Vin had probably been in a total tizzy, with war beginning, jobs changing and now a pregnant wife. Somehow it was fixed up that as soon as the Conconnans, caretakers for the convent, moved out, that Vin should get the tenancy of the house connected to his Mother's in South Hunter Street.

The Concannons had a couple of boys, who played out in the garden, Nannie said, and Mrs Concannon tired of them tramping all the soil into the house. The Corporation covered over all the yard (as it now became) with a surface of gritty concrete. Sounds echoed against the hard exterior paving, concrete and bricks. Nothing grew. Inside, the Corporation also decided to paint the hall walls and asked what colour they would like.

"Sunshine yellow" was the prompt answer, so the walls were done in glossy paint which over the years lost both its shine and its brightness.

Ironically, about this time, the Catholic Marriage Advisory Centre was set up in the evenings at the Child Guidance offices at the end of Maryland Street. Celi was roped in to help as secretary three evenings a week, Monday, Wednesday and Friday. As a sweetener, they installed a phone in the hall at number 9, with a set of levers to transfer calls from their home to the office and vice versa. Vin saw it as a complete invasion and had very little to do with it. It was all he could do to be polite with anyone who rang up to make an appointment. He never made a call out at all.

But one night (Mary missed it) he phoned up around midnight to tell Celi that he was in a car racing round Princes Park, it was really exciting and they had just driven over the little bridge that led to an island. The ornamental bridge was not designed for traffic and the only item on the island was an intriguing Wendy House celebrating Peter Pan. What a group of drunken men were doing, chasing round an empty park, was inexplicable. He was not phoning up to reassure her; like a naughty schoolboy, he was showing off. She was in bed, her hair in curlers, like Mary, all the lights off and the fire banked up for the night. As usual, it took a week or so before she told Mary about this escapade, having no one else to tell.

Another evening, he appeared at the living-room door, flinging it open, making a dramatic entrance, blood streaming down his face and onto the cream riding mac. He stood there, like a wild animal seeking refuge, looking strangely at Celi. She fled into the back kitchen and came back with a bowl of water and the facecloth and a towel to sponge the worst off. He said it was new bifocals and misjudging the kerb edge. It was about a quarter to ten and he did not think Mary would still be up so late. This, at least could not be covered up. He was totally ignorant of how they spent their Saturday evenings - bath-time, then BBC's Home Service, *In Town Tonight*, followed by *Saturday Night Theatre*, hair wound tightly round curlers and cocoa and biscuits. then, bed in the freezing upstairs with an old hot-water-bottle that caused chilblains. Thinking about the Crown of Thorns, it was something similar as the curlers stuck into her head whatever way she tried to sleep. Sometimes the odd curler came adrift and fell out, giving a lopsided result to the Sunday morning curls.

Some Saturday nights Celi took Mary to the Crane Theatre in Hanover Street, where they saw most of Gilbert and Sullivan's repertoire – *The Mikado, The Gondoliers, Iolanthe;* Terrance Rattigan's *Separate Tables* and also *Bonaventure,* where a nun in an enclosed convent solved a crime by cutting bits out of newspapers.

The mixture of styles was enlightening, and when Celi said that she and Vin had met in amateur dramatics at the David Lewis community centre, Mary found it difficult to believe. It was just as difficult as imagining him dancing in those pointed patent leather shoes that had always been in the bottom of their wardrobe. The black shiny points always waited there; and then disappeared without comment. Perhaps they had been sold to a dress agency as no one else they knew would have a need for them; they were almost historic.

Other Saturday evenings, now that Celi had a bit of extra money via the Catholic Marriage Advisory Board, she took Mary to the pictures. While the Rialto was nearest, they also went to the Smithdown Picture Playhouse coming out with people still singing bits from *Oklahoma* or *Annie Get Your Gun* as they stood in the rain waiting for the bus, having to adjust from the multi-coloured happy America to the black wet Liverpool streets and the streaming gutters. The beguiling comfort of the red velvet curtains, soft lighting,deep carpeting and photos of glamorous stars all fell away as rain seeped into their shoes and they got home to find the dog had gone to bed in the corner and the fire was out.

For reasons unknown Celi also took her to The Pavilion, or Pavvy as it was known, where a mixed crop of vaudeville acts made an inexplicable entertainment. Acrobats, conjurers, sopranos and tenors, dancing troupes, all followed each other in a mad programme. The highlight in first and second acts was a tableau, where under the excuse of The Jungle or Mexican Fête or similar, men and women stood naked in a make-believe glade, with branches, logs and subtle other barriers hid their interesting parts. The contortions some of the models had to achieve looked most uncomfortable, but luckily it did not last for long. Again, Celi and Mary came out of the theatre into rain and darkness, with Mary even more puzzled than usual as to what it was all about and why Celi would have thought it was a good evening out.

Other Saturday nights they went to 7.30 pm confession at the Pro-Cathedral, *Going to get your kettle scraped ,* meeting other parishioners on the way. Mary wondered why, once being in a state of grace, they should go and bother to live through another week and any inevitable sins. It was their duty to avoid being run over crossing Brownlow Hill. Then, into Boots at the corner by the Adelphi, a quarter pound of sweets each from their Ration Books, bath and hairwash later, followed by the Saturday Night Play, if Mother rushed the ironing. The iron heated up on the fire, tested by spitting on it, then was slipped into its shining tin shoe. The old flat iron sometimes shedded rust or soot on clothes. Father's shirts and collars, however, went to the laundry and came back on Mondays like cardboard.

They never went out together, only on Bank Holidays there was a forced march down to the Landing Stage and a trip on the ferryboat to Seacombe, perhaps strolling along the prom to New Brighton eating an ice cream. Mary looked with longing at other children who might have been friends. After dinner, the afternoon would start with Father announcing it was time to go out and Celi going upstairs for long enough to get him hot and bothered,

"For God's sake, how much longer are you going to be up there? What on earth are you doing?" Mary filled up the dog's water bowl and locked the back door to fill up the time while he fussed and harrumphed Then Celi would come downstairs with full make-up,

137

hair smoothed, wearing a different outfit and after her final glance in the mirror they would start off in the sunlight.

Now and again, about twice a year, Celi asked to be taken out on a Saturday night by Vin. This was almost a petition and not a casual question. He would consider this seriously and take her to the Roscoe Arms, always the same pub conveniently just off Hardman Street. He would invite his friend from work, Andy and his wife as ballast. It was a sign of how exciting Celi found this that she boasted to Mary that they had all come back to the house one time and had sat up late, talking even until midnight.

They had little other connection. Mary's bedroom was directly through theirs, in fact her bed would have been about two yards away through the connecting door. Usually she could hear everything, the ticking of the alarm clock and its bell at a quarter to eight each weekday. Apart from his interminable speeches when he came to bed drunk, there was no real conversation or real intercourse. One night she did hear the sound of a vigorous tussle, with Celi just saying an "Oh Vin!" that could have been taken to have several meanings, except that straight afterwards there was the clear sound of him sobbing as though something terrible had gone wrong. Another night she heard a quick rustling, like an attack with no talk before or afterwards, like absolute formal strangers coupling. There was nothing else. No chatter, no laughter, no joy. Silence.

One dinnertime, Celi told her that something important was up at the Child Guidance Clinic, but not to tell her Father about it.

" It's confidential. The police have asked Sister Beatrice for the use of her study to observe all night, because they think premises across the road are being used for prostitution." There was a deep-set doorway between a café and an antique shop, leading to two floors above. The entire set-up was like a spider's web, each part easily linked to the rest. A flamboyant figure they had nick-named Tallulah flitted from shop to café. She drove a sleek light green Armstrong Siddeley Sapphire, waving a long cigarette from a jade cigarette-holder and overdressed in flowery gowns and clattering high heels.

Mary said nothing, it made sense and obviously it was good that the police were doing something about it. She did not tell her

Mother about an instant a few weeks ago; one of those seconds of seeing more than was on the surface. Walking down Maryland Street one afternoon, she had drawn level with Tallulah's luxurious green limousine and her attention had been caught by the face of a girl sitting alone in the splendour of its pale green leather back seat.

Looking across, it was definitely Eleanor, a girl from Demonstration School days. They would both be about the same age, fifteen. Eleanor had blonde hair, quite long, and pale green eyes. They recognised each other. Her expression was a cross between intense boredom and fear, which Mary did not understand, but hoped now it was a mistake. But if Tallulah (or whatever her real name was) had been an aunt or other relative or friend, it was beyond normal for any schoolgirl not to have mentioned any connection in class or playground. They had never seen Eleanor in that car or going to the café in the past, so it did not make sense now.

Now her sad face came back clearly and Mary only hoped she was mistaken in her conjecture. Mother was excited about getting sandwiches and vacuum flasks ready for the police that night as part of her afternoon's work. Being the last typist to join the office staff, Celi was given the job of making the afternoon teas for everyone in the building.

On some Saturday mornings she took Mary to the Clinic with her and Mary had the enjoyable task of rearranging the family figures in the gigantic model doll's house. In order to assess disturbed children's problems and outlook, the doll's house had three generations of figures and several rooms to play with. Children's attitudes to their family members would be easy, then, to observe. The outstanding example was one little boy who rapidly put the entire family, with both sets of grandparents and parents and children, out in the garden, leaving only the baby resident in the empty house. Miss Geraghty would sit beside the table, making notes and asking stray questions. To add to the diagnosis (and the fun) a dog, cat, budgie and several goldfish, tropical fish, hamsters and white mice were scattered about the building in carefully segregated rooms. Of all of them, Rex the dog had the most freedom to rove around the building, though the budgie was often to be found creeping round Sister Beatrice's veil and starched white gimp while

139

talking in its tinny voice, *Hello, hello.* Her assistant, Miss Myerscough took care of the dog, usually taking him to the Hermitage at St Michael's Hamlet, as the convent could hardly accommodate Rex.

Upstairs there was a small library as many of the disturbed children had problems with reading and in fact it was often the foundation of their troubles.

"It only takes six to ten weeks to get them up to reading again, except for the severe cases,. Sometimes it's because they've missed school because of being sick, others, well, they have problems like undetected deafness or short-sightedness and then some are just not very bright," Celi said, "In some afternoons, if we're not too busy I can help them with reading practice, it's all they need, as their parents can't always do it. It makes all the difference." Her job was to type out the reports that the psychiatrists and social workers produced, and send out letters to various parents, schools, doctors and education inspectors.

The small library-room under the eaves had a collection of new books, a selection of Enid Blytons, and children's classics like *Wind in the Willows, The House at Phoo Corner*, and *Tales with a Twist,* but there was one book that intrigued Mary. It was a kind of dictionary which gave the number of times any word had been used in the classics like a Tale of Two Cities or Jane Eyre. The most-used word was 'and,' followed by 'the.' It showed the cement that glued sense together, the spaces between images and ideas. She never saw the book anywhere else. Sitting here in the carpeted and immaculate white-painted room was sitting in the ideal bedroom. The only thing it needed, apart from a bed, was an apple tree brushing against the window.

The High School was a poor girl's version of all the boarding-school stories, because they all went home at four o'clock, with no chance of midnight feasts. Sometimes the netball teams stayed behind to practise, as they had regular Saturday matches against other schools, although it was almost a secret society. On Mondays the netball team girls chattered and boasted about their performance. It was a private club, cut off from the rest of the class.

Other girls gathered by the windows and talked about heir weekends. They only had to move another inch or so and the thirty-foot drop to the concrete path below was more in view. Sitting on the window-ledge like this was a favourite game because it annoyed any teacher over in the playground or any teacher who entered the classroom. But any window-ledge that was two feet deep made its own invitation. Outside, the 'ones' and 'twos' shrieked about in clumps; the third forms were seriously at netball practice and the 'fours' and 'fives' did skipped homework or slipped into the cloakrooms to re-do their hair. High walls surrounded everything although the shrubberies, greenhouses and lines of trees hid the more obvious signs of a courtyard-prison shape.

Sister Anthony asked her if she would like to come into the studio at weekends to finish work on sculptures, as the new kiln had to be fed with enough pieces to justify firing overnight. It was an unusual experience to be able to wander round the empty building and feel the almost-ghosts of all the absent pupils and teachers and nuns. As she walked through the convent grounds, letting herself in the two gates, it was a following of her grandfather's footsteps. She had sat in the infant's school and seen him cross this same path at each dinnertime, going back to work and letting himself through these exact same green-painted wooden gates. She remembered feeling so proud of him, in his workman's blue overalls and peaked cap, crossing the playground in all weathers after calling home for his dinner.

The empty school had a sad atmosphere bereft of the crowded chattering girls. Lost belongings lay around the cloakrooms – stray shoes, hairbrushes, cardigans, exercise books, each one a sign of someone's existence. She could wander around looking at everywhere. Past Sister Joseph's study and the secretary's office were the sixth form classrooms, where the girls had their own toilets. This was the only one in the school that had a sanitary towel machine in it, for girls of 17 plus. It was far too late to be providing the facility, a type of ignorance that the sisters obviously would not have been able to explain fully.

Crossing that corridor led to the junior and senior libraries and the second years, alpha and beta. For reasons never explained the school started at classes two, alpha and beta and went on to six one and six two, the crest of the wave.

But most girls had left long before that – a type of cull occurred at the fourth form as girls ducked out of the exams and went off to work instead. Others left the fifth form after the O Levels. Only half remained for lower sixth, to do Advanced Level and some of them also mysteriously disappeared before the summer exams. Each year at least one girl entered a religious order. For questions further unanswered, there were two or three girls, grown women by now of 18 or 19, who were after some elusive exam that had slipped their grasp. Wearing ordinary clothes, they appeared now and again like ghosts, vaguely ashamed of themselves, but able to call their few teachers by their Christian names. Those who gained degrees or other honours, including joining religious orders had their names painted in gold on large boards fixed to the downstairs hall walls.

The corridors stretched past empty classrooms as she went up the little stairs up to the studio and its view of the grounds. From here there was a clear view of the Gothic Church of England cathedral with its tiara-like summit.

"Just like them," Sister Anthony said, "Thus far and no further, the crown descends!" The Protestants had won long ago, the Catholics had been defeated. The way to find out a Protestant was by listening to the end of the Our Father prayer - they had put an extra ending, "For Thine is the kingdom, the power and the glory," whereas the Catholics had only "But deliver us from evil, Amen," which made more sense.

The other way was to check the end of any Bible's New Testament - Catholics had the Apocalypse and they had Revelations. Neat. Protestants obviously tinkered about with endings. For a long time they had persecuted us. It was 1829 when the Emancipation Act gave complete civil, economic,and legal freedoms. Catholics and the Jews were only allowed into universities in the next century, and the poor Jews who lived at the bottom of Brownlow Hill called their own street "University Hill" as they watched the first students walk past.

Farmhouses in Lancashire hid priests in the times of persecution and larger halls and stately homes had priests' holes, hidden cells behind the squire's bookcases or along underground corridors. Young men were smuggled in from France with new translations of the Bible. It was dangerous and exciting and glamorous, unlike the modern plain priests who mostly came from Ireland or were austere Englishmen.

"If you like, you can go and join Sunday benediction in the Convent Chapel," Sister Anthony suggested, "You can go in to the choir seats, in the organ loft, up with the angels. Just go along the top corridor and let yourself in." It was a privilege and an entry right into the world of Fra Angelico. From the balcony, she could see how the sisters knelt, about three to a bench, a yard space between each. They drew their veils more about their shoulders to emphasise the blinker effect and cut out any distractions. They were praying machines, about eighty in all. The black habits emphasised the grace of even the homeliest, plumpest nun. Sick nuns or the wheelchair-bound were each looked after by a younger nun. Doctor Bligh said that his calls to the convent were mostly about sprained ankles from nuns slipping on the polished floors. It was standard that their black shoes had a slight heel, a nod to fashion or conformity.

It was a permanent joke at the police station about intruders in the Convent grounds. The tree-lined pathways were unlit and the surrounding walls had several unsafe levels, easy for a man to climb over. There was nothing to steal in the grounds, but a drunk could have done a lot of damage to the statues or could have broken windows.

Confirmation stole up on them gradually, it was not as exciting as First Confession and Communion. It brought a Holy water stoup present from Aunty Pat Charles, a friend of her mother, who agreed to be her sponsor. Promoted to a new white plastic stoup, it was hung next to the brown electric light switch at her bedroom door, its little sponge still clean and unused. The Bishop, who was not impressive, made them soldiers for Christ. It was already becoming a strange performance, although the extra strength needed for adulthood had to have some ritual; even the most primitive tribes had such goings-on. Here in St Philip Neri's, the preparation for further life in Liverpool was unclear. It did not have the comprehensive deal that First Holy Communion had. Being anointed with oil on the forehead was apparently the best that could be done in the circumstances.

The Holy Ghost came into play here, endowing them with new virtues, a heap of gifts – Wisdom, Understanding, Counsel, Fortitude, Knowledge, Piety and Fear of the Lord. Fortitude sounded like the most useful quality to develop as all the others sounded more or less the same except for Piety and Fear of the Lord. As they grew older, they were told that the Fruits of the Holy Ghost kicked in and they sounded much better – Charity, Joy, Peace, Patience, Benignity, Goodness, Longanimity, Mildness, Fidelity, Modesty, Continency and Chastity. Give or take a few, that described a pleasant person, a bit unassuming but someone good to have as a friend.

The bishop told them that they were now part of the Church Militant and potentially part of the communion of saints. *'Saints have the restored preternatural gifts of Adam and Eve and behold the Godhead face to face.'*

There were no other clues. They were sent out into the world to do the rest on their own.

As Mary had very little money - pocket money was sixpence each from Mother, Father and Auntie Julie, her options were limited at the weekends and she was vulnerable to any possibility. Julie was visiting relations in Barnet and so, would Mary like to come to London during the Easter holidays? Every movement had to be carefully negotiated via Father. He gave his permission and Mother bought the usual special bar of Imperial Leather soap and a new tube of toothpaste for visits and washed more white socks.

They would not have been able to pay for the train ticket and this caused unseen earthquakes, Celi always being at a loss, Vin dismissing any embarrassment by being cantankerous. Mary knew that any invitation, anywhere was an improvement on mooching round the house for yet another Sunday.

Meeting the Barnet branch of Nannie's family was a pleasant surprise; a belonging with strangers. They stayed at her widowed sister's, called Nana, as obviously they were of similar ages and both grandparents. It was a sign of belonging that the cistern above the toilet had the imprint "George Williams, Builder" confidently impressed in its surface. They visited Father Williams at Kenton, who surprisingly lived in an ordinary 1930s council-style house, not a venerable Victorian presbytery. He said the Arch-Bishop had sent him here to build a Catholic Church and develop a parish. It was unsettling to think of someone having to start from scratch with none of the infrastructure that the nineteenth-century Liverpool church builders had created.

On their last day they called into Fortnum & Mason's Food Hall as a treat on the way back to Euston Station.

"I'll get you a sandwich we can eat it on the train, now, what would you like?" Mary was more distracted by the potted palms and the sleek white counters, the strange items of what must be food though she had never seen most of these convoluted eatables. She chose a ham sandwich and the assistant was just about to wrap it up, when Auntie Julie reached out,

"No, no, sorry, you'll have to put it back, I'm sorry." She turned to Mary - "It's Friday, have you forgotten,we can't eat meat on a Friday, you know that, you'll have to choose something else." The assistant stood watching this exchange and the shamed Mary sheepishly chose a cheese and pickle sandwich instead, while Julie chose a virtuous sardine and tomato. The rules they had to follow were seldom shown up in public like this, though Mary wondered too how any Catholic would navigate social life and parties of any type, as in order to go to communion on a Sunday one had to be fasting from all food and drink except water since midnight. A Catholic would have to stand around being affable and discreet while everyone around them got drunk and made fools of themselves - although perhaps that was the idea, to test their self-discipline and save them from trouble.

145

However, it did sound like a good arrangement to spend one seventh of your life eating fish and one seventh keeping Sunday as a day of rest, as far as possible for all. Something healthy about that.

All the Everton team became heroes. Mary learnt their names by heart - O'Neill, Moore, Donovan. Farrell, Jones, Lello, Mc Namara, Fielding, Parker, Eglington, and dashing Dave Hickson. She got a photo of him and stuck it to the inside of her desk-lid. Sunday mornings she raced down to look at the football results in the back of the Sunday Express.

When they got to GCE O Levels, though, and studying *Macbeth*, he was displaced by Marlon Brando, a luscious black and white photo, where, draped in a toga, he was giving the graveside oration about Caesar. It helped, giving the dry Shakespeare words a transferred glamour.

Some of the girls in the fifth form were going out to dances on Saturday nights, to places that Mary had not a clue about. There was a schism across the classroom between the girls who were already navigating a woman's world and the flat-breasted sporty ones who were devoted to the netball team and its complicated fixtures and constant practice matches. Boys were on a distant horizon, not helped by the newly arranged inter-schools Friday-night dances. These were an invention to encourage Catholic girls and boys to get involved with each other, cutting out all others.

This new event was announced at assembly as almost a Christian duty. The dance was being held at St Francis Xaviour's, miles away. Surprisingly, she was allowed to go, as school was encouraging it. Mary got onto the tram and arrived at a big school hall, not very different from their own. The parallel bars could not be disguised, though coloured lights brightened it up. Dressed in a taffeta skirt and black top, Mary found somewhere to sit and hoped for the best. A couple of girls from school could be seen whirling round in the distance but they did not smile at her.

Miss Holton's dancing lessons were no preparation for this. The school had only two records and as the portable record-player had to be wound up regularly, one girl always had to be on duty to wind the handle and change the two records. Geraldo's "*Jealousy*" and "*The Blue Tango*" rang out again and again as they stumbled round the gym on rainy Tuesday afternoons. Like any games lesson, it was controlled humiliation for most of the class. Miss Holton gave a quick demonstration of the footwork, using a small girl as prop, and then roved around the floor picking out mistakes and only making matters worse.

Mary went home and tried to fathom out the steps from diagrams in *Everything Within,* that stood on the sideboard beside Dorothy L. Sayer's *Detection, Mystery and Horror* and the library books. The chapter on ballroom dancing had little maps of footsteps, black for the man, white outlines for the woman, with arrows to give the direction of the next movement. She moved across the sitting-room carpet attempting the steps, holding the book, while trying to avoid bumping into the furniture. This was how you got a boyfriend, how you met. This was probably how her parents met. To master this was essential. For some reason Mother was no help, which was a surprise, as she must have been good at it once, with her sister, Kay being a dance teacher at the Rialto at some time. There was a photo of Kay in a long white dress in the photo album which proved it.

It was in this state of uncertainty that Mary landed at the Saint Francis Xaviour's dance, called SFX for short. After a while sitting at the edge, feeling embarrassed, with great luck a boy asked her to dance and she managed to stumble around in the crowd. He did not seem to mind at first, being far more interested in showing her some drawings he had done already for Christmas cards. He brought them out of his jacket pocket and brandished them about while they moved about somewhere in the middle of the dancers.

"You've got to get in early, you see. I've got contacts already. So if you say you're interested in art, you're already too late for this year. I sent these off before autumn." He waffled on, frequently standing on her feet because she was going in the wrong direction. As Mary was considered tallish, she had learnt only the man's footwork in gym lessons and so was unfitted for any dancing with an actual man, as he eventually cottoned on. "You're doing all the wrong steps! You're supposed to be going backwards!" And so when this song ended, she was relieved to go and sit down and wait until her Father would come and collect her. It was raining now and they went off to the tram-stop in the cold. He was cross as they had to stand there in the rain.

"It's on an evening like this that you catch the flu." Father complained. "Coming out from a crowded hot place like that into the cold is just the way to get ill, of a November evening. You could catch your death of cold this way." And with that grim end to the evening, they sat in the tram as their rain-sodden coats began to dry on them in the comparative warmth. Her going out like this had ruined his evening and there was not much conversation on the way back. He delivered her back to Celi and hurried out to salvage as much as he could of the remnants of his Friday night.

She draped the sodden coat over a chair to dry out. The living room fire was the only source of heat for the whole house. Its door had a special draught excluder and there was often a loud whistling noise of air being drawn in under the living room door when the open fire was drawing well.

The group of shops along Hardman Street were closed down Mrs Clarke's, the tobacconists, moved temporarily round the corner into South Hunter Street, while Mr Ingham's dairy went to Oxford Street and the greengrocers disappeard entirely. It was a link with the countryside gone; the high hoppers loaded with potatoes covered with black soil, the stacks of vegetables being delivered daily. It was the first time Mary had ever seen a five-pound note, as one of the consultant's wives from Rodney Street produced a white note as big as a birth certificate to pay for her groceries.

Instead, a new building appeared, Atlantic House, a hostel for sailors. This was a Catholic hostel, to save sailors in port going to waste and ending up in trouble. Monsignor Atkins showed Celi and Mary round the downstairs rooms. The foyer led into a ballroom.

"We are planning to save any sailors from ending up in any mess," he said. They had programmes of dances arranged, orchestras booked, and a list of proper respectable girls for the sailors to dance with. "You would be just the right sort of girl when you are a little older," one of the organisers joined in. Mary thought it wrong to be manipulating men and young women like this, it did not seem either sensible or religious. But then, just as Mother was agreeing it would be exactly right for Mary, they were led to the back of the ballroom where Monsignor pushed a button, the walls divided and a complete altar came into view. It was absolutely outlandish. Their plan was that at midnight on Saturday the walls would draw back and there would be a celebration of Midnight Mass right there and then for the dancers.

Dancing with a pretty girl, miles away from home (and miles away from wife or girl-friend), a couple of drinks, soft music and suddeny, sliding walls and the full Latin Mass. If one was fasting from food and drink from midnight (when the walls opened,) technically one could then go to communion too. It was bizarre and twisted so many strands of human experience that it would probably lead to more sins, Mary thought, than if they had not bothered and the sailors had stayed in B&Bs, gone to pubs, picked up girls or tarts and went to Mass on Sunday if they wanted to.

As a mark that she was growing up, Celi cashed in an endowment policy to buy a bedroom suite for Mary. The damp cupboard was no place for clothes; she had no chest of drawers, which did not matter as she had hardly any clothes. But now there was going to be progress; wallpaper appeared, and new lino. The room was transformed. But Vin would not let the choosing of the furniture go by without his say-so. He went with them to Brown's in Clayton Square, where a light-coloured wardrobe, dressing table and chest of drawers was displayed, at £15. Naturally, he was the one to pay over the money although Celi was the one who had paid over the fifteen years. Unfortunately there was no money to buy a new bed, and so the gawky leg continued to dig into the new blue lino.

The furniture throughout the house remained static, though "We used to have the table over there once, Celi had said. Mountains away, another land. There. When. So the furniture had once been fluid in its placing.

However, this independence was only a miasma. There was no heating and the few times Mary tried sitting reading in her bedroom, her father came upstairs and told her it was "too cold up here, you'd better come down to the fire right now." She could not argue; he was right; she had sat watching her mottled arms growing more blue with each chapter.

When Auntie Julie had got her new fireplace put in, Vin and Celi decided they should have one too. It was probably rivalry more than necessity although Celi must have looked forward to a blacking-free future and a goodbye to the basket with the tin of Zebo, blacking-brushes, emery-paper and dirty gloves. But it was the same as the wallpaper situation; in spite of the beautiful designs available they chose a mottled beige affair with a line of spotted brown tiles and a stepped top ledge. It looked like the frontage of a small nineteen-thirties cinema. She could imagine little people queuing up around the coal-scuttle for a new Saturday-night film.

Although smaller than the iron range, it dominated the room as only a truly ugly object can do. Mary looked at the selection of models in the catalogues and pointed out the classic imitation marble versions of the nineteenth century fireplace in their sitting room.

"We can't possibly afford something like that! What are you thinking of!" Father was aghast. Mother said nothing. When Mary suggested that they could have a gas fire and then a separate Ascot to heat water they both looked at her as if she was talking in tongues. Whatever it was, she was talking dangerous twaddle and it would only lead to trouble.

It had been the same when Mary had got to the High School and discovered that girls took daily showers; they were the richer ones, however.

"You can't mean having baths every day, surely, (because no one they knew had shower equipment), it won't do you any good. Whatever gave you that idea? A Saturday night bath is sufficient for anyone except a coal-miner. It'll only drain away all the hot water! What other fancy ideas have you got! Too much washing and bathing like that will only weaken you! It doesn't do your skin any good." Celi, Vin and even Julie formed a chorus like a solid wall.

Pointing out that Father would not have to bring in heavy buckets of coal in the rain and snow and there would be no ashes and cinders for Mother to have rake out, and therefore no dust or smuts,

150

made no difference. And there would be no interfering with how the water was heated, no thank you. If anyone wanted to have a bath on a hot summer's day they would be continuing with having to make up a blazing fire to heat up the water in the copper tank. How else would clothes get aired and needed socks get dried quickly without being wrapped against that big copper heart in the living-room cupboard? They could not envisage such disturbance or such expense. The Corporation would only pay a small outlay on unnecessary expenses like this.

The *Laughing Cavalier* was brought in from the cold sitting room and installed above the new fireplace. He glinted a smile at them all. On either side, much smaller pictures of Corot's *Girl* and Vermeer's *Girl with a Pearl Earring* kept him company.

"She's the image of Aunty Marie, you know," Celi said and so the picture became Marie, looking over her shoulder.

The other pictures on each side of the living room door were nineteenth century engravings of Notre Dame Cathedral and, near Father's black desk, Caen Cathedral in their prudent passe-partout sticky black-paper frames.

From America, a stamp collecting colleague of Father's started to send a large Collier & Ives calendar every year, of reproductions of sailing boats, which further enhanced the corner desk devoted to papers, letters and stamp albums.

The dog, knowing only hot and cold, relished being able now to get even nearer to the source of heat and at first, misjudging the distance, scorched her front fur.

15

One Sunday when Mary had been given the freedom to wander round the art room, and all the school, at weekends, Sister Veronica waxed lyrical about the joys of belonging to the order. They had met in the upper corridor.

"All the day is dedicated to praying. We have each hour sorted out, arranged between our duties to the convent, private prayer, mealtimes, the Angelus, community at eight o'clock, evening prayers and bed. Then it all repeats, in a perfect circle." The Irish farm was behind her, the lost farmhouse, half-a dozen children, her farmer's wife-future changed into this dedication to 280 girls and the score of staff.

Sister Veronica had also been a teacher and decided inexplicably to teach Mary the exports of India, which might come in useful,

' Rice, indigo, wheat, tea, tobacco, jute, cotton, rubber, sugar cane, mica, copper, tin.' There were others, there must be, but these twelve were apparently enough to pass any exam. It was obvious that once a nun was no longer required as a teacher, she was placed further down the ranks into these housekeeping rules. Sister Monica, once headmistress of the Demonstration School was now in charge of the junior library. Sister Francis was in a little office by the side door with all the registers and mounds of silver paper from Penguin wrappers for the missionaries. She was also in charge of the milk delivery and had to count all the crates each break-time. She was like a bright little animal in its nest, surrounded by tottering piles of silver paper. It was like bees clinging together in winter, with some taking the outer, colder side and then changing places to keep the hive alive.

It was like a thunderbolt when Sister Veronica died. That large swirling guardian of the High School's front door, their interface with the big world outside, postmen, guests, deliverymen, parents, troublemakers, Her Majesty's Inspectors - she had dealt firmly with them all. In quiet moments she sat embroidering tablecloths and mats for potential sales of work, often catching Mary as she passed by to ask,

"What do you think the colour should be for these flowers here in this corner, probably asters. Or could they be marigolds? What do you think?" She laid out the possible embroidery silks, a limited choice. They would quibble enjoyably about the proper colour to use.

There was silence now, a gap. The school was taken to the convent chapel for the funeral service. As the coffin was lifted down the grand staircase, in complete silence, every nun lined the way, each with a lighted candle. The coffin was loaded into the hearse outside the big door, where the older classes went into coaches, all sitting in respectful silence, to the cemetery, where there were further prayers at the graveside. Even on the trip back there was hardly any conversation amongst the subdued fifth and sixth forms.

Little Sister Pauline was assigned a new helper but rumbustious Sister Veronica was irreplaceable.

Sunday morning and the deep lethargy that only adolescents experience meant that Mary could not manage to get up early for Mass. The minutes fled by. She heard Mother leave for half-past nine Children's Service. The next one would be eleven, which would be sung Mass and also that would mean having to go with Father, something to be avoided. As the front door shut, she hurtled out of bed, flung on yesterday's clothes, dashed down the back stairs, splashed some water on her face at the kitchen sink and managed to run up the hill to St Philip's. She caught up with her Mother in Faulkner Street, just past the chip shop, rushing up almost out of breath trying to catch up, bereft. Mary could see her, dressed in black, the only figure in the street. She called out,

"Wait for me!" Mother turned round, staring coldly as if looking at a stranger with hatred. Mary faltered, "I changed my mind and thought I'd come with you after all." Her Mother smiled a grim smile, as if interrupted in something extremely private. Mary felt as though she had intruded or accosted a complete stranger; a second of fear. Mother had been a different person just then, superior, distant.

They went to several churches, which was breaking the rules -you were supposed to only attend your own parish. The nearest church, however, was the Little Chapel, a chapel-of-ease situated in the old Liverpool Workhouse buildings along at 144 Brownlow Hill. Unchanged except for the installation of electric light, the Little Chapel was icy cold in the winter and kept the original design, with a central barrier going down the centre to keep women and men separate. Its walls were a grim mid-green, with plaster crumbling in parts.

On winter mornings their breath was visible in the icy interior, though an oil heater blazed somewhere at the back. Priests were sent up from St Nicholas, and their favourite one was little Father Byrne, a young man with the true Irish colouring of black hair and almost blue-white skin and a scattering of freckles across his cheeks. His sincerity and appealing gaucheness were that of a country lad dropped into a city, but his almost-stuttering sermons were simple and heart-warming. Every woman in his little congregation wanted to mother him.

The other priest on the rota, Father Percival, was English, red-faced, plump and cheery, often racing through the Mass and sermon, which was appreciated. His most famous line was about studying at Upholland Seminary,

"I know my way in by all of the doors – and some of the windows, too!"

The church integrated all classes of people, but mostly from the slums nearby, as outside, a group of Teddy girls stood, black pumps even in the snow, black skirts, tight-clinched Waspies, twirling their chains in imitation of their boyfriends. The boys, quicker to make their getaway, had both chains and flick-knives. Little Father Byrne was somehow blended into their lives as a Sunday fixture.

It was strange to see the two priests one afternoon walking down Lime Street past the salacious posters outside the Scala and the Futurist, both looking like Mafia hit-men, dressed in black raincoats, black boots and black fedoras, striding towards Lime Street Station.

"They are usually only allowed out in pairs, like nuns," Celi said. "And it looks as though it's their day off."

Some Sunday evenings, they would often go to benediction if Celi was not going go up to Penny Lane with Mary to visit Nana. St Vincent's on Park Lane was as far as they would go. Walking back through black streets glossy with rain, on winter Sunday nights, they still had inside them the link with something larger than all this. The gold monstrance kept shining inside them, a link with transcendence

154

that could last all week. The memory of that bursting gold monstrance, with God Himself wondrously ensconced in the middle - they had been blest with that compressed sunshine.

They crossed past Mrs Allen's tenements its clumsy thick balconies hanging over each other, often with a light-bulb missing, leaving shadowed gaps between the door-window-window-door pattern. Kent Gardens was opposite St Vincent's church, it showed how far Mrs Allen had to walk to come and clean their house. They went through Chinatown Square, treacle-black if it was raining, which was quite safe for women to walk through compared with other parts of Liverpool Eight. Here and there, an open doorway showed a Chinese man sitting at the top of the steps and a long hall behind him, a room lit at the back, a suggestion of figures hunched over a table.

"They do a lot of gambling, it's a private world but it does not affect anyone else. There's no parties or drink, very quiet they are, but we are not allowed into their world, it's all secret," Mother told her. Mary tried to stare as hard as possible, being met with the impassive half-lit face in the gloom .The only public lights came from the *Far East* restaurant which brightened up one side of the square.

And all the time they carried inside them the golden sunburst of the glittering monstrance, its threat of exploding into thousand gold splinters and at its centre, God Himself in the form of a host, centring energy and beaming it out like invisible food. It held them warm all the way up the hill home and the end of a Sunday winter evening. It was as if something important had been accomplished and this was the 'place' they reached most Sunday evenings, the weekend completed.

The unacknowledged hunger of the parishioners sated; Saturday nights - pictures or pub; Sunday nights - benediction. World and non-world, they teetered between both, contentedly.

Sometimes, if he had run out of money, Vin was at home, sorting out his little kingdom of stamps into rows and then onto special album pages; but often he was out again. They never knew exactly where and never asked. Like his actual job and his wages, Mary knew not to ask; you did not have the authority.

She went ferreting about in the little reproduction Queen Anne chest of drawers in the sitting room - forbidden territory even for her mother. Top drawer – cigarette cards, assorted according to subject: cars, boats, breeds of dogs, film stars, military uniforms. All the world, cramped into one drawer.

The next drawer was crammed to the top with yellowing cuttings from the Daily Express, the Daily Mail, The People, The Echo, The Liverpool Daily Post, all dealing with different events in the war. Blurred photos catalogued the defeats, the lists of dead, the tracks across the desert, Montgomery and Rommel fighting it out as if personally. Of course, if Vin had not been able to be in the army, how else would he be able to chat knowledgeably in the pub to any returning soldier or their relatives? These carefully kept cuttings were his private alternative diary of those five years of wartime.

The third drawer held postcards from all over the world, some of them embroidered and kitsch, others a window onto far-off cities and monuments. In the fourth drawer were his yearly accounts books, including stamp-club memberships. None of this was interesting except for a small photo from the Echo, a 'Where is this?' quiz. It showed the front door of 20 Maryland Street and asked which famous writer had stayed there. The answer was Charles Dickens, passing through Liverpool on one of his lecture trips to America. He had got up early and gone for a walk, been locked out and had sat on the doorstep (which had three steps up) waiting for the household to wake up.

There was also a page torn out of a history magazine about Compte Jean-Baptiste Martineau, 1762-1833. Emperor Napoleon had appointed him a Marshal in 1804 and he fought throughout the Napoleonic Wars. After 1815 he tactically became reconciled to the Bourbon Restoration. Retired from the army he married a dressmaker and set up a haberdashery business in Limoges. He died in Paris and was buried in Les Invalides. Here was Father's obsession that they were descended from a French count, merely because they had the same surname.

She put the papers back carefully so there was no trace that anyone had disturbed them.

Films

16

Lower sixth form. St Thomas Aquinas. Five proofs of the existence of God. As fast as she tried, the more it fell apart.
"I believe, help, Lord, my unbelief." Someone else had been here before.

It was not obviously necessary to 'prove' a tree or anything else that existed, so it raised a suspicion that something was awry if God had to be proved to exist by using rules invented by a mediaeval thinker, even if he was a saint. The five proofs worked on their own but also raised more questions. It was the same problem she had with numbers, where no one questioned what happened in the gaps between one number and another. This was something out of the wilder reaches of algebra, lace-work for its own reasons. She had yet to discover Gerald Manley Hopkins' *cliffs of fall.*

Other parts were beginning to unravel too. How did anyone dying get a quick judgement, when they were judged (by whom?) and then also get a proper general judgement on the Last Day from God/Jesus? Christ was going to say to the wicked "Depart into everlasting fire" and he would be saying to the just "Come to the kingdom prepared for you." The Explanatory Catechism of Christian Doctrine did not explain at all where these people through the centuries were being kept in the meantime, in their shady afterlife. The ones in Purgatory messed the numbers up too, as they were supposed to be able to get into Heaven once they had suffered enough to purge their sins. They would already be shuffling in, one by one through the centuries. And what about those in Hell already, suffering before the right time? Also, it called to question the proper canonised saints who should not be classed as proper saints before God/Jesus (and the elusive Holy Ghost) said so? It did not make sense.

They were sitting at last at the Sunday dinner-table, the aroma of roast beef carrying through from the back kitchen. Fresh mustard waited in its blue glass cup slipped into its silver container beside the twin pepper and salt cellars. Over the week, the mustard would dry to a crust and have to be discarded the next Sunday. Whiskey sat under the table, ready to nose for any scraps. As they began to wade through the roast potatoes, beef and over-boiled vegetables, Vin said to Celi,

"Bung us the salt," but she, suddenly exasperated, remarked,

"For goodness sake, Vin, it's *please*, less of that shipyard talk here!" and with that he sprang up, scattering his knife and fork, throwing his keys on the floor and shouting,

"You wear the trousers then! You want to be treated like a bloody queen!" and with that, he dashed out, grabbing his coat and slamming the front door.

Mary was more flabbergasted than frightened, looking down on him for such a petty response, but Celi began to weep. Mary clasped her arms around her Mother, who was leaning on her shoulder, sobbing wildly by now.

"It's all right for you, Mary, you can leave when you're twenty-one, but I've got to stay here forever, " she gasped. Mary stroked her Mother's hair. She was trapped too, in this problem with these two trapped children, held together only by the furniture and their fear of the outside world. She would definitely be going the minute it was possible. Why her Mother was accepting such a life-sentence was incomprehensible.

Of course, she realised, he had also made a complete fool of himself. Sunday afternoons, 3 p.m. meant quiet streets, everyone at Sunday dinner and all the shops and pubs closed. He had nowhere to go and he also had no keys. She knew he would merely have to walk round the block and re-emerge.

When he did knock at the door after all, it was Mary who had to open it and the Sunday dinner continued with banana and custard, the usual jam tarts and several cups of tea. The couple sat smoking and reading the papers in an unspoken truce yet again.

Mother had splashed her face with water to wipe away the traces of crying. Mary counted up that she had five years to go before leaving. Five more years of this.

Later in the week, one lunchtime the two women talked about his moods.

"I've thought of making a graph, to see if he's influenced by the moon – something like women's periods, that sort of thing, It's about every six weeks, at a guess," Mary said. Celi looked up from her library book,

"That's strange, I've often thought the same thing, but never got round to it." And neither of them started the investigation, as if frightened to invade further into a territory they were afraid of. If it was inevitable, there was no hope; it was better to leave it to this random chance, his torpedoes detonating at will.

17

September the 8th, Our Lady's birthday and the first day of Autumn term, Mary walked into the Studio with some recent drawings from the holidays, full of enthusiasm.

"What are you doing here?" Sister Anthony was surprised. "I thought you were going off to the Art School?"

"I don't know what you mean... I didn't know anything about it," Mary answered, totally puzzled. It appeared that she could have left and gone off to the college right after O Levels but no one had mentioned the fact, including Sister Anthony herself. Her parents were on a different planet and had nothing to do with the school whatever, apart from Mother coming to Open Day and looking at the work on display each summer. All fathers were at work, obviously, from the usual school hours of nine-to-four.

"Oh well, You can do Art History A Level in a year then, and go off next September. It's only a year, we can cram it all in with Advanced Religious Knowledge." Mary was beginning French, and English Advanced too, but this was more important, a goal in sight. An escape, too, from many problems.

The centre of Liverpool, late 1950s, nearly Easter and reaching exam time; early butterflies danced about the convent's rhododendron bushes in the honeyed sunlight of mid afternoon and the relaxing religious lesson. Religious lessons were easy; you just had to take notes and memorise them. They followed Jesus through the three Synoptic gospels and then had to detour through St John's Gospel for the variation, one quarter of his life presented differently. She had always preferred St John and now realised why – he was the odd one out. Mary loved the out-of-this-world Apocalypse, where St John tried to describe situations that had no way of being described, tying himself in knots of rainbow colours.

As they followed the rest of the syllabus for Religious Knowledge advanced level, the class was introduced to the deeper levels of the Proofs of the Existence of God. It was all very neatly done, and worked out like a mathematical formula:

First mover unmoved (motion)
First Cause (causation)
Contingency (necessary or unnecessary)
Grades of perfection (gradation)
Order (intelligent design in nature)

There were also vague additions like proof from morality. As they sped through this mixture of Aristotle's philosophy and St Thomas Aquinas' explorations, the entire edifice started disintegrating in Mary's mind. You did not go about proving a table; it existed in its own right, (except if it had been burnt, or lost a leg, but those were only niggling details.) The very fact that grown men had gone about trying to prove the existence of God meant that ... He could be unproven, lose his capital 'G' or 'H', or at least be in need of being proved. Daily, as fast as they learned more, more bits fell out of her mind.

Seventeen years consciously or unconsciously believing in Him, and now at this late stage they were being given this evidence of His existence. Conflicts, misunderstandings and outright discrepancies multiplied. They had skimmed through this for 'O' level exams, but this went far deeper now.

Sister St James told them " God created the world and left it in its own existence. He will not, and cannot, for instance, interfere with the law of gravity. And though God is all-knowing and can see into the future that we cannot know, He cannot change that future. It is as if you were watching a car being driven towards a cliff – you could see what was going to happen from the distance, but you couldn't stop it crashing over the edge.

Similarly, God has given us free will, so we can choose whether to do right or wrong - He does not interfere."

So much for the people in the car praying to God to save them. The back pages of the larger Explanatory Catechism had a list of eighteen of the chief heresies; many of them made sense. Each variation tried to tackle the scaffolding of belief, like whether the Holy Ghost really was a third of the Godhead. They gave various ingenious ways of dealing with the God-human-here-today-eternity problem. Down the ages people had questioned, but the lid had come down firmly, Council after Council. Everyone prayed to God, sometimes through auxiliaries, as in a family – through Jesus, as instructed, His son; through Our Lady, his daughter (or wife or daughter-in-law, if the Holy Ghost was a splinter-god) and through any saints, God's friends. It was exactly the same as life in any street or tenement. Get round the old man through a friendly face.

In no time at all after Nannie died, Auntie Julie was saying

"I was waiting for the 85 bus in Berry Street to get to school (Our Lady's Eldon Street) and it was getting late already, so I said a quick prayer to Nannie that the bus would come along soon." So Nannie, presumably already in Heaven was already able to direct Liverpool Corporation Buses. Faith made sense out of gaps; it fabricated a reality that worked in outer space but did not work in the here-and-now. Except it did work at times; it was elusive. St Augustine's heartfelt plea pulled her back in the opposite direction:

Thou hast made us for Thyself, Lord,

and our hearts are restless, till they rest in Thee.

That made absolute sense and settled it all. He stopped God from falling to pieces. They wrote the details yet again in their exercise books, to go over again for homework.

Supreme, the origin of all life; He exists of Himself; Uncaused, He is the cause of all things; Infinite with no end or limit; Perfect: Eternal, not made – He was a ragbag assembly of superb qualities, a reassurance outside of time, golden, warm and loving forever. She could almost hear Him laughing at them all and their silly questions.

To counterbalance that, they were told, now that they were in the lower sixth, about the Heroic Sacrifice. They might consider it later on. It was a practice that contemplative orders went in for, as a way of saving lost souls out in the wicked world. This was where someone both brave and noble sacrificed all the grace they had earned, or would earn throughout their lifetime, for the redemption of some sinner, like a murderer who was completely lost. It was the spiritual equivalent of giving all your money away to a gambler and hoping it would mend matters. At the moment of the Last Judgement, the person then threw themselves on the mercy of God, as their own spiritual bank-balance was completely stripped and the person who had got their grace might not have added to the store of sequins. Mary still thought of grace as sequins. But their religious education deepened rapidly here like falling off a cliff.

She began to pray *"Lord I believe, Help my unbelief"* almost daily as the entire system began to crumble and the beauty began to fade. The words of the man whose son was possessed by a demon beseeching Jesus centuries ago were as bright and as needed as ever. The spiritual underpinning of daily reality was beginning to show gaps and slippages. She was beginning to go adrift.

The art history studies were no help either. Once past the childlike innocence of Duccio and Giotto, the Renaissance blossomed into pure Vatican propaganda. As Mary leafed through E.H.Gombrich's *The Story of Art*, it was obvious that the big guns had moved in and the homosexual Leonardo and Michaelangelo had designed the structure of all future stories by manufacturing their propaganda images. They were like Hollywood producers, with an

162

army of assistants and ready financial support from the Vatican and Italian oligarchs like the Medicis. Their versions of *The Last Supper* and *The Creation of Adam* were the definitive ones; it was impossible to imagine any other arrangements. It was as if an early photographer had asked all the apostles to smile at the Last Supper and had fixed them for eternity at that precise instant. Raphael came in third place, with a steady supply of Madonnas and Childs. It was all neatly cemented into place. People did not need to think any further, a constant supply of Holy Pictures, postcards and framed reproductions kept all those images current.

It did not help her unbelief, either, to look at the Baroque sculpture of *The Vision of St Theresa* by Bernini and try to see it as expressing a mystical, and not a sexual ecstasy. Even a seventeen-old girl could see that. It was a relief to land on the safe, neutral pages of Cézanne's apples and Utrillo's Parisian streets, yet something essential had been lost.

The other extreme, however also fell down just as badly. Rationalists said that everything evolved from some primeval substance, fish-shapes formed in the sludge, struggled ashore, grew legs after centuries, climbed trees which were conveniently waiting for them and some became birds. Big birds turned into prehistoric monsters and horses. Monkeys formed and people were descended from them. All dogs were bred from wolves. Bit by bit, gradually over aeons, all of these came into existence by making an immense effort.

"But it doesn't explain a butterfly, does it, Sister? All those colours and intricate designs, they could not have just happened out of slime," Mary questioned. The rest of the class stared at her, although Sister St James mildly agreed. Those quaint six days of Genesis were a way of dividing up the stages of creation. The modern-day version of an abstract god did the whole lot in one big explosion in space - ironically imitating the beginning of the Bible. Replacing the Aslan-like benign being by a start-up explosion in outer space was a betrayal of everything worthwhile, putting fireworks versus benevolence.

163

They left this subject and turned to tracing Jesus's biography and finding any references to him losing his temper, which he did, a few times, quite dramatically.

Leaving school was balanced by the excitement of getting into the Art School. Sister Anthony arranged the interview, picked out some of Mary's paintings, lent her a portfolio and off she went to Hope Street. It was hardly an interview at all. Mr Bell, Head of the School of Painting, riffled through her work, said

"Well, you can certainly paint," and that was it, all settled, appear when term started in early October. She was out of the door in less than ten minutes.

Going to Art School after years of walking past it and trying to see through the closing doors was a triumph. Nothing else was needed in life; this was all she ever wanted.

At the same time Whiskey, the dog, was dying, with back legs dragging and no chance of healing at the age of fourteen, a good age for a dog. Mary was not as upset as expected, and outwardly seemed strangely hard, as she had wept about it in advance. The parting from the old companion was neatly timed with this new event. A vet came to the house and collected Whiskey in his car on a Saturday afternoon. The last she saw of the dog was of Whiskey sitting in the back seat, held by Father, perhaps thinking she was going off to another Heswall holiday of five years ago.

As the family came out of mourning, all black clothes were given to Mary. Luckily the French existentialists made black the trendiest colour possible. It was also a help, as one morning Mary woke to find that all she had to wear that was clean were an orange jumper, blue cardigan and purple skirt, all Aunty Kay's cast-offs, kindly brought as useful for a student who did not need fashionable clothes.

Upset at the clash of colours, Mary bought some tins of dye and managed to boil the discordant clothes black one by one in the largest saucepan that then had to be scoured back to being usable again. But now she had an entire wardrobe of interchangeable black clothes suitable for all occasions. It was annoying that her mother also joined in the fashion set by Juliette Greco and got a black leather jacket as if pretending to be an art student too.

Coming back after Midnight Mass with Auntie Julie and Mother they found Father already at home, completely drunk and tearing up the Christmas cards, nicotine stains deep on his fingers, waving his arms about. He stood on the new tiled fire-surround, with his behind in front of the dying fire smoking yet another cigarette. *The Laughing Cavalier* looked down at them with his usual unhelpful gleam of a smile. The fireside rug was covered with scattered remnants of Christmas cards as Vin shouted angrily and at the same time felt sorry for himself about life in general. It was all a waste of effort, according to him and they were stupid to keep on with the pretence that all was going well. Christmas was a total waste of time and money. They were all fools. He snatched another card from the mantelpiece and tore it up, throwing the bits on the rug, snarling at them.

It was a parody of one of the carols from the Midnight Mass, Jesus Christ the Apple Tree:
For happiness I long have sought,
And pleasure dearly I have bought:
I missed of all; but now I see
'Tis found in Christ the apple tree.
I'm weary with my former toil,
Here I will sit and rest awhile:
Under the shadow I will be,
Of Jesus Christ the apple tree.

Julie, shocked, backed away and went off through the sitting room to her own house. Celi shooed Mary up to bed and dealt with it as usual, secretly. Enough Christmas cards were saved to make the usual cheerful display. But as Mary went up to bed, she wondered how much money it had taken to get him into such a state.

165

Reels

18

College announced a trip to London at the middle of term, in November. There was no money for Mary to go, even if Father had allowed it, but Nancy thought of a plan.

"My Dad's brother-in-law works for a transport company at the docks, and they have to go down London regularly, and he said we can get a free lift that way. And, as well, I've got a boyfriend, well, of sorts in London, and we can stay in his flat too - so all the trip will won't cost a thing!" Nancy, who had all the confidence in the world, said she would come round to the house and persuade Mary's Father about it. And she did precisely that, he was charmed into agreeing without realising it.

"Hmm. As long as you two keep together and you're back in this house on Sunday night -" Because Nancy was there, sitting in the fireside chair, he could not thump the table. Somehow he managed to swallow his pride for once, which was a surprise. Celi said nothing, trying to work out which way the wind was blowing.

So, on the Friday night at 6p.m. Nancy and Mary got the bus to The Tunnel entrance and walked along to the meeting place along Waterloo Road outside Trafalgar Dock. Two lorries waited for them, lights on in the dusk and the girls climbed into the cabs. Nancy went off with her driver, Dennis, and Mary was left with George, a dark intense-looking man. He did this run several times a week, he said, and was often away from home.

" It's a different life, no one knows all about it. We've got our own prostitutes," he told her, unnecessarily, " it's all organised. Wives all stay home and scratch, that's what." He made a grab at her, stopping in a lay-by before they reached their midnight stop, and unable to fight him off, Mary endured a mauling as he tried to undo her clothes.

"What have you been doing with that one?" Nancy said later. "What have you let him get away with? My driver and him have been comparing notes and now Dennis has had a go at groping all over me, it's all your fault!" Mary was now in disgrace with both of them as the dawn broke and they arrived at the edge of London. The lorries drew up near Tuffnell Park.

"This is as far as we can go," George announced, "You know this is all unofficial, like, but we could do with a donation, you understand, we could have got into a lot of trouble about this, lost our jobs and all." As she was still locked in the cab, Mary had no escape and managed to find a ten shilling note in her handbag to give him. Then he released the door. As she was scrambling down, he hurled after her,"Of course, it would have been free, if you'd been a bit more accommodating, like, serves you right for being such a stuck-up bitch!" And with a laugh, he revved up the lorry and turned around the next corner to Brecknock Road. The two girls stood on the deserted blue-grey dawn street, shattered, bodies still shaking from the constant rattling of the engines. They wandered along Fortess Road until they found a small café that served early morning breakfasts.

"Knackered, completely knackered and we don't know where we are yet," Nancy said, as they chewed on bacon sandwiches and toast, washed down with over-sugary coffee. Mary took out the tube map and they worked out how to reach Gloucester Road and Andrew's flat. "He might be up, by the time we get there," she added."That's if we ever get the energy to stand up and manage to walk out of here."

They emerged into a comparatively bright day, for November. After the dark soot-covered buildings of their 1957 Liverpool, the buildings here were white like wedding cakes, street after street, icing-sugar white, it was a dream. After asking the way a couple of times, Nancy found the flat was nearer Earls Court after all, and they arrived bedraggled and subdued at Andrew's door. He was completely ordinary looking, Mary thought; not really boyfriend material and difficult to describe; "just ordinary" was no helpful description.

Nancy quickly disappeared off to the bedroom with Andrew while Mary gratefully collapsed to sleep on the living room couch. It was almost evening before they were up and about, with a quick meal of tomato soup and hunks of bread.

"We're going out now, come on, we're going off to the Troubadour for the evening, Andrew says it's good, hurry up," Nancy stopped her from sitting down and dropping off to sleep again.

"You'll soon get your second breath," Andrew assured Mary as they went down the stairs to go off to a Saturday night in London. It began to be exciting, to be in an absolutely new place with no connections.

She noticed him leaning against a doorway at the side, idly smiling at nothing with a relaxed laziness. Then their eyes met and he walked over to her. It had all seemed so natural, so clear.

"My name's Pete. And what's yours? Would you like to dance?" It was as simple as that. It was a relief, a triumph to be able to dismiss her parents from her mind, to exist without their presence, their questions, not to have them, invisible, looking over her shoulder at everyone.

After a few dances round the crowded floor Pete saw some friends sitting at a nearby table. A plump fair-haired man smoked a cigar, wearing a wide-brimmed hat, everything about him one size larger than normal, gold rings included, too chunky and a little loose; they slid a little on his fingers. Pete introduced him to her as Gus and the small dark man on his left mumbled an unpronounceable name. They looked glad to welcome her into their company. She felt accepted, even liked. This London was easy.

"I like to see you young people enjoying yourselves," Gus said in a Canadian-Australian-American accent. She was wrong; it was a Rhodesian accent. "I love all these English kids. I'm opening a coffee bar back home and I'd just love to take you all back and show the people what you are all like. I could offer you the first jobs there."

They went back to the dancing quickly then, meandering away from the tables.

"Do you dance this way? Back home we do it differently. Try …That's right. You're a peach," Pete hugged her and began humming "I wish I could shimmy like my sister Kate," though the group on the stage were still staunchly punching out Everley Brothers tear-jerking songs. Peach was a strange thing to have said. It was out of date for one thing, like chiffon scarves.

"Who was that man with the rings?"

"Him, Gus? A white slaver, good job I saved you!" he joked.

"White slaves transatlantic? Or was he Australian?"

"He's international, darling," Pete mocked. Obviously she had stumbled on a bit of real London here, you had to be clever. Either it was a joke, or even funnier, it was actually true. A couple of years here would sharpen wits, make you able to sum up people without asking questions. Intelligence and naivety fought bravely. Then she decided that she probably was naïve and provincial and the best way out of that was silence, a girl's best armour. After three more dances they decided to go as it was already near midnight.

"Can you take me back to your friends' for coffee?" Pete asked as the music stopped and the place began to close down. Mary had not seen any trace of Andrew or Nancy since they had disappeared into the jostling crowd.

"They might not be in yet and I haven't got a key. I don't know where they are."

"It's pretty late now. The tube's stopped you know, and it's quite a walk from here if he's beyond Earls Court Road."

"What shall I do then? The buses have stopped too. We would have to go and hang around and wait for Andrew, until he and Nancy come back." Out on the street it was quiet, as London can have moments of quiet; they walked silently together at last, more close than in the dance-cellar, as though the people there had been a barrier.

" You could come and stay at our place, then, if you like. My friends are pretty broad-minded."

"Thanks, there seems nothing else to do." She clasped his hand and they started walking in the opposite direction. He turned towards her and looked at her for a minute.

"You're different, you know. I mean, not phoney. Not like most of the people who go there. I took a friend there once, one of the bowler-hatted type, but he didn't like it. His type of people are snobs all through, they can never let themselves relax."

As they walked, Pete went on to tell her that he was a freelance journalist. He had been doing a series on youth clubs for the *Johannesburg Star* but when he wanted to include clubs that were for black youths, the Editor said no.

"So it was a matter of principle and I couldn't continue like that. I asked Basil if he wanted to come with me and we sailed here from South Africa." Mary was impressed with this idealistic and campaigning attitude. He was vague, however, about where he worked now and she thought it was at a news agency. It might have been in a café; he was not forthcoming about how he earned any money in this foreign land. It explained his golden skin and blond hair, fed on oranges and sunshine.

He took her shoulder; he kissed her gently. There was a calmness within her that was inexplicable, as if part of her mind had been smoothed away gently.

His room-mate Basil came in later.

"Hi, Pete."

"Hush, Basil boy. We have a visitor."

"Have we?" He kicked off his shoes and came over to the bed. "Can I be introduced?"

"Yes, you mutt. Meet Basil, the laziest sod in London."

"How do you do."

"How do you do." How strange to be lying in bed with one man's arm around you and being introduced to another.

"Mind if I put the light on?"

170

"Don't be long, so and so."

"Ah, shut up, boyo." Basil put on the light and came over to the bed. "Mm She's pretty." She smiled up at him, amused at such frankness but with a wry thought of 'Any girl in another man's bed is pretty.' Pete spoke up now,

"Now we've been inspected, would you kindly put the light out and for Chrissake go to bed."

"O.K. Pete-y boy." Basil went on mumbling, but she could not understand it as it was in Afrikaans. Pete laughed once or twice and threw back some remark.

"He's a great guy, Basil. We went to the same school and he came over with me on the boat from South Africa. He's just frustrated and jealous." He held her beneath him, his arms crossed around her back. She drew down his head to hers. With understanding and gentleness he tried and tried again to enter her, but it was no use. "What's wrong, honey?"

"I have never done this before. You are the first." He was lying beside her now and turned his head. His eyes looked straight into her and he kissed her warm and slowly. The effort would have to be all on his side and it might get awkward. Pete tried again. There was nothing to worry about; she trusted him, utterly relaxed.

"Is that right?"

"Yes."

"Oh, Baby!" gently, half-choked. A ring of kisses round her neck. A warm rich feeling, like red wine, blood scattered with stars, the world and the spirit at one, all painted in red. His face above her, blotting out everything else, the sky through the window, visible behind his head; for the first time, the universe obscured behind one face, yet spilling out around it.

"De tyd saal leer…" She could not understand what he was saying. He translated, looking really serious. "Whether or not…time alone will tell…" What did that mean – it left her vaguely disquieted. He was changed, inexplicably sad. Face in the half-light blue (grey clouds masking the stars.) His fair hair falling along his forehead. Cigarettes afterwards. Face in the match-flame. A particle of ash from her cigarette fell on him.

"It doesn't matter." His skin glowed gold in the flame, but in daylight he was genuinely sunburnt, a complete foreign brilliance. Pete started to talk about his favourite writer, Kipling, *"The Gods of the Copybook Headings"* which Mary thought was terribly old-fashioned but did not like to say so.

Waking in the morning was a coming back into the everyday world. The first London buses were already chuntering past in the early-morning light. How could anyone have designed a world where people were ripped away from this lovemaking and made to go out and work? She remembered a joke about a Queen asking a King if sex was the same for the peasants as for themselves and being told, yes, it was.

"Well, it's far too good for them" was the firm answer and the feudal structure was set in stone.

Even if everything else is taken away, no matter what happens, I shall have had this.

The world intruded here too, with Kathleen the housekeeper, red-haired and cheerful coming in to the room. Mary was persuaded into ironing his shirt in the utility room and chatting to her. They had coffee and toast in the hostel's dining room. Soon she was going out across Nevern Square with him and Basil in the morning, a crisp clear November day.

"I've got no money," she discovered, having left her handbag at Andrew's flat. Just a lipstick and some coins were in her pockets.

"I have ten shillings."

"No, I couldn't take that, you haven't much." But Pete insisted she should take it.

"Look, ring me at six. Take my name and the telephone number, here, it's FRE 1231. Now, you will ring, won't you? Don't fail me, honey." Written in lipstick on a scrap of paper.

From train to train. People staring The pink brocade skirt and black stockings. Platforms. Stations. Adverts. Crossing over lines. Toilets. Pennies. Polished brass toilet locks.

The Borough of St Pancras places these washing facilities at your disposal. Loitering is not allowed. VD clinics are held regularly.

Cigarettes and newspapers. This way up. This way out. Engaged. Vacant. Engaged. Exit. Excuse me, could you tell me the way? Next station. Half eleven. Happiness. People. Distance from Manchester. Sun. Cold grey black. Cream , sun, trees. Tickets please. Fre1231. It all whirled round as she wandered from toilet to toilet across London.

"I'll buy you a new dress. Red lino. Happiness. When? Six O'clock. Don't worry, you won't get picked up. I wonder if I care as much. I wish I could shimmy like my sister Kate. Basil's a great guy really. Trouble is, he's got a bad inferiority complex."

"I want to look sharp. I am going to get myself a pussy. Puss-ee. People judge you by your clothes."

" But why should they?"She had spoken up, cradled in Pete's arms. "If you're great enough as a person, you'd exist apart from your clothes and then it wouldn't matter what you wore. Only weak people depend on their clothes to make an impression."

"She's right, you know." Pete had laughed.

"Did you do a lot of horse-riding? Because I didn't find it too difficult to break your virginity and that can sometimes make it easier, all that bouncing about." She found this funny.

"In the middle of Liverpool? You must be joking! We hardly did anything outdoors, just a walk to the Pier Head every Bank Holiday, that was the ult in our sportiness. Plus our family was poor, anything like riding lessons was completely out of the question. They wouldn't even let me have piano lessons. Just think, I was the only child in Liverpool that actually *wanted* piano lessons!"

She wandered back to Andrew's flat, negotiating by the corners of street after street of cream-plastered houses. In all the rushing about yesterday, nothing had been written down, but she remembered it was a number eleven and there was a United Dairies shop next door. It would be easy to find; a milk dispensing machine was right next to it on a black and white tessellated pavement. In fact, one of those little wigwam-like milk cartons would be good to have right now.

And here it was, a black front door, some railings, a few steps up, just as she remembered it, the milk machine right next to it. Number eleven, just like her grandmother's. She rang the middle bell for Andrew's flat. A young man opened the door,

"Yes, what is it?" He was quite pleasant. Mary was surprised, but after all, Andrew probably did share the flat; it merely had not been mentioned before.

"Oh, you don't know me, but I'm staying in Andrew's flat for a day or so. With Nancy," she added, for proof. His face changed.

"There's no one like that here. Are you sure?"

"Andrew Bailey?" He looked at her more kindly now.

"Oh, yes, you're right, there *was* an Andrew Bailey used to live here, that's right, but he moved out over a year ago." She thought he was trying to hide something, but it was unlikely."You've got the right place all right, but I moved in here early last year."

"But I was staying here just two nights ago! Really! I don't understand!" He commiserated, assured her he was not hiding Andrew and there was nothing underhand going on, sorry, and then politely shut the door. Bizarre.

Unfortunately Mary had seen the film *So Long at the Fair*, where the hotel owner persuaded Jean Simmons that she had not arrived with a brother and that his room number did not exist. They had wallpapered over his door in the night; he had caught cholera and the hotel wanted to avoid the loss-making scandal. Jean Simmons was persuaded that she was deluded. The problem was solved when Dirk Bogarde turned up with a bet he was honouring, having been gambling with her brother before he was taken off to a Paris isolation hospital.

She felt totally lost now, having found the right place and the young man, whether he was lying or not, denying her any shelter or give any clue to how she could be able to reach Andrew. London was beginning to grow menacing in its complexity. Best to go off to the art galleries and find the other students who would be wandering around taking notes.

The black jacket worked well, from being a regulation school bottle-green short duffel coat it had survived being dyed black, with new buttons. Pink brocade skirt and black top; black thick tights and flatties like ballet shoes; the prefect student outfit. People stared at her on the tube. Perhaps the new confidence coursing through her veins made this difference,she sat semi slouching with a new nonchalance.

If she went to the galleries, she would bump into the other students, it was obvious. But wandering round the National Gallery, none of the art students were around, just tourists and school parties from Spain, France, Germany, Italy – all of Europe was here. For the first time Mary saw real paintings in their actual size and was mostly distracted by the dominance of the frames, with outsize gold curlicues and twists. Madonnas and Childs simpered along the walls, compared with portraits of Kings and generals. The romping flesh of Rubens was like the cream buns in Kirkland's window, soft and yielding. Her feet hurt, it was easier and neater to look at these paintings in books at home, but she dutifully went from gallery to gallery searching for favourites. Not a friend in sight, even though she went round the corner into the National Portrait Gallery too. Serious people, bottled in time, stared at her and did not help. The odd quirk, hint of a smile, searching stare, haughty look, they were all dead and gave no clues how to handle problems of the here and now. Her feet were hurting, she needed to keep going to any toilet that was available, but had to get back to near Cromwell Road before it got too late.

At six o'clock precisely Mary found a phone box and rang up Pete, who said he would be meeting her at a party after work.

"I've got to work late tonight, it's a real pity, but if you go to Earls Court Station, at eleven thirty, Basil will be there to take you to the party and I'll see you there as soon as I can get away. Bye for now." Free-lance journalism obviously often meant having to work in restaurants or pubs for a living, as his writing was not yet real employment. Over five hours to fill in between then and now. She wandered along, trying to work out if she could afford a coffee.

A young man drew alongside her and said "hello" and though she was going to ignore him, there was such an openness in his smile that Mary relented and turned towards him. His face changed.

175

"You look sad."

"I don't know where I am, really, probably totally lost!" She managed to tack a smile onto this. He became extremely formal, and offered to shake hands. "My name is Abdul, I am studying at the London School of Economics."

"So you live round here? You know London? It's all a lot to take in at once, all these roads and buildings. I came here from Liverpool on a college trip to go round the art galleries, but it looks as though I've got really lost, I can't find any of my friends from art school and the streets are all the same, I'm exhausted and my feet are hurting."

Abdul suggested they go for a coffee and as she slowly unwound he said in fact, as she was so shattered, what about going to his flat as it was so near. With the new confidence and the new tiredness, she agreed and Abdul showed her into a tidy clean room with a kitchen alcove. As he brewed up strong Turkish coffee he told her about his Mother and sisters back home. His Father had been ill for some time and Abdul was now the hope of the family.

"When I return I go back to work in some government office probably. My country needs people like me." He opened his fitted wardrobe and brought out a gigantic Turkish flag. "My Mother and sisters sewed this for me. We are very proud, I have to live up to it and honour it." She looked at him as if he was mad. But he was kindly and also brought out some sweet scones. "You can have a rest here, if you like, just here on the couch. I've got papers to see to." And unbelievably he left her on the couch after a swift kiss on her cheek and went through his briefcase ruffling out papers and notebooks.

As it grew late, Mary said she had to be going to Earls Court station to meet someone.

"Its getting rather too late don't you think?" Abdul was amazed. But the nap had restored some strength and Mary was determined to go right now. He said he would accompany her as it was late for a girl to be out alone.

"And you don't really have to make the effort, because you can stay here overnight and then find your friends tomorrow." But nothing would deter her from meeting Pete, however polite and good-looking Abdul was.

Outside Earls Court station they waited. A crowd of about thirty men hung around at the entrance. She could not have given any reason why they were there. Abdul did not speak much. He stood with his hands in his pockets. When he did speak it was usually to say again,

"But why don't you stay with me? I could sleep on the floor." An unexpected streak in her said no, wanted to be certain of meeting Pete at the party and would not be changed. "See, it is getting nearly midnight now. Your friends are not coming." A certain amount of distaste in 'friends.' No, she would not accept that; if that was not true, her mind had not planned what would happen next. Alternatives were numbed. It was a time spent in a white-hot refrigerator. No explanations. Abdul looked at his watch again. No, no, he is not going to win. Anyway, the whole thing isn't real.

But at last Basil and a small swarthy man were coming towards her and Abdul was shaking hands with her, with a curious look of questioning and reproach and without speaking, without anger, he just disappeared down Earls Court Road. She shook hands with the man introduced as Freddie. Basil also put his hands in his pockets and whistled, watching Abdul walking away. The three of them walked on to the corner, then stopped. Freddie said

"O.K. , Basil? We're O.K. We're going on ahead. See you later."

"O.K. So long," Basil nodded and then turned to her with a curious look. Then he went. Abdul had looked at her in the same way. Freddie and she went on together. She felt rather strange by now, a bit dizzy. This man was so small, he reached up to her ear and he wore such a startling red jacket with eagles on it. He talked of his job in the club up the street. She should go there some time.

"I'm only here for three days." They walked along many streets and crossed a few roads. Houses ranged on either side, no spaces. Cars parked between trees. Terraces, mansions, sleekness and London-ness At last they came to a large wrought-iron gate and went up a flight of stone steps to a cream-painted house in a large terrace facing a park. He took out a bunch of keys and opened the massive front door which had pillars on either side and balconies above.

Immediately there was a change : in him, in her and the atmosphere in the hallway. He became strangely touchy, she became numb, the house silent and hostile. The hall and stairs had red jute carpet, cheap and rough, not luxurious. Freddie went up in front of her, *shhing* her not to make a noise.

Funny, for a house with no restrictions. Up and up. Their feet scratched on the carpeting and she was too tired to count the stairs. There were no loud sounds in the house. No big party after all, just a small get-together. Pete would be sitting on the floor drinking coffee and waiting for her. They reached the topmost floor and Freddie opened the door.

The room was so small that the double bed dominated it. Beside it stood a wardrobe and a chair. Behind the head of the bed was a gas ring and a washbasin. And that was all.

Illogically, her first response was pity; pity for him, that this was all he had, that people at his job would not know that this skimpy room was what his life was made of. He was about thirty. How sad. Then the rest of he thoughts gathered together, aware that in a situation like this oughtn't she to feel afraid, startled, angry? Not merely tired. She sat at the far end of the bed on the little chair by the window and said, looking at the traffic down on the road,

"I'm not going to sleep with you, you know." Flatly, like that. No use now not recognising what all this was about. He said nothing. Then she asked where the toilet was. He said she could use the washbasin, which disgusted her and she insisted on going to the toilet down the corridor properly. How many other girls had been in this room in this way? (They would have had to climb on the bed to reach up to the washbasin, or drag that little chair all the way round – how ridiculous.) How long had it been since the last one and what had she been like?

He grunted, opened the door and stood out in the corridor for her to follow. With each footstep along the corridor, he took a footstep in time, to pretend there was only one person. No restrictions indeed. They came back together. There was a light showing beneath one of the other doors. Back into the room. It smelled stale. Bad move. She could have escaped, but that would have meant leaving her jacket behind. She sat on the chair by the window as her feet were hurting now, but kept her black coat on. Never had there been such deep tiredness as this, that stopped her mind, digging deep into the space between each thought. He must think she was stupid. So far Pete had not been mentioned by either of them. It was too obvious.

"Are you tired?"

"Yes," (Bloody fool.)

"Why don't you get into bed?"

"I don't want to."

"But don't be silly. You want to sleep, don't you?" She was still in midst of the emotional and physical upheaval of the night before, affecting her soul and identity, while outwards it also had driven her from one ladies' toilets to another all day. Sleep. That deadness was necessary. Freddie had spent a large amount of his resources, obviously and was now having to think up another move. She watched him detachedly. Now, he really was stupid but he was not tired at all. He was brushing his teeth. Now he was putting a kettle on the gas ring. There was no hot water. How sad. All these people you saw walking round the streets of London, looking all normal, and they all issued from cramped rooms like this. Their clothes were their real home.

"Look," he pointed out, "you can lie down on the cover." She disregarded this completely. How much longer could she manage to sit up on this rickety chair? It squeaked gently now. Last night was so mixed up with this, it was hard to separate the two. There were few lights left on in houses outside the window in the thousands of streets behind.

Too tired to risk walking along those streets, that staircase, rise and walk out of that door. But not sleep on the cover. It was shiny and cheap looking, whirls of orange and yellow rayon flowers.

A calm deadness took hold; an illusion of strength. A fight was going on between the real part of her, the part that separated

179

herself from others, and the arms and legs that were her body, that was the same as everyone else and the part everyone saw and labelled with her name. She was getting drunk with tiredness now. He was taking off his shoes. Brown suede, and probably smaller even than her own.

She got up and sat on the floor, her head leaning on the side of the bed. A throbbing weaving spark went round and round in her head like a late wasp on indoors autumn afternoons. Freddie came and sat beside her, his hand stroking her hair. Words were too difficult to say, to think out, to string together. She was talking inside herself but could not speak in words any more, was more on a scale of sense-experience. The stroking she could feel and not like, but without a clue what to do. Freddie plucked at her jacket.

"Take this off," he said, pettishly annoyed. How childish he was. His name was Freddie. She stood up and took it off. Some time earlier she must have removed her shoes. Automatically her arms, hands, even the fingers worked. But she had to concentrate. It was like after the sixth gin (no one had ever been able to afford any more in the drinking bets they made at college) when every care must be taken as the glass is put down and she had always been sharply conscious of the hands. It was slow, deliberate, important and she had to concentrate. She managed to walk to the bed and almost fell onto it. This time she collapsed along it, the gas ring behind her head. Freddie undressed quickly and pulled back the silky yellow cover from underneath her. His arms reached out around her and he kissed her shoulder.

She was bored, like teatime at Auntie Julie's, having to humour him. He was trying to undo her bra through her underslip and top and was not making a good job of it. He was really cross by now and becoming forceful.

This is ridiculous, she thought. It's time to do something. He was so annoying but waves of anaesthetic kept passing across. She tried to struggle against him, thinking him a silly little man. He was surprised and said in wonder,

"You are a strong *girl!* with the accent on 'girl.' But suddenly she felt so apathetic about it. She could do nothing. Run out to the corridor in a dishevelled state? What could she say? What were the other people here like – warrens of little rooms and little peevish men? And surely they would ask her why she had come here, a respectable girl did not find herself in such a situation, did not come into strange houses with strange men after midnight. And where were you last night my dearie? Somewhere else. You mean? Ah, but that was love, that was different. No, I don't know where he is, not right now. And they would shake their heads and shut the door or ring for the police, if they were respectable, or inveigle her into their rooms just the same as Freddie. She could not risk that. Where was Pete? Didn't he know where she was?

Running downstairs and out into the street and calling out for the police would lead right back to her parents and even more trouble. They would not be able to cope and Father would be apoplectic. Mummy would not be able to cope and would go all hysterical and weepy. It would become a massive lot of trouble, far worse than this and going on forever, they would all-but lock her in the house and withdraw her from college, make her wear twin-sets and pearls and make this event the be-all and end-all of both her life and the entire family's. The neighbours would talk about her and what a pity it all was , how something *awful* had happened to her years ago and she had never been the same ever after. The family would be marked forever and she would not be let out of the back bedroom until she was in her late twenties, if ever.

The scream that had almost come, she killed and a cold anger came, despising this silly man with his greasy black hair.

"I said I'm not sleeping with you," and she sat up. He grabbed her, protesting, clawing at her top. After all, that was a challenge and he had been pretty understanding so far. She had been shilly-shallying round all the past hour, nothing like he had expected.

"But I am a man!" he shouted (no restrictions about noise now, apparently) his white teeth gleaming, there seemed to be hundreds of them, all white and even , hundreds. Two small black beady eyes like an hysterical rabbit. "But I am a man!"

The stock answer to that being – *prove it!* – jokes from the boys at college rushed through her head. The unshaded light-bulb was digging into her eyes. More than anything else, the pattern on the wallpaper was important. The window. One two three four five panes. Six, if Freddie would move his head. The sixth contained his head. Now it had moved between the panes, she could see six panes. Concentrate. There are six panes, white frames, white frames digging down and crossing each other, fighting at white corners against the night navy.

She could feel, no there was a feeling of skin against her. Not even against, but mixed up with now, and poured into and intertwined with her own. Which was his leg, which was her own arm in the hundreds mixed between them? The window panes hitting hard. No, it is too much. I must go away from all this, it is demanding far too much.

"But it will not be for long and then you can go to sleep." Yes, that was where she was going to, yes she was going there, that was it, and then this thing had happened on the way. It was an interruption, it would be over soon, don't think about now, think about then. Better get it over with. It's in the Sunday newspaper all the time after all. Freddie was ripping off her knickers. Desperation was giving him extra strength. His body plunged into hers, into that part that was outside, muscles and tendons, the body that people in the street knew, the part that had a name, the skin-stuff on the outside.

The real self was up by the ceiling, fully alive, watching. Despising him and her, coldly watching these two people like the recording angel, missing nothing. She was managing to be in two places at once. Up here on the ceiling was an interesting place to be, you could see everything from here, but you could not say anything. It would not be heard. Then they slept. An absolute. In the morning he woke first and shook her shoulders until she opened her eyes.

"Get up. You've got to get up now!" He was most insistent. Good God, last night was one thing, now he was angry about something else. She sat up in bed, amazed to find she still wore a bra, slip and suspender belt. Stockings and knickers were wound down somewhere at the bottom of the bed and she reached down between the sheets to retrieve them. Now he was shouting about something. "You have made the sheets dirty. Look here and … here!" He was pointing with distaste.

There were some orangey stains, not as dramatic as blood but from her own innards after all. She was angry now. He was complaining, after using her, that the process had left some marks on his precious sheet. He was now accusing her, twisting the entire situation around so that it was she who was the accused. He was still pointing at the stains, had pulled the top sheet off as though the bed were sodden with cat piss.

"Dirty!" Freddie said, now in triumph.

"Well really, I can't attend to your laundry problems. Soak it in cold water. I'm leaving London today." By this time she had swivelled her skirt the right way round, finished dressing and washed her face with cold water using her hands as facecloth.

Freddie was still dramatising around the bed. Some light blood traces had spotted his yellow rayon coverlet too. Life did have its subtle revenges.

Mary wandered back to the main road and tried again to make out where Andrew's flat would be from here, but it was no use. She had no money spare for the tube now. After finding Earls Court Road she tried out various ways and reached The Troubadour again. Here in the daylight it did not look as glamorous as the night before last. Late morning sunlight showed up the wooden floor and the walls covered with posters of past happenings. She could afford only one coffee and must work out how to get to Victoria coach station as easily as possible.

It would have to be walking, however exhausted she felt now. Food was more important; after all, she had all day to walk that far. She had to manage it. And with this new fatalism, Mary sat and looked at the dust-motes swirling in the shafts of sharp November sunlight.

With the precision of a film-shot, Nancy and Andrew walked in at just that instant. Their shocked faces were out of place now.

"We were just going to the police about you!" Nancy squawked. Andrew looked at Mary sternly.

"We didn't know what to do. What did you mean by waltzing off like that? You left us with no message at all!" Telling them about returning to what looked like his flat and it turning out to be a duplicate, so surreal, was brushed aside. It was definitely not the time to tell them what had really happened. When she told Nancy privately later some of what had gone on, swearing her to secrecy, all Nancy said was

"Well, now you know what it's all about, then." So she did not tell her all the details of what had really happened the second night and left it at an apparent two-night tryst, of sorts. They walked back to the flat, which appeared, in its uncanny way to be exactly where it was before. Its location was an exact duplicate of the place she had gone to a day ago. Mary tried to justify her absence.

"But I came to exactly the same place and there was no trace of you! The shop next-door, the milk-machine, the black and white tiled paving, it was all exactly same! Except of course, it wasn't." They treated her much as her parents would have, with disapproval and a complete lack of wanting to know the details.

Mary could still see clearly those four bells and the black front door opening and the man saying that yes, she was right, Andrew had lived here over a year ago but had moved he knew-not-where and wasn't it funny how these things happened and how she felt trapped in one large conspiracy and unable to reach out into the real world. Perhaps it was that shock which had softened her up for what happened later that night.

Andrew went with them to Victoria Coach station, kissing Nancy goodbye and shaking Mary's hand formally. As some students were staying on in London for a few more days there was plenty of room on the coach back. Friends-of-friends gave them the unused return tickets and the driver knew no different.

"Thank God that's over! I could hardly stand him by the end!" Nancy complained but was not very talkative after that and Mary, shattered fell into a deep and blank sleep.

She walked into the house a different person. Her hips swung with a different power. She knew for definite that her parents had nothing like this and it was impossible to think they had ever had the same experience, nor that she had been conceived from such a powerful event, such a starburst.

The next week, going down town to the Picton Library, Mary took out a Teach Yourself Afrikaans and managed to cobble

184

together a letter to Pete, on the lines of how could you think I was such a *slet*, to go and trap me with Freddie, and returning his loan of the ten-shilling note.

Back at college it was the usual round of non-stop life-drawing, a boring mapping of naked bodies on half-imperial size paper with red conté crayon to make them look more authentic by mimicking Renaissance drawings. Lunchtime they went off to the Pack of Cards café and as Nancy, Len and Mary sat down with their usual toasted cheese sandwich and black coffee thickly laced with sugar, a new song came over the jukebox.

It made her speechless. Bitter-sweet and comforting, Tommy Edwards assured everyone that *It's All in the Game*. The good advice tumbled out. He was the only one who understood. The underlying masochism was unacknowledged. His voice slid down like treacle from a spoon. It was like a personal message, an invisible telegram. Mary fell into the song as if it was a cushion. It told her that suffering was usual, it was 'The Game' and she was just at the start. By being so miserable, it made what she had been through normal. You gave yourself into these songs; you gave up. There was no compass.

It had nothing to do with rolling round the bedroom floor, terrified that a baby would soon be living there with her. Nothing was going to 'fly away' - it was all in the here and now, on the bedroom's dull plain blue lino in the cold December afternoon.

There was a remaining problem; pregnancy, the dreaded result of anything stronger than a kiss, it seemed. Debbie at college had told them anecdotes about how her uncle, a doctor, had women coming to him for help to get rid of unwanted pregnancies or bring on late periods

"These women turn up in the surgery, with cobs of Daz or Omo stuck up their innards. Or pieces of soap get lodged in there. They are all desperate not to have a kid. He has to get them out of the mess they've made of their tubes and see if he can do anything about the pregnancy. Sometimes it's too late."

It was all turned into a joke. Slippery elm was mentioned, some herb, but how did she get hold of anything like that? Did Boots sell it? Sophisticated Tracy had talked about a pint of gin, a mile run and a hot bath, but Mary was unsure what order to do the things in and could not afford the gin and knew she could not manage a mile run, especially round the nearby streets. Someone might stop and talk to her, plus she did not have the stamina to do a mile. Did walking back, tired out, count as part of it?It would only attract a lot of attention if she ran around these streets in the cold. Their fire did not produce really hot water anyway, so the hot bath part might not work either.

Days overdue. Three, five. Slow quiet panic set in.

She rolled around desperately on her bedroom floor, trying to reach inside the tubes and channels that led inside her. Fingers could only reach a part of the way; the rest was blocked off. All a complete mystery. Women also used crochet-hooks, she knew about that, but worried that she would just rupture the walls inside, ruin her stomach and bleed to death. The choice was getting worse by the day; it was going to be either a child of Pete's, who she could after all love, or a child of the unknown South American - or whatever he was - with the ugly face. She would have to live with that face and look after it all her life otherwise, a replica of Freddie.

Looking round the bedroom, it would have to be brought up here. Her parents, after the initial shock (she would not tell them everything, until the colour of the child became obvious) would accept the situation and life would go on. No, it wouldn't. It would get worse. They wouldn't ever let her out of the house again. She would lose all of college, all friends, any hope of earning any money, stuck here babysitting forever.

A cold dread took over and allowed her to act as though nothing was going wrong. She was totally frozen. Ten days overdue. Swinging between life and death. This new blue lino, the striped Regency wallpaper, the being here and all the hell going on inside the bloodstream. Living here, in this bedroom with all the anger and disapproval that would avalanche down and not even liking the baby. Perhaps a toothbrush would be a better idea than a crochet hook? What about asking Tracy about going to an abortionist – but then, she had no money. Father had tight rein on everything and there was no grant until next year, she had been too young, a month under eighteen at the start of this term.

186

Outside, the men from Blakes Garage went on playing football in their lunch hour and soon the inevitable football would come over their yard wall. Sometimes one of the men would climb over the wall (how did they do it so easily, back and forth?) and other times there would be a plaint of "Can we have our ball back?" from the lads in the street. And sometimes Celi would go out and bring the ball in and not return it, keeping it under the stairs with other rubbish, while Mary always dashed out from the lunchtable and threw it back. It was their only way of having a good time and she liked to hear the men shout and cheer as they played. The girls from Berwick's Toy Company opposite hung about the garage doorway and sometimes joined in the game too, they were all young after all and full of high spirits.

One day Celi let her return all the balls and the men were overjoyed and both sides of this little civil war were satisfied. Father, on the other hand was near to going over to complain to the boss, but as there was no games on a Saturday the lads were safe.

Random reminders of the night with Pete were spread all around Liverpool. On a doorstep a piece of paper, a headline, torn with only one name – Pete, although it was really an article on the Johnny Dankworth Orchestra. A letter in the paper from a woman in London, a Mrs Peters, complaining of the taxi fare from Cromwell Road to Nevern Square. A publicity drive for South African Cape apples. A holiday company's window with a poster of Johannesburg. Basil's picture of the mountains in a shop window. A lion on a tin of Tate & Lyle's syrup. Samson and Delilah. Out of the strong came forth sweetness. Yes, out of the strong. Sweetness? Yes. But not now.

And at a party, the same record turned up again: through the deep red walls, a whitewashed wall and some boys singing like the Everley Brothers. Cigarettes? A packet of twenty. Only tens left and those, only Woodbine. Whitewash? Eyewash! And suddenly, tears.

Each day she was in a type of amnesia which alternated with a strange euphoria. Moodswings. Thank goodness for names and identity on the outside, the clothes that kept a person together so that all this chaos could go on, unremarked, inside. Fifteen days now. Choice was getting less and less. Mother would have hysterics and Father would go off his rocker. A neat suicide would be a way out, but she did not know how to do that either and would have to get some medical books out of the library. It was not the sort of thing you could ask anyone about. Aspirins were supposed to work. You needed a hundred of them, but some people vomited the lot up. That would be embarrassing and even harder to explain. She would have to buy several hundred then, from several chemists around town, in order to be able to try again when no one would notice.

Luckily after three weeks her tense body decided to let out the delayed blood which caused a stew of emotions, all illogical, grief, hope, regret, relief,fear, broken-heartedness. Each emotion came into play, all at once.

Spring again. And Summer. Autumn. Another person now, many pictures had shifted like screens between what had happened and her.

The nuclear bomb was paramount. Nancy said she could come and watch the J.B. Priestley programme on their TV at home in Woolton. It was disturbing, it was vital, but when she began to talk to her parents about it they backed away into trite excuses. As long as the communist Braddocks were kept off the council, that was as far as their public responsibility went these days. Probably worn out by the war, they had no psychic energy to confront this new issue that demanded even more attention.

Father did make a small scene however, when Mary was going to a concert at the Philharmonic where Paul Robeson was appearing. Several of the students from college were going, a mixture of music appreciation, rebellion and idealism.

"Another one of those communists, they're even coming over from America now. You just be careful you don't get caught up in something serious after this." The downfall of Christianity, direct from the stage of the Phil itself; he managed to take all the anticipation out of it. Luckily Theolonius Monk proved enough distraction, plus Art Blakey thrashing life out of and into a stack of drums. The heartfelt songs of Paul Robeson affected a different corner. She slunk back into the house trying to look as though it had been a boring evening.

However, Mary was now stranded at a crossroads just as important as the pregnancy scare. The superb experience with Pete was, in religious terms, just as venal as the assault by Freddie; it was a mortal sin. The two nights were both equally mortal sins. Sex outside marriage was an absolute, there was no way of pretending it had not happened and so there it stayed, a bright black mortal sin simmering away and blocking her entire spiritual landscape and future destiny. There was no way of reaching towards God from her now. But she refused to confess it as a sin; it would be defiling a hurtling into space and a richness that was a complete parallel of her First Holy Communion. It would be betraying the most wonderful thing that had ever happened to her. Putting sin around it would be a type of vandalism..

But without going to confession, she could not go to communion; it would be a sacrilege to do that, it was probably yet another mortal sin. Like a bad chess game, she was cornered.

And so it began, slowly at first, going to Mass and having to stand aside as others went up to the altar-rails for communion and received God into their body and soul. She began to get panic attacks and could only kneel in the back benches to be near the door. It was the same in every church. And now she had to avoid going to Mass with her mother, who would notice the lack of taking communion. She was exiled on all sides. It came to a head at Christmas, that dangerous time for so many people.

By now there were no more distractions to try. Mary had counted all the cathedral's pillars she could see (eight) and their arches (six) and women wearing navy hats (three) and as many of the floor tiles she could make out beyond the benches (twenty-seven). Now she could try colours – how many things were gold or brown, for instance, or sizes – which stones in the arches were really the largest? But none of these efforts were successful, the rising feeling of panic in her stomach had not gone away. Now she needed to go to the toilet as well. The faint beginnings of a need to vomit joined in. It was surely impossible for one set of innards to be working in so many different directions at once. Now real panic set in.

Midnight Mass at the Basilica had got as far as the sermon and the Archbishop would be speaking from the pulpit, alone, for hours. Once they got into a place like that, they went on regardless of the people in the benches.. There would be total silence apart from the shuffle of feet. Not many babies appeared at Midnight Mass in the Cathedral, so there should be no piercing yells or screams to mess things up. Once a moderately intelligent and not too unhappy child had discovered the wonderful echo, it was only natural to experiment with the sound, until the parents, embarrassed or furious would have to retire or cause a worse scene by trying to gag it or hit it. Any smacks also echoed.

But there were no babies or toddlers. And now the archbishop was gliding across the sanctuary towards the pulpit. She realised there would be no life-saving distractions now. With mounting panic, she stood up and shuffled past the other parishioners to the end of the bench and walked down the aisle just as the archbishop trod the five or so stairs up to his decorated pulpit.   The cathedral was packed, but orderly. Unlike the other churches in town, there was an extra-large space at the back for latecomers, who were standing in ranks by the door. her entire family was there, their shocked faces ranged in size – Father, Mother and Auntie Julie. They looked like Ensor's painting *The Entry of Christ into Jerusalem* – faces stacked up in lines and groups.

She went into an empty side-chapel and sat on a bench. The main performance continued on her left. After the sermon, it was all lights and carols and activity; it was really tempting. The queasiness had entirely disappeared – she did not need any escape any more. For a minute there was a great temptation to go back and join in again but she left at the beginning of the Last Gospel, although it was her favourite, to avoid the crowd and having to encounter the family yet again.

She was home already, of course, when they appeared. Auntie Julie said something about had she been unwell? but it was more out of politeness and obviously something that was not really believed. In fact Auntie disappeared without even a glass of sherry and went off next-door to her own house, most uncharacteristically.

As soon as Julie was gone, they both laid into her.

"Well, what was all that about?" asked Father. "You've gone and insulted the Archbishop in front of everyone." It was no use to say that she had felt sick, but Mary tried.

"I felt sick, Daddy."

"You were drunk, I could see that," he interrupted her.

"Oh dear, this is terrible," said Mother from the sidelines, more in disapproval than shock.

"Did you go off with Greta and Lucy drinking before the Mass? Where did you say you were going? They weren't with you!" he went on.

"I went up to Greta's parents because they live right opposite and I wanted to be early. We all had a tiny glass of sherry, that's all, to celebrate – they don't have much drink anyway, they're far too poor. And then I got a bit worried about the time and so I left and Greta and Lucy said they'd turn up later. But it was ages too early so the ushers gave me a seat right at the front." It was never going to happen again. She would never take a front seat at any function, ever. It cut off your line of escape. If there had been a seat at the back, then none of this would have happened.

And suddenly it had all got so bad – even worse than the Christmas when he had torn up all the Christmas cards – that a ration of courage came and she was saying

"I feel sick in churches because really I don't believe in God, that's the trouble. I have to go to church, but it doesn't work. I just feel as though I want to run out of church all the time." No mention of all the other underlying reasons. She had quickly, and quite uncraftily, grabbed at the first reason and that had luckily been the safest. They might accept a disbelief in God – it made sense and was abstract. Any hint about sex or love or a man would have shattered everything to smithereens. Even so, Mother gasped,

"Oh, no!" and Father lunged and tried to grip Mary by the shoulders but she became hysterical at this point and dashed out of the room escaping him, running across the dark sitting room and into Auntie Julie's hallway and up the stairs. Auntie had not gone to bed and was sitting with a cup of chocolate and surrounded by wrapping paper and string. She looked up as though she understood and did not react with a scream or much astonishment to see Mary and Vin and Celie all chase up the stairs and burst into her living room at getting on for half-past twelve on Christmas morning.

"I, I, can't… don't let them, Auntie, can I stay here with you please? I, I "- the gulps and sobs made the words nonsense.

"This has all got to stop" Father said. Vaguely out of his territory (though it was only his sister's upstairs living room, after all and it had a strong aura of their Mother in it still,) he did not want too much of this shame to be discussed even here.

"What is the matter?" asked Auntie Julie mildly. For once, she was being superb. Perhaps under all the layers of silliness and stupidity this splendid lady was buried. She did not offer to put the kettle on.

"I'm awfully sorry about this," said Mother. "It's not right that our dirty linen should be in public like this." Mary turned on her, in the middle of tears.

"This isn't public! This is here!" They were both trying to keep her on their little island so that even Auntie Julie could not know what went on.

"I've said it before and I'll say it again, she's got the wrong friends and spends too much time away from home. She should start coming home for lunch, for one thing," Father said heavily. By saying it, it became true.

If they could teach all art by post then I would not need to leave the house at all except to go to Mass and confession, Mary thought, still in the middle of tears.

"Mary is just not feeling well at all, she's rather upset," said Mother trying valiantly to sweep the entire heap under the lino.

"Auntie Julie, please, can I stay here tonight?" Mary appealed from beside the grandmother clock.

"Your place is in your own room," said Father loudly. No escape.

"You can't let your family down like this," said Mother just as firmly. Betrayer. She had sat down by the window. Father remained standing.

"What is the matter, Mary?" asked Auntie Julie as the entire drama was being played out in front of her without any clues being given. Mary continued to cry. By now her handkerchief was sodden all over. She moved it from corner to corner but it was covered in wet snot.

"I, I don't believe in, in God," Mary sobbed. By now it had become the uppermost thought. Everything lost, all those years of grace and belonging with other Catholics, all jettisoned.

"There, there," said Auntie Julie, coming across to her and putting a hand on her shoulder. In the past three-quarters of an hour this was the first show of any sympathy and showed that Mary could still be considered a human being. For a second the still-perceptive part of her mind decided that Auntie Julie's religion or God came out much better than the religion-God of her parents. Yet Auntie Julie spent even more time in the strait-laced department of the church.

"Now, just settle down, don't get all het up about it," said Julie, becoming more and more wonderful by the minute. Father said,

"Well, it's enough of this nonsense. It's time to go to bed. Come on now, you'd better start to do as you're told."

"I can't go back. I want to stay here. Please, please, Auntie, let me stay," Mary became completely hysterical now and was hugging the sides of the grandmother clock for support. It was the only dependable thing in the room. She could see that Julie was weakening under Father's threatening glare. Mother got her hankie out and began to weep gently, saying

"This is the worst thing that has ever happened to me in my life." Again, a matchbox corner of Mary's mind snapped back that it wasn't much fun for her either and she felt a real betrayal by her Mother. Instead of standing by her and trying at this desperate moment to defend her to her Father, Mother had retreated into her own emotional terrain.

Mary clutched the soggy bit of cloth to her eyes and nose. She was exhausted and very frightened. She could hear them, in the distance it seemed now, discussing what to do with her. Julie said she could sleep in one of the several beds in the house, though none of them were aired. In the morning, though, she would have to go back to where she belonged, next door. The kettle was put on, a hot-water bottle filled. Father and Mother went away and then Mother, with pursed lips, reappeared with a nightgown and washing items.

"I shall see you at nine o'clock in the morning, than, and we'll start all over again. It's Christmas Day after all," and trying to ignore Julie totally, she went out of the room.

Small and shattered, Mary accepted whatever Julie did and whichever bed she was sent to and fell into an exhausted sleep.

Christmas Day passed in dutiful blankness. Potatoes were peeled, sprouts put to boil, Julie did the bread sauce and Mary spent a lot of time, just as in every year, passing from one house to the other through the sitting room with graters or little bottles of essences or metal polish for the silver napkin rings. By three o'clock Father had carved the turkey, swearing and cursing as he did every year and they listened to the Queen's speech in respectful silence. There was no escape from families at Christmas.

Until the pubs opened and Father disappeared, the day functioned as normal. The three women washed up all the crockery and pans and equipment, sorting out in a mild bickering way which pans or forks or plates belonged to which house. The presents, never anything exciting except from Julie, were done with. Father always gave money, as he said he did not understand shops or what sort of thing anyone wanted. The money was always given raw, a crisp ten shilling note not in an envelope or card and they always said 'Thank you, Vin' (or Father) in a surprised sort of way, as though it was unexpected.

He received socks, handkerchiefs and his once-a-year cigar, which stank out the living room but had to be put up with because it was Christmas. Mother would give Julie something unwantable like an embroidered hot-waterbottle cover and Julie would give some splendid gift that they really needed and couldn't even think of getting such as an electric iron or letter-headed notepaper for Father.

With Father eventually out of the way and Julie off to visit a nearby friend for a walk to evening service, the real discussion began. Mother started to mend something from the never-ending supply in the needlework box.

"So what's this all about? I said you shouldn't have gone to that art school. Your Father and I wanted you to go to the University, you know."

"It would have happened at University, then. In fact it really happened at school. We were taught that we were saved because we had been baptised and I looked out of the window onto Rodney Street and all the people who hadn't been baptised and who weren't Catholics, and it seemed unfair. Why should we be safe, and them left out?"

"But that's what Christ and the church teach, love. You've got to take their word for it, and not just rely on *your* fine ideas."

"But I can't believe it's all true. I even really do go to Mass when you see me going out on Sundays – I don't just walk round the streets, like I could, I could have gone and deceived you all. I try to keep all the rules but it just doesn't work." It was useless to discuss with her Mother the time-bomb ticking away beneath all this; the surface story was bad enough. "I just can't go on any further." Mother looked at her speculatively, as if at a scientific experiment.

"There's a chaplain at the University, now I come to think of it. He's used to dealing with things like this. Perhaps you could go to see him." It was reassuring to know that other people went through the same crisis and yet this proved her very point. If intelligent university students up the road had also reached the same conclusions, then perhaps the entire scheme was a fake? If you put your brain to work on it, then it all fell to pieces.

Perhaps it only worked if it was swallowed whole, like medicine. As soon as she had begun to question even a corner, the entire work of art had unravelled like a loose piece of knitting, faster than she had ever imagined. And this was happening to university students too. Entire mind-worlds were being demolished.

195

"I might see about that." A lie. Now she was telling lies as well. Obviously, if he were any kind of chaplain, then his job was to shove people back into the church by whatever sleight of hand he could manage. He would certainly not be drawing his pay on an honest basis if he spent most of his time easing people out of the church in as painless a way as possible.

"The next Mass is being offered for Joan Smith, who is just leaving the faith. We also ask your prayers for Bert Jones, who has given it all up as a bad job and has gone off to become a pagan. For him and all the others like him, atheists and agnostics, we ask a blessing, most heavenly Father." The only blessings or prayers were for people already firmly on the right road – those getting married, dying or becoming ill within the faith.

Instances where the faith itself was in fact the illness were not admitted to exist. A sin against the Holy Ghost. That dove, in the long run, was the most powerful of the three and kept everything together. Only encountered as a first-class carrier pigeon in the Gospels, it carried more clout in the here-and-now than the rumbustious God the Father (never as wild again as in the Old Testament,) or the likeable God the Son (nice, fanciable but unfortunately unavailable, presently sitting next to God the Father up in heaven, past aeroplanes and sputniks.)

Years ago she had found an old Holy Picture in one of Nannie's prayer-books where the Holy Ghost was represented as a white-bearded old man, the same as God the Father. They were sitting next to each other on thrones and Jesus sat in front of them, three men together.

"Wouldn't be allowed now. They've changed him into a dove, changed the rules," Grandpa said dourly. The Holy Picture disappeared soon after that.

It was getting frightening. No, it had been frightening ever since she had reached the blockage, as it became in her mind. Juggling with God, sacrilege, the Church (vague),the local church (their priest, the rest of the people in the parish), most of the people she had known since childhood and her family, plus this driving truth of her own was frightening. As each part came to the front, the others died back – but then it changed.

Auntie Julie could no longer ask her about the sermon or who had been at half-past nine Mass. She could nip in the back of the church after Mass and get the *Universe* or the *Catholic Herald*, but people would know she had not been at the service.

Now, her bedroom. What could be done about the altar? It seemed rather extreme to demolish it especially as in the middle of it all she still trusted Our Lady. Definitely the rosary beads were not going to be thrown away either. Her Sunday missals, the three different versions, stayed in the sideboard drawer with the other ones. Mother went to Mass alone, as she had sometimes done already. Father went on as though nothing had happened. It did not threaten his routine at all; only his authority had been affected. But without the added bonus of the church's rules he did not know how to deal with a pagan in the house.

The milk-bill and paper-bill money were no longer left on the windowsill in the hall, in case she stole it, as she had borrowed it once before and he had seen that as theft although she had paid it back before the weekend. As some undeclared punishment though, no new clothes were bought for her at all and she had to ask for the money to get a new pair of shoes when the current pair started to let in the rain. Luckily the rest of the family came out of mourning for Nannie and Auntie Cappy at this point. It was not a formal decision, just that the black clothes they had bought specially over five years ago and worn ever since (because of the money spent) had become boring and so they passed them on.

Jumpers, skirts, a jacket and a wide swinging tent coat. One bright orange jumper stood out from the rest. Aunty Kay called in one night with two carrier-bags-full. As another outcast in the family, she understood what it felt like. In Mother's view, all that side of the family had fallen away from the faith and Mary's cousin Lucy had stopped going to church some time ago. Prayers were needed all round. Aunty Kay said nothing about the scandal – perhaps she had learned of it via Nana, the only person Celie confided in apart from Mary herself. Mother was an island within an island.

On the rare occasions – once a year - when Mother really lost her temper, Father sat round like a chastened little boy and Mary was astounded to see the balance altered. The strength came from nowhere, had an immediate effect, subsided and then Mother became the same efficient self-effacing person as usual. It hurt that at this point Mother had not bothered to use her strength to help out.

She remembered the dog, Whiskey and missed her now. With an animal's true instinct it always knew that something was going badly and licked the tears off Mary's cheek whenever they were that close. Otherwise the friendly wet nose would be there nuzzling her knee at dinner and the left paw would come up to show Whiskey wanted to be taken notice of and stroked and fed snippets. A bundle of fur and yet such a bulwark of reassurance and love. Auntie Julie and the dog were the best, and everyone thought they were both stupid.

The terrible crime of Spiritual Pride was about. It was Mary versus the entire Catholic church. Apart from George Bernard Shaw (dead) and Nathaniel West (also dead,) various other writers, musicians, actors and artists and some unspecified students in the same city, she was out on her own. The introductions to GBS's plays were a shock, especially the one where he challenged God to strike him down with a bolt of lightning and nothing happened. Mary did not know whether she was reassured or disappointed.

Atheism was hard work and much of it was impossible to keep up with. Being unable to pray for anyone who was ill, you had to go and visit them and leave the rest to the doctors. Anyone going in for an exam, you could lend them books or go over questions with them (and who would want that sort of interference and what if you had several friends going in for exams at once?) If there were any family or personal difficulties, you had to weigh in with advice and perhaps make the problem worse by interfering. All of the possibilities spread out from prayer were now impossible. It all went cold. It was impossible to send your Guardian Angel on a helping mission to someone else's Guardian Angel to give someone encouragement in a difficult time. (She had invented this idea but thought it was feasible and God would agree.) The Guardian Angel hovered about, like a best friend who was being ignored and was difficult to get rid of. She had not realised how sophisticated the dismantling would be at this point and so left the angel to its own decision what to do. There was, of course, no God now, so the entire horizon was blank. It had all gone; it was permanent frost. Nice Jesus, that good friend, was nowhere about.

There was no extra fund of strength either physical or moral to draw on, you were totally alone and separate from both the living and the dead. Holy Souls, Saints known and unknown, those in Limbo, Purgatory and those in Hell did not exist. There was nothing. You just died and that was it. Emptiness. You might as well go out and rob a bank; there were no eternal repercussions except getting caught in the here and now by a passing policeman. Any accumulated grace had totally disappeared. Everyone was on their own, there were no supernatural connections. Those still in the church - or any other religion, were all wasting their time, deluded.

She was absolutely cornered.

Yet there was God, behind it all. There was this human yearning and without God there was nowhere for this yearning to go; it would have to remain, a pain that hid behind everything.

Now that the drama had simmered down, Julie was back to her usual boring silly self. The magnificent Boadicea had disappeared. She addressed Father with due deference and was extremely polite to Mother. There was no hint of superiority, that they had lost face. Nor was there any hint that Mary would have divided loyalties. Perhaps Mary would like to go over to Birkenhead Market next Saturday afternoon if that was all right? The question had to be asked in three directions at once. Father had to give a vague consent, though it was no skin off his nose.

Mother had to see if she needed any help carrying extra shopping and Mary herself had to say if she wanted to go. Julie navigated all this deftly. Things would be back to normal soon if everyone was nice to each other and pretended nothing had changed.

19

4th February 1959 Buddy Holly died. The news spread round the Art School canteen and it was as if one of themselves had died. The music lot were absolutely shell-shocked. They felt as if a sure future had been ripped away; the map had gone and they were stranded now. He had gone. Their dreams would have to find a new shape now.

That summer there was a college trip to Paris and as quite a few students in the same class were going, Mary was, amazingly allowed to join the trip. Mr Ingham, had who owned the dairy and greengrocer's on Hardman Street signed her new passport papers. These days he had moved to a corner on Oxford Street and was a JP. The original shops had been demolished and rebuilt as Atlantic House, a Catholic hostel for seamen. She had a most unflattering photo taken in a booth at Lewis's. The amazing amount of fifteen pounds was allowed from her grant via Father. Monetary controls did not permit much more to be taken out of the country, even for a week abroad.

Coming back from Paris at the end of August, in contrast to the French trees that were already baked into crisp orange, London trees were still obviously rich with some late greenery. It was a chance that might not come again - Mary went along to Cromwell Road, found the right door, but there was no 'Moscardi' any more in the nameplates. Perhaps he had gone back to South Africa, perhaps he was working on a London newspaper. Gone. There was no way of tracing him any more.

Father wanted to know did she go to Les Invalides as he had asked her to? Yes. The tomb of Marechal Martineau? Yes. And had she gone to church on the Assumption of 15th August, a Holiday of Obligation he wanted to know? She truthfully said she had not managed it, she had genuinely forgot in the middle of so many things to attend to. It was as if he wanted to control the trip, make it his instead of her own. He snapped that her mother should make sure Mary went to Mass, they should go together.

For once, Celi stood up for her, saying
"I will not be her jailer."

200

No way was she going to mention going off to the Cité Universitaire camp site with a Dutch boy called Theo and spending the night with him in his tent. They had met on the Place du Tertre amongst the scattered artists' easels and found that they were both artists with similar tastes in painting. His friends gave them a lift to the camp where they had hired tents for the summer.

"We can get through here, saves walking miles around," Theo said as they scrambled through a hedge. Climbing over the fence she tore her sleeve. "Don't worry, I can give you a shirt to cover that," he said to reassure her. But they parted the next morning as he was going off to Spain with his Dutch friends, it was arranged already.

"I should not be doing this, I am a Roman Catholic" he said as they began to lay together and strip off their clothes.

"So am I. But it is not wrong, if you mean it," she said, already having passed that crossroads and turning into his arms. It was real, here in the green tent and in new surroundings a fresh life could start without any rules. They could stay here. For a few seconds it was a serious temptation to go off with him, but the next year at college, the final exams, were too important to risk throwing away. She did not have any more money either for travelling further round Europe. They parted the next morning after walking along the long tunnel of the Porte D'Orléons station, its wall plastered with well-designed posters and getting back to the Place.du Tertre.

This was nothing she could discuss with her parents.

20

Mad or bad? That was obviously it. If everything around her was pointing one way and Mary was the only one going in a different direction, then she had to be either mad or bad. She would take whatever any results came up with the truth. Celi rather begrudgingly arranged for her to see a psychiatrist via her Clinic connections, as of course to ask for any appointment warned of family trouble. Taking the afternoon off college, Mary arrived early at Sefton General. Five other people, elderly men and women sat in the corridor outside the consultant's office. Dr Grosvenor said he had fixed her appointment as a special favour to her mother and what was the matter?

Mary was at a loss to explain the mess. She was not going to tell him about Pete and the Cromwell Road night or the night after. Nor did she feel like having an intricate discussion on theology with him. He was already impatient and she felt awkward.

"I am not happy at home and I can't change how I feel."

" Does your father pay the rent? Does he go out to work?"

"Yes, but that is the least he can do. Anyone does that."

"Well, do your father and mother throw chairs at each other?" His level of understanding was already at nil, she decided.

"No, but there are his bad moods that last for days and it is a strain to live like this. I don't feel right."

"Does your mother feed you, cook you meals, then?"

"Well, she has to cook for herself and Father anyway, so obviously ..." At this he lost his temper. So far his rapid-fire questions had showed an irritability, and at this answer, he stood up, becoming red in the face, both hands on the desk. If he could, he would have hit her.

"Well, yours is a happy home, then, and you should not be wasting my time here. There are people outside there "- he pointed to the door "who have real problems and you are just feeling sorry for yourself. This interview is at an end." He was almost at the point of throwing the desk at her. She had a vision of the family she did not have yet, or maybe would never have, a home of warmth, happiness, jokes and hope. Clear gold.

Mary returned to the corridor, feeling different now, observing the seated assortment of docile patients, withered with age and mental health issues, waiting to be processed by a man who did not have a clue about life. Throwing chairs indeed. She wanted to tell them to go home while they still could. She was neither mad nor bad, but very alone. Total submissive faith was needed in religion, psychiatry, politics and families.

It was late winter afternoon now and growing dark. South Hunter Street was even darker than usual, as an aerial extension had been built across the street form one floor of Blakes Garage to Berwick's toy factory. Materials could be lifted up and trundled across the walkway, but the tunnel took light away, like a lid across the street. It was raining as well. She crossed the gleaming blue-grey cobbles towards home, realising that somehow she was right and there was definitely something going wrong in the house. There was a vague suspicion that Dr Grosvenor could have been another of Celi's admirers and would not want to hear anything against her marriage set-up. Everything had to be perfect and Mary was the only one objecting to it all.

She helped to lay the table, brushing off the smuts of soot from the tablecloth and sat down to dinner. Something had died but she had to go on living.

Lynn was expelled from college later that year as she was in an obviously expanding pregnancy. She received a formal letter saying that under the circumstances it was better for her to leave and consider other options. Ed did not mind as he had a new post in a grammar school, the were married and they had moved to a better flat in Chatham Street. This was another decrepit building which strangely had a doctor's surgery in the front room and a dirty waiting room with a toilet that the residents also used.

"We'll be covered with germs by the end of the week," Lynn joked, "and if we survive, we'll be invincible." The little boy was a joy and she manage to keep on painting at home, plus she encouraged Mary, Nancy, Bella and others to call round with the latest College gossip in their lunch-hour. Occasionally one of them would baby-sit in the evening.

It was only gradually that Mary realised something was wrong. Lynn usually bouncy and cheerful, was often still in her dressing gown at midday when they arrived, bags of chips in hand, ready for a cup of tea and with cigarettes to share.

"Preggers again," Lynn told her. " But Jem from up Myrtle Street knows someone in a chemist's and I've got these pills to take. We can't afford another child, Ed's has only just got this new job and we're holding on by our fingernails. I can't ruin it all for him. A blue pill a day keeps the midwife at bay " she joked. Mary took in this bit of information but it had not really lodged, as though Lynn would be taking pills forever and there would be no trace of anything happening. It would all fade away. She usually called in at the chippie and bought extras for Lynn too, like today. There she was, standing at the flat door with two helpings of vinegared chips, the smell livening up the shabby hallway. The door was slightly open already.

Lynn was lying on the floor on a plastic mac spread underneath her. It was one of the clear ones, the kind they laughed at old ladies for wearing over a thick coat. For no particular reason she was wearing a thin coat too, but there was a pool of blood caught in the folds of the plastic mac. Elsie, the woman from the upstairs rooms was kneeling down beside her. Both Lynn's baby and Elsie's little son were playing on the carpet nearby as if nothing was happening. Elsie looked up, relieved at Mary turning up.

"She knocked on the ceiling with the brush to get me to come down, and look at her, I'm really worried now. Don't know what to do. I mean, there's the doctor's here, but he won't be here until after six tonight." Mary knew now what all the pills had been about; this was the crunch. No delicate fading away. Lynn was moaning and twisting from side to side. Her skin was turning green and amongst the flood of blood was a small lump in the folds of plastic. Lynn could die, she thought, this is actually happening, it's real. It's like watching a murder, this could end up with Lynn dying right now and we'll both be responsible.

Mary's mind kicked in, something directed her what to do.

"You go back upstairs, Elsie (Elsie's hair was stuck to her forehead with sweat) and take the kids upstairs. I can say I turned up and it was all like this, so you're not involved at all." The scandal of all this happening in a doctor's premises would lead to all kinds of other trouble, with them all ending up in court. Elsie's husband was a bus driver and they lived in just two rooms above, they could not afford to get involved in a scandal like this. Relieved, she hugged the two infants, coaxing her own son to climb the stairs and went upstairs, leaving Mary to phone for an ambulance.

There was a payphone in the hallway. It was not exciting to phone 999 after all; it was ordinary.

"Just get a bucket, then, and bring all the bloods into the ambulance, the hospital will need to see it," the ambulance service operator instructed her. Two sturdy men appeared, bringing a wonderful down-to-earth reassurance in the drama. By now Lynn was definitely completely out of it, just giving slight moans as the men lifted her. Mary lifted up the flooded mac and poured it all in an enamel bucket, trying not to vomit. Then she dashed upstairs with the baby's bottle and the keys to the flat. Looking over the bannister she could see the bright red blanket as the men carried Lynn on the stretcher along the hall and into the ambulance. Elsie said she'd ring Ed at his school.

"Yes, Lynn gave me this number to ring earlier on before you turned up." Mary scrambled onto the ambulance and sat with the bucket of blood and the homunculus as big as a fist swirling round at her feet. Lynn was still a strange colour and was totally silent now. It was worrying how much time it had taken to get help.

Unfortunately *Carmen Jones* was on the Scala recently and Mary had seen it twice in the afternoons, with different boys, being popular that week. Black V-neck sweater, tight red split skirt, black peep-toe shoes, long swinging earrings – she knew she looked tarty. But the fear that they had been playing round with life and death right now sent her back to the Rosary. She still thought that Lynn could die. As the ambulance speeded along, Mary started desperately saying the Rosary as an anchor to reality or to have something good to hold onto. *Hail Mary, full of grace, the Lord is with thee. Blessed is the fruit of thy womb.*

The Rosary, however, began with the Annunciation, the actual agreement of a young woman to become pregnant, then the Incarnation, then the Nativity - all the cleaner ideaLucyed versions of what she was sitting in the midst of right now, Lynn unconscious, a bucket of blood and the person who caused the pregnancy out at work. The Rosary gave a complete journey through life, the crises of adulthood, pain and shame and loss and defeat, and then the entrance into a higher plane where rewards and peacefulness abounded, with the ending of Our Lady, as Everywoman, being crowned Queen of Heaven and the glory of all the saints. It was a long way from sitting in the back of an ambulance but the prayers formed an invisible ladder.

Name, address, husband, phone number, Mary helped fill in the necessary forms. She also rang Ed's school and told him what had happened so far and which ward Lynn was in at the Maternity Hospital.

"Oh, she'll be much happier now," he said blithely, shocking her. So much for married life. "Elsie rang me about it earlier."

In spite of it all, Mary found herself sitting at dinner precisely at six o'clock as if nothing had happened. It was not the sort of thing she could mention to her parents. Having left the chips somewhere on the table in Chatham Street that afternoon, she had nothing to eat all day, but could not finish the meal even so. Celi did not comment.

On Sunday afternoon Mary went up to Oxford Street to visit Lynn, still in hospital, Elsie looking after the baby. Ed was already by her bedside and Lynn was sitting up, wearing a new dress, not an ordinary nightgown, a bow in her hair, lipstick and eye makeup on, and looking really happy. They were holding hands and Mary felt like an intruder. No talk about all the danger, the near-death, the bucket. Nothing. She was intruding on a private twosome. Lynn was giggling,

"They call this the naughty girls' ward. They know what's up, but they can't prove anything and have to seem sympathetic. I'll be out tomorrow, thanks for the perfume." There was no way to discuss what had happened; even in the bohemian world there were walls as strong as those in her parents.' Each tribe had its own rules; the problems came if you moved between the different groups.

21

One by one the students got their grants. Each week there was a celebration in The Crack and it was drinks and cigarettes all round. A bit of an exaggeration and optimism made it seem as though as soon as one term's treasure-chest was emptied, it was time for the next term's cheques to be rolling in. Reality was, however that there were slack weeks when the only drinks came from merchant sailors landing in, pockets full of money, and for some strange reason wanting to spend their day drinking with art students. Sometimes Doris, the landlady herself, would glide into the bar and chide the students,

" You shouldn't be joking with them like this. These men haven't even seen their families yet, so you better not keep them here wasting their money." This did not make sense; it was their own free choice and a couple of halves of bitter and a twenty packet of Senior Service was hardly a small fortune. But they accepted the moral tone of her rebuke and yet did not know how to stop the sailors from turning up. Art students were amusing, witty and entertaining; it was their nature, they were well-trained bohemians. College constantly instilled in them how to become Impressionists in lifestyle, on the way to becoming art teachers; there was no other system. Fashion designers and graphic designers were trained differently from the start, to achieve work.

As the weeks passed, Mary sensed something was wrong. Friends asked about it too. Her Autumn grant had not appeared yet and it was already late October. Everyone else had received theirs, including Alastair, whose parents, he ruefully told them, were so rich that his grant was only half-a-crown per term. But he bought them cigarettes and a round even so, for fun.

This grant cheque was going to be important because reaching twenty-one was the ultimate moment, each person's Mount Everest,

I've got the key of the door,

never been twenty-one before.

Mary was going to say that she thought it was time she handled the money herself and it stopped being merely a process of endorsing the cheque each time, three terms a year, as it went straight away into Father's bank account. Standing in front of him and having to ask for the money for a new bra was bad enough at nineteen or twenty; after twenty-one it would be her own fault. The performance would go like this; she would stand beside the table while he sat surveying his stamp collection:

"Daddy, I need a new bra, the elastic's gone on this one." Rustle of papers, slide of sheet of stamps or some other fussy don't-interrupt-me-gesture.

" How much money does that mean?"

" Eight and six."

" Hmmph. Arrange that with your Mother, then, and I can sort it out with her later."

"Thank you, Daddy." Humiliating. Her friends were going down Bold Street and buying scarves and jumpers and handbags.

Tonight, Friday, was one of Celi's evenings at the Catholic Marriage Guidance Service, which meant she would not be home until after half-past eight. He suddenly produced the cheque and brandished it at Mary.

"Here, sign this." He stood over her as she sat reading in the fireside chair. This was the time to make a stand. It was as if he had waited for when they were alone. How long had the cheque been hidden in his desk? What was he doing about it?

"I thought it was about time that I managed my own money, Daddy, and it went into my own account, with me paying out a weekly amount for my keep."

"Sign this!" He thundered, waving it at her and producing his fountain pen. It was a do-or-die moment.

"I'm not going to." He grew angry now and was shouting at her that it had to be done, now. The room was full of his ranting voice. A red explosion happened behind her eyes and filled up all the room and at the same time a thrill of stars ran up her spine, giving her all the strength in the world.

"I won't, *I won't*," she screamed and he made a grab for her. But Mary skewed round, dashed out of the living-room, grabbing her coat from the hall and ran out of the house, down the street, slowing to a walk round the block. By the time she cautiously walked up by Back Maryland Street, the living room light, just visible above the yard wall, was off. He had galloped off to the pub as usual. The cheque was nowhere to be seen. She did not mention the scene to her Mother, not knowing what to do next as that wonderful influx of strength had vanished.

Because of their two staircases there was no need to meet each other the next day. On Saturday morning Celi went off to work at the Child Guidance Clinic to deal with the post and Mary went to Windsor Street Library to get out of the house. Luckily, after a very late breakfast he did not bother to come back for lunch and after going down-town shopping with her Mother, general cleaning up, going up to Myrtle Street for the weekend joint, a late tea, Mary left for Jill's flat and joined her other friends in The Crack for that Saturday night. They knew it was her birthday on the Wednesday and Jill, Doug, Ginny, Ben, and Nancy were already at a table cluttered with used glasses.

"So, what did you get?" Nancy asked. Her parents had given her a travel clock, with, as Jill had said, the unwritten message 'Don't travel' and they were laughing about that and about good-natured Alastair's minimal grant of half a crown because his parents were so rich. and other funny goings-on, when Mary turned round to see her Father marching into the bar-room. He stood out because he was tall, but also because almost everyone was young here. It was made worse by the fact that he was calling out her name quite loudly.

Jill was sitting underneath the large engraving *The Battle of Waterloo,* opposite *The Death of Nelson* and could see the door. "Good God!", she spluttered, "Here's your Father!"

"Mary! Mary!" The foghorn voice was different here. He struggled through the crowd. He had already been drinking, in fact it was getting on for 10 pm.

"It's her Father," people explained to each other. All merriment ceased. Mary stood up as he approached. Even strangers in the crowded bar went quieter and lowered their voices. This was a proper scene. He started. It was a mishmash of everything.

"Right, I've got you here now and I want to talk to you. And I want that key to your wardrobe, for one thing. What are you hiding inside there? I want the key!" She looked at him with shock.

("He goes into your room whenever you're out, Celi had said. "Don't leave anything private about. Get any letters addressed to college. Leave them there, or he'll read them")

"No, you can't have the key." She had to make a stand although there was nothing particularly provocative in the wardrobe. He got a bit angrier. Another glass of gin appeared at her right hand. And beyond that, another gin was lined up. While Vin grew madder and angrier, she grew calmer and more distant, pickled in gin.

"And another thing, you say you don't believe in God! What's that all about! Explain yourself!" He pointed up to the nicotine-cream ceiling and Doris' flat above, with God above that. "Who's giving you all these fancy ideas? Well, God's watching all this carry-on, young lady, and you've got to start going back to church! Give me the key to your wardrobe! Now!" He kept on pointing upstairs to Doris' flat above, where God was a witness Someone slid another glass of gin along the table to her and others took up the baton too, until Mary stood there trying to reason with him while having a constant glass of gin in her other hand. It was a silent vote of sympathy.

He then became maudlin, a turn that she always despised and mistrusted. She was certain that she had read a scene just like this in Dostoevsky's Crime and Punishment, allying herself with Raskolnikov's ethical dilemmas, sinking into the rich Christmas-cake of his prose.

"You say you want to write as well, now we didn't want you to go to that Art School. We only had you, but I wish we had a dozen like you." How on earth would he have coped then, she wondered, the sentimental liar. Luckily the place was so crowded that he was still trying to reach her and make a grab, but the bodies in between made a barrier. Doris then appeared, glamorous as ever, accusing Mary of the row.

"Now, if you want to talk to your Father, would you take this outside? We can't have this sort of thing going on here." The last thing Mary needed was to get isolated outside with this grim angry man, already half-sheets to the wind. He must have been drinking all day, upset that anyone had stood up to him, and his daughter at that. Now he was near to getting her banned from her favourite pub. Her hand was shaking. Doris was determined. Father was determined. Another glass of gin, about the fifth, appeared. She was going to get crushed between their opposing wills. Twenty-one years was disappearing in an instant. This chance would not come again. She took another sip of the gin.

A small man appeared now at her left elbow - lithe enough to have made his way through the small packed bar. He turned to the man hovering above him and tapped Vin on the arm, looking up at him.

"It's Vin, isn't it? Don't I know you? Vin, we used to work together at Lewis's remember?" And with this, her Father crumpled into a sentimental wierdo, almost falling into the man's arms.

"Harry! Harry Chambers. Well I never!" and he became a normal person again as this Harry manoeuvred him across to the seats while her friends and acquaintances made a wall of bodies so that Vin was in one triangle of the small room while Mary was in the other. There was a hedge of people, friends Mary did not know she had, forming a diagonal. With shaking hands she managed to light another cigarette.

"Well, I've always thought you were exaggerating about him but I believe you now, seeing all this" Jill said, shoving a sixth glass of gin at Mary. She was in such a state that they were having no effect except perhaps as some kind of anaesthetic.

Mary squeezed out of the bar, along the passageway past the front bar and out into the street. By this time she was running down Rice Street, hysterical. The rain was cool and covered the ground like varnish. If she kept running like this the problem would be that she would hit Pilgrim Street and have to decide whether to turn left or right. The ghosts of both grandmothers led each way. Even that did not matter. Everything led to the Pier Head and the Mersey. She would decide then.

Little Ginny ran after her and said,

"Look, you can come and stay at my parent's house overnight, if you like. We've got to go soon though, to get the last bus to Hale Village. Come on with us." Her boyfriend, Ben was running on her other side. This was freedom - friends on either side, guarding her. Father was still trapped behind the wall of people; it would not last forever. Here was a chance to escape. They dashed after her out to the darkness of a rainy October night. Mary began to cry now, seeing safety and she ran down Rice Street as if it was going to stretch for miles, right into Pilgrim Street as if it would never end. It began to rain more heavily now. She wanted to run like this forever and tomorrow to never arrive.

They had already missed the bus and instead got her into a taxi. Ben was dropped off at his bedsit in Canning Street and they continued off to Ginny's house out in Hale Village. Money did not seem to be a problem in the panic.

With the strange calm of some adults, Ginny's Mother took the arrival of this sniffling and bedraggled friend of Ginny's as almost normal at this time of night.. She was remarkably unfazed.

"Yes, you can have the spare bed in Ginny's room. But you must ring your Mother first." The voice of reason. Something to do with the cloud-grey carpet that covered all the floors of this modern bungalow, all calm and quiet. Ginny's Mother was sitting on a rug beside an open fire, logs hissing, as she stroked a red setter. "My husband will be in later and he can run you home tomorrow afternoon, but right now you must definitely phone your Mother so she knows where you are. I'll look out some nightwear and a spare facecloth and toothpaste and so on." It was as easy as that; no drama.

At least they had a phone at home, courtesy of the Catholic Marriage Guidance Council. It would be about eleven o'clock by now and Mother would definitely be at home. The phonecall was formal. Mother was distant.

"I'm just staying the night at Ginny's, at her parents out in Hale Wood. They said I could stay."

"It's rather late. I hope you are going to be all right." There was deep disapproval in her voice. She was not pleased about this event. This was washing their dirty linen in public and Mary was breaking several rules at once. "Right. I don't know what's going on, but as you're there now, there's nothing that can be done, is there! Do give Ginny's Mother my thanks for putting you up and then we can have a talk tomorrow and perhaps there'll be less of all these goings-on." Father was unsaid between them. Sleep was deep and immediate, there was the silent dark of the countryside all around.

Sunday brought a crisp October morning and the two girls took the glossy red setter for a walk along the edge of the fields. Men were planting daffodil bulbs even though it was the weekend. It was a world away from last night's mad dash down the rainy black streets. This was the first morning of freedom. There was the bright yellow of the future daffodil fields to look forward to. She remembered it as if it had already happened, a view of golden fields.

"Those fields are full of daffodils in the spring, it's all yellow as far as you can see. I meant to do a picture of it for litho, but I'm moving to textile design next term instead. What are you going to do?"

"I've applied to do the teacher training year in London at the Institute of Education, as a chance to make a fresh start. It'd solve a lot of problems, somewhere to live as well, there's a students' hostel near Malet Street." Ginny agreed.

"I'll be doing the same, good you reminded me. It's getting exciting. It's the big world!" On Sunday afternoon Mr Fortescue motored them both into Liverpool where Father was strangely absent and after a quick chat and cup of tea, Celi went off for her usual Sunday afternoon rest. Mary wandered into Julie's as if nothing had happened.

As the late October afternoon grew darker, she made up her mind what to do next. Creeping back into their own hall, she got her coat, called a quick

"Goodbye for now, just going out a bit" and fled off to the bus stop. Getting out at Penny Lane, Mary went off to Aunty Frances' and Uncle Sef's. He was there on his own. Listening to her story, he shook his head and said it was impossible to put her up in the empty bedroom above the front door.

"We all know what it's like, Mary, but we can't interfere like this. It's between your parents and yourself, we can't get involved, I'm sorry." It was raining really hard by now and the streets were deserted. She would have to give up college right now and get a job as a shop assistant, get a cheap bedsit in Upper Parliament Street; there was no other way out, there was nothing else she could do. But she remembered that Nana lived round the corner, and they had an extra bedroom too, these terrace houses were all the same design, each with a small bedroom over the front door. By now the rain was getting into her shoes, another expense to worry about. This was the last place she could think of – her friends in town had no spare places at all.

Nana was glad to see her, which made her burst into tears immediately. Sitting on the living-room couch, Mary spluttered out the mess that she was in. Nana got up from her rocking chair. She stood up and stretched out her arms across the room, the old black cardigan sweeping out like a big black crucifix and her arms went round Mary, round like strong black coils of rope, hugging Mary close.

"You can stay here, Mary, of course you can. We've known something's been wrong for years. Your Mother would never talk about it, even to me. She'd hint now and again, let things drop, but never told me what was really going on."

For the first time in years Mary felt safe. It was a new feeling, she did not know exactly what was different. Ragged edges had dropped away and there was now this warm centre. The last time she had felt like this, Nannie had been alive. The other bookend. Nannie and Nana. This is what she had lost when Nannie had died.

There was no ceremony. She phoned back home. Her mother sounded fed up, non-committal. Nothing special happened. For that night, Mary slept on the couch in the living-room. An old nightdress was produced and an assortment of sheets and blankets and someone's under-pillow. Safety. When Kay came in from her job as barmaid at *The Swan*, she slipped off her shoes and saw as she opened the door, by the light from the hall, the body on the couch. Mary was flat out.

On Monday Celi arrived with some clothes. Shamefaced, shocked, disapproving. But now there were allies - Nana, Kay and Lucy. The truth that she had never let anyone know was now spattered out for all to see, the empty husk of their marriage. The façade of the family, the secrets that she had protected from outsiders, even her own mother, were now right out in the open.. Mary had let her down. Rules had been broken. But Mary was not going back. It was their marriage, not hers. She was tired of being both the battleground and the smokescreen.

Some late twenty-first birthday cards arrived. There was also a letter from Father enclosing £10. All it said was

"I have done as I said I would, here it is. £10 enclosed." He signed with his full name, Vincent Robert Martineau as if they were strangers and as if it were a legal document. So, in a way it was, She had won. The Liverpool Education Committee grant cheque for the term was enclosed, still made out in her name, still unendorsed, for £40.

Homeless, on Nana's couch, courtesy of Kay and Lucy, a cuckoo in their tidy nest, with Mother aghast and Father brooding – this was what freedom cost. It was uncomfortable on the two seater couch, neck bent, knees bent in the short space. But there was peacefulness in the house.

By midweek Kay and Mary cleared up Lucy's old bedroom. Bed, chair and chest of drawers. Coat hung on back of door. As there were no dresses, the couple of jumpers and skirts Mother brought later went in the same long drawers as the bits of underwear. She went back to the house and brought up her little artist's paraffin stove to warm up the hall. (A rare taxi ride, with painting equipment and books.) A contribution to the house. She gave the ten pounds to Nana. It was unclear how, all these three years, he had only managed to save that small amount from her grant. She had not cost much to run after all. A weekly amount of £2 was settled on as board, this left £1 for everything else. Safety, with a large gap where home had once been. The front door key in the back of the drawer. Don't go back. Don't use it. Learn to use this new key instead.

The little bedroom over the hall still had the pink polka dot wallpaper of Lucy's childhood years. It did not matter that Mary had displaced her and she slept with her Mother. They had already been doing that for months; her clothes mixed with her Mother's in the same wardrobe from St James' Road, their make-up and costume jewellery scattered together on the dressing table, their haircurlers and intricate female things nestling together in the drawer. Mary had a look - they told her to experiment with the lipsticks and she found strange items like eyelash curlers which looked like something out of the Inquisition.

The minute the Lady Chatterley trial opened, a Penguin copy appeared in their make-up drawer. This, in a house where Kay and Lucy hardly read any books and were often out until five in the morning. Why read up on what you were doing anyway? Mary did not understand it. They would have learned more from reading Dostoevsky. Father's theatrical scene in The Crack was right out of one of his novels.

It unsettled her that they should have chosen to sleep together. Why had Lucy left her own room, leaving a space, for Mary of course, but why had it been left empty for so long?

They welcomed her with uncomprehending kindness. They gave her their old clothes which were not really old, far more glamorous than anything at home and only three months out of fashion. The house revolved round clothes and wardrobes.

They all did something amazing; they changed their clothes every time they came back into the house. Proper, smart outfits for the world, slightly shabbier dresses from the minute the front door was shut. They ran upstairs to hang coats and jumpers and skirts on hangers, Nana too, a little slower. From the bedroom, also, a constant flurry of material came down - to be washed, hung to dry, ironed, zips mended, taken in, let out, hems highered or lowered, buttons, snap fasteners to be added or taken away. The top-class items were sent to the cleaners and reappeared wreathed in tissue paper. Even more important clothes were bought on weekly payments, or quarried out of second-hand clothes agencies, cleaned, renewed.

These were passed on to Celi. It might have been better if they had not. Then her true state would have been made obvious.

January 1961, the start of a new term. Wandering into the upstairs studio, Mr Burton told her that she was wanted immediately in Mr Stevenson's office.

"Something important, serious, I think," he gave her a strange look and turned back to talking to Bernard.

Summoned into Mr Stevenson's office - literally on the carpet, a small Persian thing in front of his desk, she felt like the stalwart little boy in W.F.Yeame's painting *And When Did You Last See Your Father?* except that Mr Stevenson was not cajoling. He was livid. His face was bright red. The painting showed only the beginning; it probably ended like this too. Now she was inhabiting old paintings, a double-life.

"You have gone and let the College down. You have insulted this College by not turning up. You did not turn up for your interview at the Institute of Education in London." After a while he accepted that she knew nothing about it, that the letter had been sent to the wrong address and that nothing could be done.

Apparently the official letter inviting Mary for interview had been sent to her parents' address as they did not recognise that she was living at Nana's.

"It was sent before Christmas, yes, to your original address." He ruffled papers. Explaining their mistake made no difference, he said. In place of going to London, her fifth year was going to be arranged here, no escape. He was adamant that the arrangement could not be changed or challenged.

"No, they will have informed the students already which ones have been accepted and you cannot disrupt that now." Like a chess game Mary was trapped between Nana not wanting to put her up any more, parents who were moving nearby to Penny Lane, meeting at the bus stop or worse, on the buses. She would not be able to earn enough in the evenings to support herself as well as being at college all day.

Mary dashed home at lunchtime and lifted everything from Father's desk. Mother's eyes looked everywhere, but she admitted

217

that a letter with the Liver Bird crest had arrived over Christmas time and the last time she saw it was on his desk. She implied she did not know what was in it but looked embarrassed. Mary searched through the papers in his waste-paper basket but there were only envelopes with a January postmark; no trace. Her Mother watched, aghast at this disruption. Mary wildly riffled through the piles of philatelic magazines on his desk, even lifting the lid of the Holy of Holies itself and rooting about inside. She was past caring about niceties by now.

Celi would have to explain this invasion later when he noticed this disorder. He managed to keep these secret places; Celi would not ever have looked in here, or into the drawers of the little reproduction Queen Anne chest in the sitting room, where he kept his monthly account books. Celi probably did not know even now how much was in his weekly pay-packet..

"So what's all this about?" Mother asked, pouring out another cup of tea.

"It's a letter inviting me to an interview in London for next year's teacher-training course."

"London! Do you have any idea of what you'll be walking into? How would you cope there?"

" They've got proper hostel places for their students and it'd be a real chance of a fresh start away from all the coffee bar zombies, but of course, he wouldn't let me be the judge of that would he? Oh no! Being twenty-one makes no difference to him!"

Celi went on being concerned, shocked and seemingly far more stupid than she really was. Tonight she would have to tell him that Mary had been round going through his papers but with any luck she would be able to set them all neat again and avoid a row.

Mary called back at the house one lunchtime, putting the old Yale key in the lock. Mother was there, sitting embarrassed beside the teapot, with the tea-cosy made like a little cottage, a brown felt roof, flowers glued to the sides of the little felt windows. It was the only time Mary had seen her embarrassed. It was a good job the dog was dead or matters could have been worse. All up the slight hill the Maryland Street houses had been pulled down.

Piles of bricks, flagstones from backyards and stacks of front railings were all higgledy piggledy, left exposed to the elements. It was as bad as the war and because it was so extreme there was no way of asking where the neighbours had gone to. Their indoors doors were now formed into a stockade all round the destroyed yard walls – a mixture of cream, brown and green living room, bedroom, larder doors; all the private lives of the families stacked here like exhibits.

Typically, Father was the last person in the street to be budged. He would not move. While never being a protester about any planning or political matters, now he was holding on here out of sheer crassness. Or perhaps it was naked fear. He was being ripped apart from his nest. He would not relinquish his childhood home just because the Corporation wanted to demolish it. This was a battle of wills. He had the upper hand because they could not de-house him without going to court and wasting both time and money on legal procedures. It was an all-round disaster, with Celi trapped in the middle of it all, embarrassed, still dusting and washing dishes and cooking dinners and hoping keeping to routine would triumph over the emotional and practical chaos.

It had got worse suddenly. Julie next door had said she had got a flat in Rodney Street and had moved out the previous Saturday. If it was awkward between them all the years before, it was open war now. He was not on speaking terms with her for leaving so suddenly. All the furniture from his childhood, including the bulky iron wringer with its three clanking wooden rollers had been taken away in vans. Only the over-large bookcase in the downstairs parlour had been left behind as it took up so much space. Damp issues of Arthur Mee's *Children's Encyclopaedia* slumped together on the bottom shelf, but Joe's silver aeroplanes had gone with her.

Every night Vin still went through the shared door through their green-carpeted sitting room to the echoing hall of number eleven and walked through the empty house, checking its emptiness. The lino-covered stairs echoed his large footsteps. On the middle landing, the framed *Boyhood of Raleigh* had left its outline on the wall. All the rooms were double-sized now. Up on the top floor the two iron bedsteads that had been Joe's and his own were left in the front bedroom, with the view over the school playground trees. The discarded bedsteads showed signs of rust.

The ghost of his Mother stomped around with her constant chant,

"We've been tenants of this house over forty-five years - we've paid for it time after time by now." He had thought, though not consciously, that this would all continue forever, like a stately home. As Hitler had not managed to raze it, it was perverse that Liverpool Corporation itself was now demolishing it. The mix of threat and embarrassment was strong. This empty house next-door leached warmth and, while not holding any valuables, looked like a solid temptation for burglars.

Every night like this he went in, checking the lock of the downstairs parlour door, checking the lock on the cellar door and the bolts on the top and bottom of the gigantic front door as if these could all have been tampered with from the outside. The electricity was cut off; he had to use a torch.

Letters from the Convent added to the urgency. In February Sister Superior sent a last-ditch message.

Could you come to our assistance in vacating your house as soon as possible? We do appreciate your feelings about leaving, but I think you know we have been forced to build in Maryland Street.

The position now is that the Maryland Street building will be at least six months behind schedule. That is bad enough for the running of the new College, but what is harder still is that every week behind means an addition to the original cost. Already we are to find over £120,000 for the debt.

At a recent meeting of the Architects and Contractor with ourselves the Contractor stated that now the work was almost at a standstill. We should be grateful if you would help us. As soon as

you vacate we will send the grant of which the Ministry is paying
75%. Hoping that you can help in this way,
  I am,
    Yours sincerely,
      Sister Peter, Sister Superior.

At some instant the convent had become intermediary landlords and they also wanted their former altar-boy out of their premises. This was a surprise, as the rent-book that he finally held now, had the Corporation's name on it. Even the rent-man was grumpy as he also had been told to put on the pressure. Everything was falling into pieces.

"I can't keep anything clean," Mother said, as if by keeping out any dust the outside world could be kept at bay. "All the brick dust gets blown up the hill." There was also the dust of a hundred and fifty years being disturbed and spreading into the air. Ripped-up floorboards, smashed rafters, broken fireplaces, shattered sinks, toilet bowls and baths all added to the clouds of dust approaching the one inhabited house. Broken black and red tiles from everyone's kitchens shoved out from mounds of garden soil like futuristic plants.

Celi sat in the living room which looked out into the yard.

"I'm frightened to go out to the bin, or to bring in any coal from the bunker unless your Father is here." Mary could see why, as the surrounding house doors leaning against each other looked fragile and ready to fall down. The entire yard walls on all sides had been pulled down, all the strong brick walls that had kept them safe all those years.

Instead, like a joke, a haphazard barricade had been hastily constructed, made of interior wooden doors roughly patched together with cross-boards here and there. Like a crowd of drunks, the bedroom door from Mrs Evans, the larder door from the Nugents, Molly's living room door, Miss Etherington's kitchen door – in all the colours imaginable, with gloss paint or dark graining, the entire street's private rooms stood surrounding their house. Doorknobs, finger-plates, latches and locks were still on them. It

221

was as if the neighbours were ganging up around them, their lives exposed in a raw and yet comical way. All dignity was gone.

The memory of Sunday dinnertimes came back, all the carving knives being sharpened on back steps, the sound of the scraping carrying up Back Maryland Street. There was one benefit though, as Celi had always said there was little strength in the gas stove on Sundays because they were at the top of the street and it had to come up in the same pipe, feeding all the houses on the way. Now there was no one left but the two of them.

Kitchen ranges, gigantic cast iron edifices, had been wrenched out of cellar kitchens and pitched among the rubble. They reached up like old shipwrecks out of the heaped soil and bricks.

The massive amount of £200 was given by Sister Peter, the Sister Superior, as an inducement to speed their departure, a suitable amount for the deposit to buy a house. Of course Vin accepted this with bad grace but did not contest it. Not liking any part of the process, he hated going round looking at suitable houses found through the Liverpool Echo. So it was a particularly rainy October night, the Sunday before Hallowe'en that he lost his temper, for once in a constructive way.

"We'll take this one then, they're all much of a muchness," he said to the bemused estate agent. "It's pouring rain and I'm tired of all this malarkey, this'll have to do." Celi said nothing. She was delighted. Her own Mother and two married sisters lived nearby, off in Cassville and Berbice Roads and now a great step had been taken. And, even better, Mary was now just up the road staying at her Mother's too. At last they would be living in a proper residential area where houses did not get knocked down.

It was ironic that only five years earlier an important letter had arrived from Liverpool Corporation.

'This 1811 property constitutes an historical building and is under a preservation order. No changes whatsoever to the structure will be allowed from this date. Tenants are advised that internal changes to the layout of rooms, alterations i.e. putting up shelving are forbidden. Any further work must be given an official permit which can be applied for from the Town Hall office.' It went on, giving warnings and threats of fines or imprisonment for those who fell foul of this edict.

They had nothing to worry about at number nine. Father, who was not that way inclined anyway, now had an official permit to not do anything towards the upkeep of the house. Not a shelf had ever been put up by him; Celi and Mary had wallpapered the hall on their own. Robinsons the carpenters across the road lent them ladders and planks. He walked past them on his way out to the pub.

"This is a dicky heart, here," he pronounced, patting his breast pocket. "I can't take any strain." He managed to make them both feel ridiculous. Disapproval oozed out of him. They were both struggling with be-glued hoops of wallpaper, trying to keep their balance up the ladder, to desperately slap the top fold of wallpaper onto the wall and smooth the rest downwards as he left for The Roscoe.

Luckily this new terrace house was more or less decently decorated and needed no adjustments, no extra work. He had done the right thing; holding on had led to success and Sister Stephanie's cheque was in his Midland Bank account, for the time being. It had all taken so long that a new Sister Superior, Sister Stephanie, had been elected in the meantime.

Spring term meant the final exams at College were looming already. There had been a seal-cull after their second year and many of the more interesting students had gone.

"You just have to paint like this," Burton and Ballard said, "as long as it gets you through the exams, then you can paint however you like after that." The danger was, though, that perhaps the original self would not be waiting untouched under the academic facade. It was a risk to take. But Mary usually blended the two styles together. For their fourth year composition painting exam, the subjects were dire: An orchard with apple harvesting, A childhood scene, Farm machinery or a workshop, and Your outstanding emotional experience in the past year.

This last subject leapt out of the exam paper as Mary drew on that lasting view over the bannisters, her looking down at the red blanket, with Lynn half-dead and the sturdy men lifting her round the hallway towards the ambulance. Here was the chance to expunge that vivid harshness and change it into a bright picture, with an excuse to use vermilion paint raw from the tube, which seldom happened. Red was a fugitive colour: you had to be careful how it was used.

It was lucky that from the landing she overheard Nana and Aunty Kay down in the hall talking about how she really should go back now and live with her parents in their new (and ominously nearby) house. Perhaps they meant her to hear it. Cornered. Mary looked up summer jobs in the Liverpool Echo for any waitress or chambermaid situation as far away as possible. Writing to an hotel in Cornwall, the owner replied, her references from the previous summer accepted and all was set. The tickets for Lime Street entailed a change at Euston, with a separate ticket onward to Cornwall. There was just enough left in her Post Office Savings book from last year's savings to dig into for this trip now.

Sitting in The Bridge Café beside the train bridge over Smithdown Road, Mary was still deciding whether to go or stay. The jukebox was playing *I'm Going to New Orleans* plaintively. All her dreams were in that song. A lanky boy wandered past her table and put in his sixpence and it turned into Adam Faith with *What Do You Want If You Don't Want Money,* a siren call from London. It was difficult to detach from Nana, Kay and Lucy but it was obvious that she could not stay here much longer without causing another family ruckus. They wanted her returned to her parents and it looked as though being twenty-one had not changed anything after all. It was the only way out. The train to London battered overhead to Mossley Hill. Right. Another week. Time to go. Their important end-of-year National Diploma exams were over too. The café perked up. Now it had the value of something being left behind. She looked round the walls, searching for something to remember.

Calling back at the embattled house in South Hunter Street while Mother was at work, Mary took the Baby Jesus from the nativity set, with his moving head. The plaster had broken, leaving a wire centre that helped the head to move round as if alive. He was kept in the brass box on the mantelpiece along with oddments of jewellery. She also took the blue butterfly's wing silver pendant with its eternity-like zooming blue. Mother had said she could have it one day, though technically this was stealing. There was nothing else worth taking into this new life. The little ivory elephant delicately carved from a tusk went on guarding the mantelpiece.

Looking up at the gigantic clock above the Lime Street platforms, the name of the clock-makers, Joyce Whitchurch caught her eye; perhaps that would come in useful if she ever needed to use a false name.

Getting out at the Euston terminus, a moment of crisis, excitement, destiny – the second ticket in her hand, right here in London, Mary decided to go for it, never to take that onward change at all. She got onto the tube almost in a trance. Stations fled past, Northern Line - she chose southbound, as so many friends from Art School had already moved to Hampstead and her parents would look there first. Soon there were only a few more stations to choose from. Morden was the end of the line; it sounded fatal and foreboding. She did not fancy Balham either. Slow panic set in. Waterloo. Kennington. What were these places like?

She got out at Clapham Common and into the warm summer light, the suitcase not as heavy as expected. It was a sultry summer rush-hour and she had no responsibilities. Traffic swished past as she walked semi-aimlessly along Clapham High Street, where she found a B&B and booked in for the night. It took fifteen shillings out of the five-pound note she had left and from there it was a constant leapfrog from quick, dispiriting jobs to quick dreary bedsits found from Post Office display cards with all of life's complexities sorted out neatly into *Wanted* or *For Sale* or *To Let*.

After

This dream had more colour than normal life. She was with Thaddeus and they were walking out of the Rosslyn into the summer drama of a thunderstorm. All down Rosslyn Hill the sky clattered with sharp stabs of lightning turning it into something exciting. She was joking about his new dark navy donkey jacket.

"Have you got all that plastic-leather stuff across the back?"

"Ah," Thaddeus laughed, "You'll just have to look and see, won't you?" and she dashed behind him to check. The black shoulder inset shone in the rain as she reached round to laugh at him. And at that second she woke up and saw Thaddeus disappearing into the bedroom carpet, his face blending with the patterned roses. She leant out of bed, trying to catch him but he faded, still smiling.

From there on she was trying to get to Ireland. If it was possible, then she would take the opportunity to rejoin the church. It was a straight bargain with God.

A night boat to Dublin and seasickness that turned her inside out; luckily there was no one else in the cabin to witness the contortions. It was the cheapest way to reach Ireland for a few days. Then, a B&B out at Clontarf and the next day, off to Marlborough Street and the Pro-Cathedral, gearing up for confession, a giant step, a challenge, herself versus herself.

Calling into a nearby shop, she bought some wooden rosary beads as a beginning. Going up the steps to the cathedral, beggars sat on the steps, so that the faithful could practise their charity and gain some grace. Mary decided to give them something when she came out again. Moving towards the confessionals, a sign said that confessions began after Mass. That meant staying through an entire service. The new rosary beads were a help and furthermore, the owner of the combined chemists and reliquary shop was also at Mass, he was kneeling further along the same bench.

The service was about to begin. A dark green toad-like figure appeared at her right side, the classic form of a devil. Dark, slimy and without defined form, it blocked out the light.

226

"You don't need this rubbish. You're cleverer than this, you already know that. Don't get involved again. You can escape, you know, come with us. Nothing's settled, you are still totally free." Mary tried to escape this and turned away from the apparition, to her left side, where a black entity, drawing all light into it and killing it, stood malevolently beside her.

Of course, the real Devil *would* appear on the sinister left-hand side. She was terrified. He said nothing. He did not need to. She could feel his power, a black warmth drawing her nearer. It was all the more shocking because by now the priest had appeared and was at this very second ascending the steps up to the altar to begin the Mass. It showed the terrifying power of the Devil, that he could be present right here in a church.

Mary held on to the new rosary in her pocket and prayed, or tried to, Dumbstruck, faltering, she stumbled over the name '*Jesus*.'

"Jesus help." It took all her strength to say the faint name. And with that, both the Devil and his henchman disappeared as fast as they had arrived. Mary followed the Mass in a haze of relief, although it had all changed from the Latin Mass of years ago and was near to a shambles.

But the confessionals were not yet open. Another Mass had to be got through. She knew that if she left this building now she would never recapture this momentum. At last, nearly two hours after coming here, she went over to the benches where the people waiting for confession clustered, and knelt down.

"You're in the wrong place," a woman hissed, "You should have knelt down at the end of the other bench." It was as if these obstacles were being doled out one after another, giving her one chance after another to give up and walk out. But she stayed and arrived at the darkened booth, where a young priest welcomed her. He was intrigued about blessing the rosary,

"Hmm, it's one of those scented ones." She had not noticed and though it was rather vulgar to be manufacturing perfumed rosary beads. He was obviously more tolerant.

Coming out of the confessional, reborn, utterly cleaned out, she had to tell someone, and went up to a woman lighting a candle at the side altar.

" Excuse me, I've got to tell you, hope you don't mind, that I've just come back to the church after about thirty years, it is so wonderful." The woman grasped her hand and smiled broadly,

"That's wonderful news. My daughter has just left the faith, isn't it strange?. Perhaps you could explain it?"

"It will take time, she will have to work it out through a long time, just keep praying and hoping. I can't really explain it myself, it all came back with a rush, it may happen to her." And as a sign of thanks, Mary lit a candle in front of Saint Anthony's statue and went out into the hazy sunshine of a Dublin afternoon.

Julie wandered into, waddled, into the dining room. It was exceptionally noticeable that she was waddling because she was naked. No clothing to camouflage flesh into the accepted public shapes. She stood there stock still, a public statement, with a rosary round her neck.

The nuns were appalled and the other residents looked on disapprovingly or shocked, or, in the case of the more abstracted ones, merely puzzled yet again. Some went on eating their dinner. The shepherd's pie was good this week, the onions cooked through enough and the mince not stringy.

Julie stood there. A gesture of faith that no one so far had noticed. Everything else has been taken away from me. I have nothing else, but I have faith. See this rosary round my neck. I thought you would recognise this.

They did not, they only saw the outrage to good taste and good behaviour. She was in disgrace. Sister St Martin threw a coat over Julie and shuffled her out of the room. By five o'clock the convent arranged for her to be moved to another home, for the deranged and intractable where all sorts of behaviour might be tolerated or dealt with in more severe ways.

228

"This is a home for gentlewomen, we can't be expected to manage such unreasonable or shocking behaviour," Mother Superior protested on the phone to Greystones House. "We can get her ready now. I'll have the paperwork seen to immediately."

But Julie died soon after, saving everyone the trouble. At her funeral Mass a black cat crossed the sanctuary like a last joke or a modern ghost.

Mary had inherited all the past, almost intact.

Getting the assorted items home on the train was out of the question. The furniture Mary wanted was all placed in the comparatively safe hall, with luggage labels tied on. There was nothing needed from upstairs; Aunty Kay could have the dressing table with its Walt Disney curled cream legs, the bedside light and whatever else she fancied from the jumble of the past. The keys remained with her for the removal men to collect.

Mary sat on the train with the photo album on her knee, smiling at this totally-forgotten item. Surely there was a memory of what was inside it? All her childhood, that large volume on the green covered card-table in Nannie's downstairs sitting room had looked like an important treasured family bible. But opening it now, it revealed only photographs, and not many of them, either. Most of the pages were empty, the stiff gold-edged windows blank, giving no clues. It was as if the story had juddered to a halt at some point and the long-gowned sepia women and proper-suited sepia men had left the stage.

If only someone had bothered to write names on the back - but each one was unlabelled. They knew each other and did not need anyone else in the future. The figures posed confidently, knowing who they were and quite confident that everyone would know them. This anonymous future was not what they had ever envisaged.

A week later ("Those moving men of yours made a terrible row, you know. They went off and got drunk and came back very late and slept in the van, making a right racket, you could hear them all over the street" Aunt Kay phoned her.) the bureau arrived with boxes of plates and papers. A clutch of black prayer-books fell out. One was certainly the one from Nannie's bedside table. Its black morocco-bound cover as strong as ever, golden-edged, it stood in fantasy with the large wooden crucifix, the maroon rosary beads, the minute photograph of her dead husband and the box of jet-black cough sweets. Each night these items stood in the glow of the bedside lamp, melded together in its honey light.

One of the In Memoriam cards fell out. Unlike the others with their trim black borders, this one had a white lace edging, looking expensive and quite clean even now.
Judith Martineau died on Whit Sunday 1882, aged 76 years, at an address in Blake Street, Liverpool. Born, Mary counted on her fingers, in 1806 in Ireland. Foreign and far away. Outsiders in time.

Documentaries

Him

The important life of the furniture.
He had kept everything. The receipts for an entire life were in envelopes labelled Income Tax, Pension, Insurance. One large envelope named 'receipts,' held the beginnings of their life together. Many of the bills had postage stamps (with the King's head) added over the receipts. Anything over £2 had to have a £2 postage stamp with the King's head on it, as if he had to be included in any transaction.

W. Wright Ltd 22nd September 1937 - the day after Celi's thirtieth birthday. Diamond and sapphire Ring 18ct and platinum, £6.10.0

Turner & Sons, Auctioneers 19 Mount Pleasant
27th June 1938 Three piece Bergère suite £20.00
25th August lot 183   £4.0.0
!st September 1938 lot136/145/146 Dining Room set £15.10.0
24th September 1938 Walter Bentley, 8 Thomas Street, Coffee
table £1.3.6
20th December 1938   Turner & Sons Auctioneers 19 Mount
Pleasant Dining table £1.5.0

Schierwater & Lloyd Christmas Eve, December 24th 1938
22 ct Gold wedding Ring £2.10.0
Closed Saturday at 1 p.m.
Ha nover Hotel Hanover Street Liverpool 1 (central for all
    railway stations) 26th December1938,
Wedding Reception for 16 people @ 3/6d each, with the addition
of Whisky and Wines @ £2.14.0., Cigarettes @5/-, a License
Extension @5/- and Flowers @5/- came to £6.5.0

An entire home, bought of Taylor Bros.,Wholesale and retail
ironmongers on Dec 9 1938:

1 pr Lattice steps 5/-	1 Galvanised Bucket 9d.
1 Mop Bucket 2/-	1 Mop complete 9d.
1 Hand Brush 1/-	1 Sweeping Broom 2/3
1 Shovel 4d.	44 Stair Eyes 1/6d.
1 Pkt .Tacks 3d.	1 O'Cedar Mop 2/-
1 Meat Tin 1/6d.	4 Yds. Picture Cord 1/5d.
½ doz. Moulding Hooks	33' 6" Curtain Wire 1/-
1 Frypan 1/-	4 doz. Ruflette Hooks 1/-
3 Aluminium saucepans 7/9	

Dec 23rd 1938   2@ 2way Adaptors 2/6
Dec 31st 1938   1 Bell Battery 11d
                4 Glass plates & Screws 3d.
        6 @ 9" Holdfasts & Screws 6d.
        1 @ 5cwt. Coal Bunker £1.17.6
Jan 5th 1939   1 premier Elect. Iron 7/2d.
                1 Enamel Bowl   10d.

231

All paid for on the 17ᵗʰ of January 1939 at a total of £3.18.11, carefully typed out on a typewriter with jumping figures and purple ink.

Furniture had been mounting up too, starting with the bedroom suite at £28.10.0 from B&S Cabinet Works, Ltd, Wholesale Furniture manufacturers.

On 7ᵗʰ September 1938, 'on account on Mahogany suite and bedstead, £2.0.0.' The bill went to his parents' home at 11 South Hunter Street.

26ᵗʰ October 1938 1 Mahogany suite and bed £25.0.0
        1 Mahogany pedestal £2.5.0 (probably a tallboy)
        1Mahogany stool £1.5.0
        Walter Bentley Ltd Furniture Manufacturers
21 December 1938 to 315 East Prescot Road
        Two Chairs @37/6 , one Lloyd Loom Gold £2.2.6,
total £4.17.6

From there on, it became a spending spree as they dashed from shop to shop. They were both working and both living at home, so their disposal income was as high as possible, never to be repeated again.

He had kept Celi's visiting card, now a weathered cream colour, Celi McGivern, *43 Huskisson Street, Liverpool 8, tel. Royal 6292,*

10ᵗʰ December 1938 Lewis's, One Carpet £6.10.0

14ᵗʰ December 1938 Blackler's Stores, Linen £2.1.6

17ᵗʰ December 1938 T.J. Hughes, a table protector in three sections, 5/- to 11 South Hunter Street

17ᵗʰ December 1938 T.J. Hughes,London Road, 1 Bath Rail 3/11

17ᵗʰ December 1938 T.J. Hughes 33 yards, Stair Carpet £2.4.0

17ᵗʰ December 1938 Blackler's Stores, Elliott and Charlotte Street, a Wool Rug £1.9.6

19ᵗʰ December Dorondo Mills Photographers 49 Lime Street, order Wedding group photos 2-4, £2.2.0

21ˢᵗ December 1938 Harrison & Jones, Purax Mills, Vauxhall Road , deliver to 315 East Prescot Road, a 4'6" Feather Bolster & Pillow Set 16/0 net

21ˢᵗ December 1938 Harrison & Jones, a 4'6" National Mattress and C.E. Base £10.11.3
21ˢᵗ December 1938   Geo Henry Lee, Bassnett and Houghton Streets, Down Quilt £5.5.0, Bedspread £1.14.6; total £6.19.6
29ᵗʰ March 1939   The Cathedral Glass Co, 28 Berry Street,
One bevelled mirror 202x162 supplied and fitted to own frame 9/6 Re-fitting lead back own BS 30"x18" 6/6

And then, the removal from this false beginning to the real thing, on the 11the December 1939 as Bakers', 56 Tunnel Road, removers, took the furniture from 315 East Prescot Road to 9 South Hunter Street, cost £2.10.0.
Nowhere was there any trace of the costs of setting up for a baby with cot, pram, nappies, baby clothes etc.

An insight to the difficulties of a new baby did show up, however, as on 28ᵗʰ May 1940, Mrs Cecilia Martineau had to take out a hire purchase agreement for a Wringer with Rubber Rollers. Hire purchase price £4.7.6 (cash price £3.19.6) with ten shillings deposit. The days of paying cash were over.
Though there was one last gasp, from Turner's Auctioneers, 23ʳᵈ (May ? undated)1940, a nineteenth century Chinese carved Chair, priced £1.10.0

And then all this furniture fell into disgrace with Vin's moving into a home in 1992. Sent to the auctioneers, the entire lot came to £585 after fifty five years. The Bergère suite, Celi's pride and joy, came to a grand £240 pounds. Out of the house, in broad daylight, it looked almost sleazy, its green brocade faded and retiring from the light. Outhwaite & Litherland's list mimicked the original hopeful setting up bills.
A three-piece walnut bedroom suite (magically changed from its original mahogany state) made only £5
Two occasional tables, (one circular) coffee table, footstool, table lamp and smoker's stand £28
A carved oak 6' sideboard and a walnut sideboard £40
A large drawleaf table on bulbous legs £140

A set of six oak dining chairs (four and two carvers) £120
A quantity of glass,plates, vases and various glass etc £12
A three seater three-piece bergére back lounge suite £240
Total sold £585.00
And a sad addendum,
a Remington typewriter sold for £5, the kind gift from Nana
when Celi needed to get back her typing speeds in the nineteen
fifties for the Child Guidance Clinic secretarial job.

All their furniture, cast out into a wild world now, the
furniture that had held everything together, with the parents like
bewildered children not knowing quite what to do.

Her

Mother's diary

Mother's diary was on the dressing table in the back
bedroom. It had been left there, naked in the sun, for years. A
subtle mink-grey velvet; but when Mary lifted it the back cover
showed that it had been really a rich royal blue. Strangely, it had
been left, neglected, to bleach in the daylight. On this October
morning it seemed unlikely,the sky was also dun grey, lacking
all spark of light .If Mary remembered the trigonometry they had
learned at Art School, she could have worked out the exact angle
of the sunbeams as they had worked all those dead summers to
reach this surface.

The drawers were almost empty, all her jewellery had gone.
A couple of handkerchiefs, Christmas bath salts unused, a pair of
cotton summer gloves. Not much. She lifted the book up,
expecting nothing. But, out of it, fell her identity card,
registration 17th May 1943 and the title page from an old
passport, showing a sultry portrait,most unlike any passport
photograph she had ever seen. She looked like Mary had tried to
look at 21.

The validity of this passport expires 20 May 1931 unless renewed.

On the first page of the diary she had written: A present from Magda, Christmas 1978, in her round, sympathetic and warm handwriting.

It began with two deaths: January 1979 Michael Sinnott died suddenly. Cremated Springwood, Allerton, Friday 5th aged 24....Young Michael Murphy aged 19 died suddenly. Buried 5th. Snow, ice bLucyzards, gales, most dreadful weather for a decade, if not this century, according to some papers. Also strikes, petrol shortage, no milk etc. Not very good. Carrots 18p lb!...

From there on it was a mixed fabric of family visits, neighbours, religious devotions, house improvements, letters, birthday and Christmas presents, more deaths and encroaching illnesses.

Burst pipe in outside toilet....First physiotherapy session. Deepheat 15 minutes. In hospital over an hour. New Liverpool Royal Hospital. Frozen shoulder....Fridge arrived. G.E.C. Coldspace £45....

Hydrangea and peach trees chopped down!...Hems to take up for Joan. 3 silk jersey skirts....Confession St Anthony's....Wall work finished and paid for....Vin to Wrexham. Me to see Mrs Evans. To Royal L hospital 9.30 appointment. Discharged. Keep up exercises.... Confession. St Anthony's....Easter Sunday Mrs Murray, Grant Avenue, died. 82....Jim mended burst in outside toilet. Cut out only.... Confession Fr Jarwall.... Hairdo at Mops £1.45   Bus fare home 28p.... Confession   Fr. Richard.   Borg wins tennis final.... Frances broke her arm. Slipped in Calderstones Park   Mrs Evans here for the day. Dinner and tea. Worked out all right.... Vin has found a decorator. Going to do lounge and dining room? Kitchen ceiling....Frances' birthday. Took card and present. Away. Left note and Readers digests. Wrote to Marie. Not a long letter.... Mass St Philip Neri's. Took Pious List and goods for charity shop.... Missed Mass. Felt rotten. Palpitations, tightness.... Confession.... Peter started the decorating.... Peter finished work. Good job all round....Vin gone to pay off mortgage finally.... Strained heart... ME. ILL. 2 weeks in bed.... Confession St Philip Neri. Fr Cowley still very ill.... Easter Sunday. Holy Communion St Philip's....Vin's birthday. Magda and Frances....Whit Sunday Vin put down the underlay in the sitting room.3 rolls. Too much for us to use. Cut down hedge during the week....Monday went to town. Trying to buy shoes. Hopeless....Confession at St Philip Neri. Father Taafe, new parish priest, I think. Confessional locked. Electricians at work... Holiday of Obligation – the Assumption. Communion at St Philips. Saw M.Woods.....Fr Crowley died Thursday. R.I.P....Lucy comes out of hospital! All cancelled!....Frances went into St Pauls for eye operation. Said to be "satisfactory" today.... Frances "comfortable" in Ward 3....Thoroughly enjoyed my 73rd birthday! Cards from my friends and relations!! pleased with Aristoc stockings "Pacemakers" 89p Support....Took carving knife to butcher for sharpening (Tom at Thomas's) 25p....£5 from V on acc of my birthday and another £5 received. Bought bottle of Ponti Vermouth.... Hairdo.Trim, shampoo and set £2.40 and 10p.... Stan Robertson from the dairy round the corner, died of pneumonia very suddenly. Everybody very upset, especially Lucy. He helped her in many ways. We will miss him....Dr Gold came to see me re ankle swelling....Posted card....Vin bought the weekend joint. Half shoulder of lamb, blade end , beautiful. I suddenly begin to feel better, not quite so breathless, D.V. .... Dr Gold called. Put me off salt. Said much improvement. Ankle and leg/foot swelling gone down.... Hairdo at Lucy's. (Easter Sunday will be April 18th, Ash Wednesday March 4th)....Bill Moore died. Wrote note to Doris. Gave Kay the jumper patterns from Wynne. 2 weekly magazines returned....Confession Fr Taafe....Mass and Holy Communion St Philips.Mrs Mc Mahon, Willie Mayne (caretaker of the Dem School.).... Had a perm at Carolines, Greenbank Road....Vin's birthday. Shampoo and Scotch! No thank you....Kay came to tea, brought strawberries and cream. Small bottle of whiskey. Lovely day but cold....Snow and bad weather. Very cold..... Wrote to Marie. Kay called a.m. Vin out at stamp meeting. I'm waiting for the bath to fill. Lovely warm day....Planted clematis cutting from Wynn.... Rang Marie from Alvastone Road p.m. Bad line....Wrote to Marie....Confession St Philips. Bacon from Cann's. Very nice....Holy Communion 11.30 Mass. Wynn called.... Visited Cassville Road. (*Julie*)....Royal Wedding. Watched it in colour at

Wynne's. Lunch on trays. Riesling, very nice. "The Sound of Music" etc. Gave her the garden spray/hose.... *J.* on bus. To Mass together. *(She could not mention Julie's name in case he saw it?)*....Wrote to Marie....Enjoyable day at Heswall 12.45. Bought hot sausage rolls 60p. Home 8.45p.m. Via underground to Lime street. Tom's place broken into. Nothing taken....Bought kettle - of necessity, £2.5 Recent watch repair £2.50 Clock from Lucy....Suddenly to Marie's at Northwich. Smashing week there, lovely weather. Home late Sat afternoon....*J* to Women's Hospital. Hysterectomy. *(Julie again; no mention of visiting her in hospital.)*.... My birthday. Had a most enjoyable day. 74....Thursday Kay had fall, broken? elbow In Royal New Hospital for operation..... Confession. Fr Taafe. Statues of Saints Anthony and Joseph stolen quite recently....Confession. Letter to Marie....Me with bad cold. Vin takes over the shopping. Dr Marchant called. I have to stay in bed..... Dr Marchant came again. Some improvement, she says. Bronchitis.....Kay arrived, bless her. Dr Gold came. Stay in bed....Dr Gold. I can get up. Been up and dressed. In bed 10 o'clock.Feeling better but not energetic.... Confession Fr Taafe...*J. called. Spoke to V....J.* to hospital.... Kay called with her watch for repair. ...No Mass. Paid £3 to have Kay's watch repaired by Cliff Ogden...Perm. Glynol. Mrs Evans £5   3 hours!...Rings for curtains for Lucy.   10 for 18p....Bought carpet from Hellers for living room. Vin put underlay and carpet down. Very good job. Shared cost....Frances to Fazakerley Hospital...For X-ray. Sef and Kay.... Mass. Corpus Christi. Curtain rings 4p each....To see Frances. Kay and Lucy....Confession.... Communion. To Kay's for lunch. Sef & V....Very cold, windy, rainy day Bought vests for Frances, £2. Took them round with note. Pres. note for Dr M....Bin duties over to Vin as from today....Lucy's birthday. Kay called. Cancel hedge cutting....Mass. Jim called and we had a nice evening with them. Pauline has a daughter. Gerard's wife Barbara has a son. Hairdo during week. Cut and set £2.75! Not pensioners' time....Home. Friday p.m....Called on Frances and Sef. Gave Rosary beads and change 50p. Bottle of sherry from Lucy. *"Rage of Angels"* by Sidney Sheldon....Sent my Giro book to be written up....Kay at Mass. St Philips. Dinner and tea here....   New moon. Vin in a tizzy, all about the TV. Lost picture....Eyes tested. Passed

O.K. "In abeyance" Mr Gower-Perkins....Lourdes water from Mr Melia, newly home from Pilgrimage. Bless him....Murphy family just set off for Pen y Groes....Confession....Frances back in hospital 17th....Visit to Frances. Lucy and Kay. Gave pyjamas....Frances out of hospital....

Eddie Davies' funeral just left, hearse covered with flowers. Big crowd, lots of cars....Magda's birthday, sent card. Bought notepaper and envelopes and shopping list/notes. Ache in shoulder. Brisbane games in progress -we are doing well....Knights of Saint Columba Mass. Full house. Marvellous singing....Called to see Frances. Very ill. Lost weight. Kay helping a lot...Mrs Mc M gave me £1 for sewing....Wrote to Mrs Graham.... Bought Teachers £6.99!...Confession. Kay called. Frances' birthday tomorrow. Pill box present....Mass and Holy Communion. Pious list in....Mass 12 o'clock....Frances died in the early hours of Thursday morning. God rest her soul. Funeral Mass Monday....Thunderstorm. Lightening plus.....Confession Fr Taafe. First time on bus since December. Buses full of Easter shoppers....Polling Day. Vin as cranky as ever!...Kay called. We got our new bus passes yesterday. Strawberries!...Lucy and I bought a Dustette. According to her he offered it at very much less than the price he had asked. He has now given me fittings which make it a normal vac cleaner. Not a success....To hospital October....Fr Boylan. Bless him. Absolution and Holy Communion. Ward 6X... From hospital.... Paid Vin £30 and £20=£50. New curtains £11.50....Fr Joseph. First Friday. New cotton nightie....Fr Joseph anointed me, briefly, after communion....

Vin bad cough. Almost collapsed coming downstairs. No doctor till he says so....Both legs a mess. Nurse coming to dress one. Dr Endbinder called unannounced at about 9.15 a.m. Us not up yet. Ointment and 5 days' course of tablets. Vin fed up running round after me and who could blame him. Wrote to Mary on Monday....Telephone put in.734-5506 Push-button style....Meals on wheels delivered. 4/2p each. Stew dinner and delicious sweet. Baked sweet roll and custard, apple pie and so on. Today, Saturday, individual meat patties, broad beans, rice pudding and peach slices....

Harvest festival gift of fruit from children of St Anthony's. Via Mrs Lawrence....Lucy back home! Did not like the people...First Friday

and All Saints. A nun brought me Holy Communion. Deo Gratias. Dr and Sister Jones both here. Margaret did the laundry. My leg quite painful....Some improvement. No more blisters. Rang Mrs Graham and Marie... Dr Mullet will see me in 2 weeks' time, 20th Dentist will get in touch....To see Mr Nind, dentist in hospital 26th Nov Monday, 8.30 to 10 a.m. via Ambulance. Mr Malik has arranged for Mr Nind to discuss what is to be done....Letter from Marie with cheese.... Schwarzkop palette pure silver from Boots.... Dr Mullet took blood specimen. Change treatment....
Fell out of bed. To the hospital on Saturday a.m. Lovely day. Vin and Kay came. New white cardigan. Weak, faint...Catheter removed. Painful process.

Foggy weather

It trailed off here, the writing falling down the page towards her death a few days later. Then there were all the blank pages, leading to the confident listing of all the names and addresses of everyone mentioned all in that neat warm handwriting.

But on the final page, after the very last address, were some numbers added in a shaky pencil line, a last thought. Mary's own unused phone number, the last entry in the book, their voices not touching or meeting, except in the pencil lines, as always.

The convent had gone, all the sisters and their yards of black linen and serge. Julie had attended the closing ceremony where the convent chapel had been de-consecrated. No more gliding sweet-faced Sister Austin. God kicked out. New rules. All one big mess, covered by strange new ceremonies and the acquiescence of people like Julie, who had no other alternative and had to agree.

"Oh, it's Greencastle, County Down, I thought you knew," Aunty Kay said.

Northern Ireland! No one had ever mentioned that. The fairy-story Ireland did not exist after all, they were the other side of the border, they would be Northern-Irish Catholics with all that implied. They could be dead, injured, compromised, political pawns. It all turned on a heartbeat. The Ireland they had known was before partition, a different reality. All those years of romancing and she had never gone to a map to find the truth, just taking it for granted that the scenery and the butter and not being in the war was enough. They had never had the money to go there again; it was strange.

"And she couldn't have left him anyway, apart from all the Catholic church's rulings – she couldn't have gone out to full-time work and supported herself and you, because she only had one lung. Yes, the TB was serious and she had the operation after you were born, the doctors advised her not to have any more children at all."

"And Celi said you stayed at the Stevens' house in Woolton for so long that you used to call Uncle Fred 'Daddy', crawling after him down their hall. Yes, when he had to go off to sea, he was a captain, you were really upset. Aunty Doris was from your Mother's office days, they were firm friends, and as she had a little boy about the same age as you, she volunteered to take you in." Complete shock, no memory of any of it. But it explained a hunch, that she had had a brother somewhere, a lost soulmate, there had been a real companion once.

Now and again, Mother had taken her on the tram to Woolton, to Manor Crescent and a 1920s semi to visit friends. Aunty Doris and Uncle Fred were both good-looking, dark haired, with almost sallow skin. While rationing was on, Doris kept hens in the back garden and was generous with gifts - they returned home with eggs, rhubarb and more magazines. Their only son, Ian, was also good-looking but a complete stranger by now, they had no connection. The house was luxuriously carpeted throughout and was always highly heated,

"It's because Fred's used to the tropics, and he gets ill otherwise, he's become absolutely vulnerable to Liverpool winters!" Doris said, as if apologising. Fred often brought strange fruits back including pomegranates and pineapples, which were troublesome to eat and not half as convenient as their tinned versions, although such tinned fruit was hard to get hold of for several years.

"And you could never have turned up at the door, not at all - he would have gone berserk, that's why you had to meet her at my house instead. They almost separated after you left, but couldn't manage it. His temper was as bad as ever, she used to worry that the people next-door would hear him shouting. Yes, even right at the end, when she weighed only about five stone, he still wanted to keep her at home."

Video

The web was wonderful. You could be in places you weren't. You could go back. There was a news item, a video about a suspected terrorist, right there. A flick of buttons and the pictures opened. A black car came down the street. It crackled with pixels crashing against each other. Red rubbish wheelie bins, yellow rails of traffic barriers. The trees mimicked where previous trees had been – surely these were not the same ones that went in stately gaps all the way down Maryland Street?

She remembered the lopping crisis, when the trees had all been viciously cut, their fallen limbs lying along the pavement. No one had told her that the trees would re-grow, they looked defeated, maimed. And when that winter came, she had been so struck with the stark silhouette of their arms against a snow-covered street that she had gone into the school studio and

241

painted the Three Wise Men processing up Maryland Street on their camels under the remaining black branches; the influence of Raphael and all the other Renaissance painters on a plain Liverpool street.

Someone walked past, the 'always' bystander who haunts violent happenings.

A policeman with white short sleeves. A dash of yellow as a van came into shot. Two policemen walking in opposite directions. It was as slow and as deliberate as a chess game. Even the paved street had convenient lines painted across it like a chessboard.

An April evening. Suspected terrorists at the students' centre. A blurred figure being dragged out. Fear, hysteria, public unrest. The controlled hysteria that the arrival of the police always brings, with their blue tape to confine the action, the theatricality of it all.

Just out of sight, a group of children and a black and white dog played round a lamp-post, waiting for a turn on the haphazard rope swing. The sunlight sloped down the road as it neared sunset. Almost time for the Angelus. A student nun from a different order came out of one of the houses and with the rhythmical slap of her sandals, walked past them to the school gate, letting herself in with a key and shutting it carefully. Timed just right, she would reach the convent chapel just before the evening prayers began. The children knew they had a little more time left before parents came to their doors and shouted for them to come in and get washed and ready for bed.

On evenings like this the bedroom curtains let in the light and they would not get to sleep until late. It did not matter. There was still lots of time left, oodles and oodles of it until they heard the convent's morning bell, its note somewhere between lah and tee, its deliberate high tinkling note binding it all together. There were all the other evenings of summer waiting, golden and complete.

About the Author

Pat Jourdan was born in Liverpool, where she studied painting at Liverpool College of Art. She has held exhibitions of paintings and given readings of poetry and short stories in London, Norwich, Dublin, Galway and Vienna. Winner of several prizes, including the Molly Keane Short Story Award and second in the Michael McLaverty Short Story Award; widely published in magazines, the latest being Short Story Magazine, University of Texas.

Member of the Society for the Study of the Short Story, and Editor of The Lantern Review, with a blog at
     patjourdan.wordpress.com
and a website at patjourdan.co.uk

Most of the people in this book have passed away; as far as possible they have their real names and very little is fictitious.

A child's viewpoint may have caused some inaccuracies.

Acknowledgements

The cover photograph of the corner of Maryland Street and South Hunter Street 1912 is reproduced with thanks from Ged Fagan's Liverpool history website, inacityliving.

50R00148

Made in the USA
Charleston, SC
13 October 2015